PCs For Dummies, 4th Edition

Stuff you have to write down anyway

Windows login/network ID:_____

CompuServe account number:_____

Prodigy account name:_____

AOL login ID:_____

Internet address: _____

Internet Provider's phone number:_____

Helpful hints for using your PC

Always quit Windows properly. Choose Shutdown from the Start menu; press Ctrl+Esc, U. Click OK. Never just turn your PC off.

Click on the Start button to pop-up the main Start menu. You can also press the Ctrl+Esc key combination.

Start any program in your PC by using the Programs sub-menu on the main Start menu.

The desktop is the background you look at in Windows, the thing icons and windows float on.

The taskbar along the bottom of the screen contains buttons, one for each program or window you see on the desktop.

☒ Close any window or quit any program by clicking on its little X close button.

Use My Computer to familiarize yourself with disk drives, folders, and icons — the way Windows shows you the information inside your computer.

 The Help key! Your keyboard lacks a proper Help key, but Windows uses F1 as the Help key. To drive this point home, clip out the little Help key cap to the right and paste it over your keyboard's F1 key. There. Now you have an official, *PCs For Dummies* Help key.

...For Dummies: #1 Computer Book Series for Beginners

**COMPUTER
BOOK SERIES
FROM IDG**

PCs For Dummies, 4th Edition

Cheat Sheet

My PC stuff!

Fill in the following vital information about your computer.

Make & Model: _____
Network name (if any): _____
Microprocessor: _____
RAM: _____ MB
Hard drive capacity: _____ MB
Graphics: _____
Serial number: _____

Drive A is my first floppy drive!

Drive A is a: 3 1/2-inch   5 1/4-inch

Drive A is on: Top   Bottom

Drive B is my second floppy drive!

Drive B is a: 3 1/2-inch   5 1/4-inch

Drive B is on: Top   Bottom

I have no drive B!

Drive C is my hard drive!

I have other drives in my computer. They are:

Drive D is a: Hard drive   CD-ROM   _____

Drive __ is a: Hard drive   CD-ROM   _____

Drive __ is a: Hard drive   CD-ROM   _____

Here are other drives I use on the network:

Drive letter   Network PC   Pathname

Drive __ is on: _____ _____

Drive __ is on: _____ _____

What plugs into what?

Circle the following items as they apply to your PC.

My mouse plugs into: COM1 COM2 COM3 COM4

My modem is on: COM1 COM2 COM3 COM4

My printer plugs into: LPT1   LPT2   LPT3

Important phone numbers

Fill in the following information for your PC hardware.

My dealer: _____

My sales rep's name and extension:
_____

My dealer's tech support line:
_____

Operating system tech support:
_____

Fill in the following information for your software. Type in the application name first, and then the tech support number.

Application: _____
Tech Support: _____

Application: _____
Tech Support: _____

Application: _____
Tech Support: _____

. . .For Dummies: #1 Computer Book Series for Beginners

COMPUTER BOOK SERIES FROM IDG

References for the Rest of Us! ®

Are you intimidated and confused by computers? Do you find that traditional manuals are overloaded with technical details you'll never use? Do your friends and family always call you to fix simple problems on their PCs? Then the *...For Dummies*® computer book series from IDG Books Worldwide is for you.

...For Dummies books are written for those frustrated computer users who know they aren't really dumb but find that PC hardware, software, and indeed the unique vocabulary of computing make them feel helpless. *...For Dummies* books use a lighthearted approach, a down-to-earth style, and even cartoons and humorous icons to diffuse computer novices' fears and build their confidence. Lighthearted but not lightweight, these books are a perfect survival guide for anyone forced to use a computer.

> *"I like my copy so much I told friends; now they bought copies."*
>
> **Irene C., Orwell, Ohio**

> *"Quick, concise, nontechnical, and humorous."*
>
> **Jay A., Elburn, Illinois**

> *"Thanks, I needed this book. Now I can sleep at night."*
>
> **Robin F., British Columbia, Canada**

Already, hundreds of thousands of satisfied readers agree. They have made *...For Dummies* books the #1 introductory level computer book series and have written asking for more. So, if you're looking for the most fun and easy way to learn about computers, look to *...For Dummies* books to give you a helping hand.

7/96r

PCs

FOR

DUMMIES®

4TH EDITION

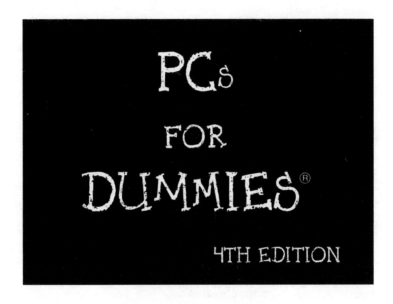

PCs FOR DUMMIES®

4TH EDITION

by Dan Gookin

IDG
BOOKS
WORLDWIDE

IDG Books Worldwide, Inc.
An International Data Group Company

Foster City, CA ♦ Chicago, IL ♦ Indianapolis, IN ♦ Southlake, TX

PCs For Dummies®, 4th Edition

Published by
IDG Books Worldwide, Inc.
An International Data Group Company
919 E. Hillsdale Blvd.
Suite 400
Foster City, CA 94404
http://www.idgbooks.com (IDG Books Worldwide Web Site)
http://www.dummies.com (Dummies Press Web Site)

Library of Congress Catalog Card No.: 96-75402

ISBN: 1-56884-634-7

Printed in the United States of America

10 9 8 7 6 5 4 3

4B/QT/QR/ZX/IN

Distributed in the United States by IDG Books Worldwide, Inc.

Distributed by Macmillan Canada for Canada; by Transworld Publishers Limited in the United Kingdom and Europe; by WoodsLane Pty. Ltd. for Australia; by WoodsLane Enterprises Ltd. for New Zealand; by Longman Singapore Publishers Ltd. for Singapore, Malaysia, Thailand, and Indonesia; by Simron Pty. Ltd. for South Africa; by Toppan Company Ltd. for Japan; by Distribuidora Cuspide for Argentina; by Livraria Cultura for Brazil; by Ediciencia S.A. for Ecuador; by Addison-Wesley Publishing Company for Korea; by Ediciones ZETA S.C.R. Ltda. for Peru; by WS Computer Publishing Company, Inc., for the Philippines; by Unalis Corporation for Taiwan; by Contemporanea de Ediciones for Venezuela. Authorized Sales Agent: Anthony Rudkin Associates for the Middle East and North Africa.

For general information on IDG Books Worldwide's books in the U.S., please call our Consumer Customer Service department at 800-762-2974. For reseller information, including discounts and premium sales, please call our Reseller Customer Service department at 800-434-3422.

For information on where to purchase IDG Books Worldwide's books outside the U.S., please contact our International Sales department at 415-655-3172 or fax 415-655-3295.

For information on foreign language translations, please contact our Foreign & Subsidiary Rights department at 415-655-3021 or fax 415-655-3281.

For sales inquiries and special prices for bulk quantities, please contact our Sales department at 415-655-3200 or write to the address above.

For information on using IDG Books Worldwide's books in the classroom or for ordering examination copies, please contact our Educational Sales department at 800-434-2086 or fax 817-251-8174.

For press review copies, author interviews, or other publicity information, please contact our Public Relations department at 415-655-3000 or fax 415-655-3299.

For authorization to photocopy items for corporate, personal, or educational use, please contact Copyright Clearance Center, 222 Rosewood Drive, Danvers, MA 01923, or fax 508-750-4470.

Trademarks: All brand names and product names used in this book are trade names, service marks, trademarks, or registered trademarks of their respective owners. IDG Books Worldwide is not associated with any product or vendor mentioned in this book.

 is a trademark under exclusive license to IDG Books Worldwide, Inc., from International Data Group, Inc.

About the Author

Dan Gookin

Dan Gookin got started with computers back in the post vacuum tube age of computing: 1982. His first intention was to buy a computer to replace his aged and constantly breaking typewriter. Working as slave labor in a restaurant, however, Gookin was unable to afford the full "word processor" setup and settled on a computer that had a monitor, keyboard, and little else. Soon his writing career was underway with several submissions to fiction magazines and lots of rejections.

The big break came in 1984 when he began writing about computers. Applying his flair for fiction with a self-taught knowledge of computers, Gookin was able to demystify the subject and explain technology in a relaxed and understandable voice. He even dared to add humor, which eventually won him a column in a local computer magazine.

Eventually Gookin's talents came to roost as a ghostwriter at a computer book publishing house. That was followed by an editing position at a San Diego computer magazine. During this time, he also regularly participated on a radio talk show about computers. In addition, Gookin kept writing books about computers, some of which became minor bestsellers.

In 1990, Gookin came to IDG Books with a book proposal. From that initial meeting unfolded an idea for an outrageous book: a long overdue and original idea for the computer book for the rest of us. What became *DOS For Dummies* blossomed into an international bestseller with hundreds of thousands of copies in print and many translations.

Today, Gookin still considers himself a writer and computer "guru" whose job it is to remind everyone that computers are not to be taken too seriously. His approach to computers is light and humorous yet very informative. He knows the complex beasts are important and can help people become productive and successful. Gookin mixes his knowledge of computers with a unique, dry sense of humor that keeps everyone informed — and awake. His favorite quote is "Computers are a notoriously dull subject, but that doesn't mean I have to write about them that way."

Gookin's titles for IDG Books include *Real Life Windows 95*, the best-selling *DOS For Dummies*, *More DOS For Dummies*, *Word For Windows For Dummies*, and the *Illustrated Computer Dictionary For Dummies*. All told, he's written over 40 books on computers and contributes regularly to *Maximize Windows* magazine. Gookin holds a degree in Communications from the University of California, San Diego, and currently lives with his wife and four boys in the as-yet-untamed state of Idaho.

ABOUT IDG BOOKS WORLDWIDE

Welcome to the world of IDG Books Worldwide.

IDG Books Worldwide, Inc., is a subsidiary of International Data Group, the world's largest publisher of computer-related information and the leading global provider of information services on information technology. IDG was founded more than 25 years ago and now employs more than 8,500 people worldwide. IDG publishes more than 275 computer publications in over 75 countries (see listing below). More than 60 million people read one or more IDG publications each month.

Launched in 1990, IDG Books Worldwide is today the #1 publisher of best-selling computer books in the United States. We are proud to have received eight awards from the Computer Press Association in recognition of editorial excellence and three from *Computer Currents'* First Annual Readers' Choice Awards. Our best-selling *...For Dummies®* series has more than 30 million copies in print with translations in 30 languages. IDG Books Worldwide, through a joint venture with IDG's Hi-Tech Beijing, became the first U.S. publisher to publish a computer book in the People's Republic of China. In record time, IDG Books Worldwide has become the first choice for millions of readers around the world who want to learn how to better manage their businesses.

Our mission is simple: Every one of our books is designed to bring extra value and skill-building instructions to the reader. Our books are written by experts who understand and care about our readers. The knowledge base of our editorial staff comes from years of experience in publishing, education, and journalism — experience we use to produce books for the '90s. In short, we care about books, so we attract the best people. We devote special attention to details such as audience, interior design, use of icons, and illustrations. And because we use an efficient process of authoring, editing, and desktop publishing our books electronically, we can spend more time ensuring superior content and spend less time on the technicalities of making books.

You can count on our commitment to deliver high-quality books at competitive prices on topics you want to read about. At IDG Books Worldwide, we continue in the IDG tradition of delivering quality for more than 25 years. You'll find no better book on a subject than one from IDG Books Worldwide.

John J. Kilcullen

John Kilcullen
President and CEO
IDG Books Worldwide, Inc.

**Eighth Annual
Computer Press
Awards ≥1992**

**Ninth Annual
Computer Press
Awards ≥1993**

**Tenth Annual
Computer Press
Awards ≥1994**

**Eleventh Annual
Computer Press
Awards ≥1995**

IDG Books Worldwide, Inc., is a subsidiary of International Data Group, the world's largest publisher of computer-related information and the leading global provider of information services on information technology. International Data Group publishes over 275 computer publications in over 75 countries. Sixty million people read one or more International Data Group publications each month. International Data Group's publications include: **ARGENTINA:** Buyer's Guide, Computerworld Argentina, PC World Argentina; **AUSTRALIA:** Australian Macworld, Australian PC World, Australian Reseller News, Computerworld, IT Casebook, Network World, Publish, Webmaster; **AUSTRIA:** Computerwelt Osterreich, Networks Austria, PC Tip Austria; **BANGLADESH:** PC World Bangladesh; **BELARUS:** PC World Belarus; **BELGIUM:** Data News; **BRAZIL:** Annuário de Informática, Computerworld, Connections, Macworld, PC Player, PC World, Publish, Reseller News, Supergamepower; **BULGARIA:** Computerworld Bulgaria, Network World Bulgaria, PC & MacWorld Bulgaria; **CANADA:** CIO Canada, Client/Server World, ComputerWorld Canada, InfoWorld Canada, NetworkWorld Canada, WebWorld; **CHILE:** Computerworld Chile, PC World Chile; **COLOMBIA:** Computerworld Colombia, PC World Colombia; **COSTA RICA:** PC World Centro America; **THE CZECH AND SLOVAK REPUBLICS:** Computerworld Czechoslovakia, Macworld Czech Republic, PC World Czechoslovakia; **DENMARK:** Communications World Danmark, Computerworld Danmark, Macworld Danmark, PC World Danmark, Techworld Denmark; **DOMINICAN REPUBLIC:** PC World Republica Dominicana; **ECUADOR:** PC World Ecuador; **EGYPT:** Computerworld Middle East, PC World Middle East; **EL SALVADOR:** PC World Centro America; **FINLAND:** MikroPC, Tietoverkko, Tietoviikko; **FRANCE:** Distributique, Hebdo, Info PC, Le Monde Informatique, Macworld, Reseaux & Telecoms, WebMaster France; **GERMANY:** Computer Partner, Computerwoche, Computerwoche Extra, Computerwoche FOCUS, Global Online, Macwelt, PC Welt; **GREECE:** Amiga Computing, GamePro Greece, Multimedia World; **GUATEMALA:** PC World Centro America; **HONDURAS:** PC World Centro America; **HONG KONG:** Computerworld Hong Kong, PC World Hong Kong, Publish in Asia; **HUNGARY:** ABCD CD-ROM, Computerworld Szamitastechnika, Internetto online Magazine, PC World Hungary, PC-X Magazin Hungary; **ICELAND:** Tolvuheimur PC World Island; **INDIA:** Information Communications World, Information Systems Computerworld, PC World India, Publish in Asia; **INDONESIA:** InfoKomputer PC World, Komputek Computerworld, Publish in Asia; **IRELAND:** ComputerScope, PC Live!; **ISRAEL:** Macworld Israel, People & Computers/Computerworld; **ITALY:** Computerworld Italia, Macworld Italia, Networking Italia, PC World Italia; **JAPAN:** DTP World, Macworld Japan, Nikkei Personal Computing, OS/2 World Japan, SunWorld Japan, Windows NT World, Windows World Japan; **KENYA:** PC World East African; **KOREA:** Hi-Tech Information, Macworld Korea, PC World Korea; **MACEDONIA:** PC World Macedonia; **MALAYSIA:** Computerworld Malaysia, PC World Malaysia, Publish in Asia; **MALTA:** PC World Malta; **MEXICO:** Computerworld Mexico, PC World Mexico; **MYANMAR:** PC World Myanmar; **NETHERLANDS:** Computer! Totaal, LAN Internetworking Magazine, LAN World Buyers Guide, Macworld Netherlands, Net, WebWereld; **NEW ZEALAND:** Absolute Beginners Guide and Plain & Simple Series, Computer Buyer, Computer Industry Directory, Computerworld New Zealand, MTB, Network World, PC World New Zealand; **NICARAGUA:** PC World Centro America; **NORWAY:** Computerworld Norge, CW Rapport, Datamagasinet, Financial Rapport, Kursguide Norge, Macworld Norge, Multimediaworld Norge, PC World Ekspress Norge, PC World Nettverk, PC World Norge, PC World ProduktGuide Norge; **PAKISTAN:** Computerworld Pakistan; **PANAMA:** PC World Panama; **PEOPLE'S REPUBLIC OF CHINA:** China Computer Users, China Computerworld, China InfoWorld, China Telecom World Weekly, Computer & Communication, Electronic Design China, Electronics Today, Electronics Weekly, Game Software, PC World China, Popular Computer Week, Software Weekly, Software World, Telecom World; **PERU:** Computerworld Peru, PC World Profesional Peru, PC World SoHo Peru; **PHILIPPINES:** Click!, Computerworld Philippines, PC World Philippines, Publish in Asia; **POLAND:** Computerworld Poland, Computerworld Special Report Poland, Cyber, Macworld Poland, Networld Poland, PC World Komputer; **PORTUGAL:** Cerebro/PC World, Computerworld/Correio Informático, Dealer World Portugal, Mac*In/PC*In Portugal, Multimedia World; **PUERTO RICO:** PC World Puerto Rico; **ROMANIA:** Computerworld Romania, PC World Romania, Telecom Romania; **RUSSIA:** Computerworld Russia, Mir PK, Publish, Seti; **SINGAPORE:** Computerworld Singapore, PC World Singapore, Publish in Asia; **SLOVENIA:** Monitor; **SOUTH AFRICA:** Computing SA, Network World SA, Software World SA; **SPAIN:** Communicaciones World España, Computerworld España, Dealer World España, Macworld España, PC World España; **SRI LANKA:** Infolink PC World; **SWEDEN:** CAP&Design, Computer Sweden, Corporate Computing Sweden, Internetworld Sweden, it.branschen, Macworld Sweden, MaxiData Sweden, MikroDatorn, Nätverk & Kommunikation, PC World Sweden, PCaktiv, Windows World Sweden; **SWITZERLAND:** Computerworld Schweiz, Macworld Schweiz, PCtip; **TAIWAN:** Computerworld Taiwan, Macworld Taiwan, NEW ViSiON/Publish, PC World Taiwan, Windows World Taiwan; **THAILAND:** Publish in Asia, Thai Computerworld; **TURKEY:** Computerworld Turkiye, Macworld Turkiye, Network World Turkiye, PC World Turkiye; **UKRAINE:** Computerworld Kiev, Multimedia World Ukraine, PC World Ukraine; **UNITED KINGDOM:** Acorn User UK, Amiga Action UK, Amiga Computing UK, Apple Talk UK, Computing, Macworld, Parents and Computers UK, PC Advisor, PC Home, PSX Pro, The WEB; **UNITED STATES:** Cable in the Classroom, CIO Magazine, Computerworld, DOS World, Federal Computer Week, GamePro Magazine, InfoWorld, I-Way, Macworld, Network World, PC Games, PC World, Publish, Video Event, THE WEB Magazine, and WebMaster; online webzines: JavaWorld, NetscapeWorld, and SunWorld Online; **URUGUAY:** InfoWorld Uruguay; **VENEZUELA:** Computerworld Venezuela, PC World Venezuela; and **VIETNAM:** PC World Vietnam.   10/22/96

Publisher's Acknowledgments

We're proud of this book; please send us your comments about it by using the Reader Response Card at the back of the book or by e-mailing us at feedback/dummies@idgbooks.com. Some of the people who helped bring this book to market include the following:

Acquisitions, Development, and Editorial

Project Editor: Bill Helling

Product Development Manager: Mary Bednarek

Technical Reviewer: Jim McCarter

Editorial Managers: Kristin A. Cocks, Mary C. Corder

Editorial Assistants: Constance Carlisle, Chris H. Collins, Jerelind Davis, Kevin Spencer

Production

Associate Project Coordinator: Regina Snyder

Layout and Graphics: Cameron Booker, Linda M. Boyer, Kerri Cornell, Todd Klemme, Jane Martin, Ron Riggan, Kate Snell, Marti Stegeman, Gina Scott, Angela F. Hunckler

Proofreaders: Melissa D. Buddendeck, Henry Lazarek, Sandra Profant, Christine Meloy Beck, Gwenette Gaddis

Indexer: Sherry Massey

General and Administrative

IDG Books Worldwide, Inc.: John Kilcullen, CEO; Steven Berkowitz, President and Publisher

IDG Books Technology Publishing: Brenda McLaughlin, Senior Vice President and Group Publisher

Dummies Technology Press and Dummies Editorial: Diane Graves Steele, Vice President and Associate Publisher; Judith A. Taylor, Brand Manager; Kristin A. Cocks, Editorial Director

Dummies Trade Press: Kathleen A. Welton, Vice President and Publisher; Stacy S. Collins, Brand Manager

IDG Books Production for Dummies Press: Beth Jenkins, Production Director; Cindy L. Phipps, Supervisor of Project Coordination; Kathie S. Schutte, Supervisor of Page Layout; Shelley Lea, Supervisor of Graphics and Design; Debbie J. Gates, Production Systems Specialist; Tony Augsburger, Reprint Coordinator; Leslie Popplewell, Media Archive Coordinator

Dummies Packaging and Book Design: Patti Sandez, Packaging Specialist; Kavish+Kavish, Cover Design

♦

The publisher would like to give special thanks to Patrick J. McGovern, without whom this book would not have been possible.

♦

Acknowledgments

I would like to express my thanks and appreciation to Andy Rathbone for his contributions to the previous editions of this book.

Thanks to Maryann Yoshimoto for her medical assistance with the text.

On behalf of the true writers of the United States, I'd like to acknowledge the contributions of Barbara Feinman toward a recent bestseller.

Contents at a Glance

Cartoons at a Glance

By Rich Tennant • Fax: 508-546-7747 • E-mail: the5wave@tiac.net

page 333

page 259

page 309

page 5

page 153

page 91

page 53

Table of Contents

· ·

Introduction

●●●

Welcome to *PCs For Dummies,* the all-new nearly completely rewritten 4th Edition. This book answers the question "How does a computer turn a smart person like you into a dummy?" Computers are useful, yes. And a fair number of people — heaven help them — fall in love with computers. But the rest of us are left sitting dumb and numb in front of the box. It's not that using a computer is beyond the range of our IQs; it's that no one has ever bothered to sit down and explain things in human terms. Until now.

This book talks about using a computer in friendly, human — and often irreverent — terms. Nothing is sacred here. Electronics can be praised by others. This book focuses on you and your needs. In this book, you'll discover everything you need to know about your computer without painful jargon or the prerequisite master's degree in engineering. And you'll have fun.

About This Book

This book is designed so that you can pick it up at any point and start reading — like a reference. There are 30 chapters, plus a handy Glossary. Each chapter covers a specific aspect of the computer — turning it on, using a printer, using software, kicking it, and so on. Each chapter is divided into self-contained nuggets of information — sections — all relating to the major theme of the chapter. Sample sections you may find include:

- Your Basic Hardware (A Nerd's Eye View)
- "The Manual Tells Me to Boot My Computer: Where Do I Kick It?"
- Learning which buttons you can ignore
- "My taskbar is gone!"
- General Commands for All Reasons
- Exiting a program
- Turning off the computer

You don't have to memorize anything in this book. Nothing about a computer is memorable. Each section is designed so you can read the information quickly, digest what you've read, and then put down the book and get on with using the computer. If anything technical crops up, you'll be alerted to its presence so you can cleanly avoid it.

How to Use This Book

This book works like a reference. Start with the topic you want more information about; look for it in the table of contents or in the index. Turn to the area of interest and read the information you need. Then, with the information in your head, you can quickly close the book and freely perform whatever task you need — without learning anything else.

Of course, if you want to learn additional information about the topic or learn something else, you can check many of the cross-references used throughout this book or just continue reading.

Whenever a message or information on the screen is described, it looks like this:

    This is a message on-screen.

If you have to type something in, it looks like this:

    Type me in

You would type the text **Type me in** as shown above. You'll be told when and if to press the Enter key.

Windows menu commands are shown like this:

Choose File➪Exit.

This means to select the File menu and choose the Exit command. You can use your computer's mouse, or you can press the Alt key and then the underlined keys, F and then X in the preceding example.

Key combinations you may have to type in are shown like this:

Ctrl+S

This means to press and hold the Ctrl (control) key, type an S, and then release the Ctrl key. It works just like pressing Shift+S on the keyboard produces the upper case S key. Same deal, different shift key.

What You Don't Need to Read

A lot of technical information is involved with using a computer. To better insulate you from it, I've enclosed such material in sidebars that are clearly marked as technical information. You don't have to read that stuff. Often, it's just a complex explanation of information already discussed in the chapter. Reading that information will only teach you something substantial about your computer, which is not the goal here.

And Just Who Are You?

I am going to make some admittedly foolish assumptions about you: You have a computer, and you use it somehow to do something. You use a PC (or are planning on it) and will be using Windows 95 as your PC's operating system or main program.

This book is specific to Windows 95. Whenever you see "Windows" discussed, it's referring to Windows 95. For information on the older version of Windows, you can get *PCs For Dummies, 3rd Edition* or *Windows 3.11 For Dummies*. Information on DOS is offered in *DOS For Dummies, 2nd Edition*; information on running DOS in Windows 95 is offered in *DOS For Dummies, Windows 95 Edition*. These books are available from IDG Books Worldwide, Inc.

Whew.

How This Book Is Organized

This book has seven major parts, each of which is divided into several chapters. Each chapter covers a major topic and is divided into sections, which address issues or concerns about the topic. That's how this book is organized, but how you read it is up to you. Pick a topic, a chapter, a section — whatever — and just start reading. Any related information is cross-referenced in the text.

Icons Used in This Book

 This icon alerts you to needless technical information — drivel added because I just feel like explaining something totally unnecessary (a hard habit to break). Feel free to skip over anything tagged with this little picture.

This icon usually indicates helpful advice or an insight that makes using the computer interesting. For example, when pouring acid over your computer, be sure to wear a protective apron, gloves, and goggles.

Ummm, I forgot what this one means.

This icon indicates that you need to be careful with the information presented; usually, it's a reminder for you not to do something.

Where to Go from Here

With this book in hand, you're now ready to go out and conquer your PC. Start by looking through the table of contents or the index. Find a topic, turn to the page indicated, and you're ready to go. Also, feel free to write in this book, fill in the blanks, dog-ear the pages, and do anything that would make a librarian blanch. Enjoy.

Part I
Introducing the PC (If You Don't Yet Own One)

In this part...

1t's entirely possible to be a very bright person yet not
know a thing about how to use a computer. The truth is:
no higher education is required, no math is necessary, and
you definitely don't need to master the thing. Those who
feel the desire will. The rest of us can just use the beast and
quickly turn it off when we're done. No problem.

This part of the book will get you up to speed on some very
basic computer concepts, even if you don't have a computer
or are just setting out to buy one. Or maybe you just bought
a shotgun and need to know what to shoot at. Whatever the
case, this part of the book is just for you.

Chapter 1
Say Hello to Mr. Computer

· ·

In This Chapter

▶ Understanding what a computer is

▶ Understanding what a computer is not

▶ Knowing what a PC is

▶ Recognizing basic computer hardware

▶ Finding drive A

▶ Reading PC hieroglyphics

▶ Getting to know software

▶ Discovering a final PC fact

· ·

Don't be fooled. Computer's aren't easy to use. They can be fun. They can be aggravating. They can be enlightening. And they can most certainly be intimidating, which is where all the *dummy* stuff comes about. It's just too bad computers don't pop out of the box, shake your hand, and give you a hug. If that were true, this book wouldn't be necessary.

In a way, computers are like babies. They come packaged with a lot of potential and with the right care and handling will achieve wondrous things and make you very proud. Like babies, computers require you to get to know them, to learn their moods and which buttons to push. It's a mutual relationship. And one that, fortunately, doesn't involve any drooling or diapers to change.

It's Just Another Electronic Gadget

A computer is that thing on your desk that looks like a TV set illegally parked by a typewriter. Call it whatever you like, it's basically a computer. But, because you may also have a computer on your wrist, in your car, or in the toaster, a more specific term is required: What you have on your desk is really a *PC,* a Personal Computer.

✔ Computers are essentially calculators with a lot more buttons and a larger display. They organize. They help you work with words and numbers. They can educate and entertain.

✔ Computers are not evil. They harbor no sinister intelligence. In fact, when you get to know them, they're really rather dumb.

✔ Computers have the potential to be very friendly. Because you can read information on-screen, many computers give you a list of options, provide suggestions, or tell you what to do next. The microwave oven can't do that. Or maybe it can but refuses to.

✔ Computers don't flash 12:00 after a power outage.

✔ Perhaps the most important thing to remember about a computer is that *you* are in the driver's seat. You tell the computer exactly what to do, and it does it. The problem here is that computers obey your instructions no matter what — even when you tell the computer something goofy. The art of dealing with a computer is a precise one.

✔ Please refrain from whacking your electronics.

What is a computer?

A computer is truly just another electronic gadget. Unlike the toaster or your car's carburetor, which are programmed to do only one thing, a personal computer can be *programmed* to do a number of interesting tasks. So it's really up to you to tell the computer what it is you want it to do.

✔ In a way, the computer is the chameleon of electronic devices. Your phone can only be used as a phone, your VCR only records and plays videos, and your microwave oven can only zap things (food, mostly). But a computer's potential is limitless.

✔ Computers get the job done by using *software*. The software programs the computer, telling it what to do.

✔ No, you never have to learn programming to use a computer. Someone else does the programming, and then you buy their program (the software) to get your work done.

✔ Your job, as computer operator, is really to tell the software what to do, which then tells the computer what to do.

✔ Only on cheesy sci-fi shows will the computer ever tell *you* what to do.

✔ Software is only one-half of the computer equation. The other side is *hardware,* which is covered in the next section.

✔ Computers can't clean up the house; they lack eyeballs and arms and legs. What you need if you want your house cleaned is a *robot*, which scientists haven't yet perfected for domestic use. When they do, buy *Robots For Dummies*.

Some history you don't have to read

Not long ago, personal computers were referred to as *microcomputers.* This term came from the *microprocessor,* the computer's main chip. The big "I want to control the world and foul up your phone bill" computers were called *mainframes.* Smaller, corporate- and college-sized computers (which only fouled up paychecks or grades) were called *minicomputers.* According to the geeks who ran the mainframes and minicomputers, *micro*computers were hobbyists' playthings — toys. However, the features available on the personal computer — the microcomputer — that you can have on your desk today exceed many of the features of the early mainframes. So there.

What is not a computer?

Your children. Real estate. Most livestock. Durable goods. Books and music. Fine art. The firmament. Condiments. Bicycles. Anything with a knob. Cat litter. Volleyballs. Shrunken heads. Everything in the *Potpourri* category on *"Jeopardy!"* Sushi. Anything Martha Stewart does, creates, or touches. Martha Stewart herself. Martha Stewart's dog.

Hardware and Software

Computers have two parts, hardware and software.

Hardware is the physical part of the computer, anything you can touch. Hardware is nothing by itself but potential. It needs software to tell it what to do. In a way, hardware is like a car without a driver or a symphony orchestra without music (and at union wages, that can be pricey).

Software is the brains of the computer. It tells the hardware what to do and how to work. Without the software directing things, the hardware would just sit around and look formidable. You must have software to make the computer go. In fact, software determines your computer's personality.

✔ Computer hardware isn't anything you'll find in your local True Value store. With a computer, hardware is the physical part — the stuff you can touch, feel in your hand, drop on the floor, lug through an airport, toss out a window, and so on.

✔ Computer software is the brains of the operation — the instructions that tell the computer what to do, how to act, when to lose your monthly report, and so on.

✔ Computer software is more important than computer hardware. The software tells the hardware what to do.

✔ Note that although computer software comes on floppy disks, the disks aren't the software. Software is stored on disks just as music is stored on cassettes and CDs.

✔ Without the proper software, your computer is a seriously heavy paperweight.

So Just What Is a PC?

PC means Personal Computer. It was the name IBM gave to their first personal computer, the IBM PC. That one computer was essentially the Model T of all computers. Even though it was made in 1981, many of its design elements are included in today's models — much to the frustration of PC owners and manufacturers everywhere!

✔ The term *clone,* and later *compatible,* was once used to describe any computer that used IBM PC-like hardware and could run PC software. Those terms are rarely used today as the standard PC has become more generic. In fact, computers are sold today based on what type of operating system they support; see "The operating system (or "Who's in charge here?")," later in this chapter.

✔ The only personal computer that's not a PC is the Macintosh. Its owners prefer to call them Macs instead of PCs. Lofty folk, they are.

✔ By the way, this book doesn't touch upon the Macintosh at all. If that computer is more to your liking, rush out and buy *Macs For Dummies* by my pal, Computer Magician to the Stars, David Pogue.

✔ The original PC wasn't created to start a dynasty, even though it did. Had the designers known how successful it would be, things might have been different (meaning *worse!*).

Your Basic Hardware (A Nerd's Eye View)

Figure 1-1 shows what a typical computer system looks like. I've flagged the most basic computer things you should identify and know about. These are just the basics. The rest of this book goes into the details.

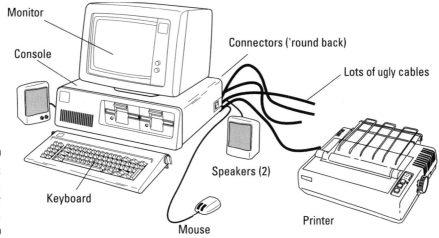

Figure 1-1:
Basic
computer
things.

Monitor

Console

Connectors ('round back)

Lots of ugly cables

Speakers (2)

Keyboard

Mouse

Printer

Monitor: The TV set-like thing that typically perches on top of the *console.* The glass part of the monitor is the *screen,* which is where the computer displays information or offers you insults or rude suggestions. Monitors are covered in detail in Chapter 13.

Console: The main computer box, also called the *system unit* by geeky types. It contains your computer's guts on the inside, plus a lot of interesting gizmos on the outside. See the section "Stuff on the console," later in this chapter, for information on the greeblies pasted on the console.

Keyboard: The thing you type on. La-di-da. Chapter 15 cusses and discusses the computer keyboard.

Mouse: Not a fuzzy little rodent, but a computer mouse. These things are especially helpful in using all that graphical software out there. By the way, the mouse is pointing the wrong way in the figure. I did that so you can see the two mouse buttons. Refer to Chapter 14 for information on proper mouse orientation and button info.

Speakers: Most PCs can beep and squawk through their own speaker. But if a computer has a special sound card (indicating that *multimedia* thing), it will have a set of stereo speakers on each side of the monitor.

Printer: The printer is where you get the computer's output, printed stuff, *hard copy.* Foray off to Chapter 16 to increase your PC printer knowledge.

Connectors: Behind your computer are a bunch of holes, each of which is named Jack. Into these *jacks* you plug various peripherals and other devices the computer controls — such as the printer, shown in Figure 1-1. Some parts of Chapter 11 are devoted to the various PC connectors on a computer's rump.

Lots of ugly cables: One thing they never show you — not in any computer manual and especially not in the advertisements — is the ganglia of cables that live behind each and every computer. What a mess! These cables are required to plug things into the wall and into each other. No shampoo conditioner on earth can clean up those tangles.

✔ These parts are all important. Make sure that you know where the console, keyboard, disk drive, monitor, and printer are in your own system. If the printer isn't present, it's probably a network printer sitting in some other room.

✔ Part IV of this book covers all computer hardware in detail.

✔ A computer really exists in two places. Most of the computer itself lives inside the console. Everything else, all the stuff connected to the console, is called a *peripheral*. See Chapter 18 for more information on peripherals.

Stuff on the console

The console is really the most important part of your computer. It's the main thing, the Big Box. Every part of your computer system either lives inside the console or plugs into it. Figure 1-2 shows what a typical PC console may look like. I've flagged the more interesting places to visit.

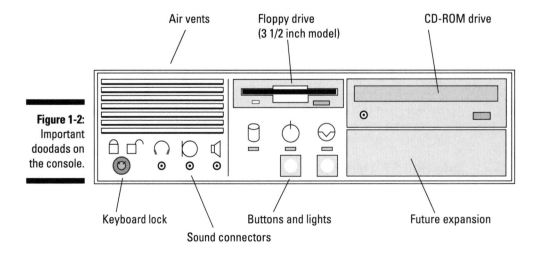

Air vents   Floppy drive (3 1/2 inch model)   CD-ROM drive

Figure 1-2:
Important
doodads on
the console.

Keyboard lock   Buttons and lights   Future expansion

Sound connectors

Air vents: OK, this isn't truly important, but most consoles sport some type of air vent on the front. The thing has gotta breathe.

Floppy drive: This is the slot that eats floppy disks. There may be one or two floppy drives, and they can be of the slim $3^1/_2$-inch variety or the wider $5^1/_4$-inch type. Mostly you'll be using the computer's hard disk, which dwells in the PC's innermost places. Part III of this book uses several chapters to discuss all the whatnots of disks and drives. It's a big spinnin' deal.

CD-ROM drive: This is a high-capacity disk looking exactly like a musical CD though containing computer information. Chapter 7 covers how you use and abuse CD-ROM drives and disks.

Future expansion: This is usually a blank spot on the front of your computer that allows you to add even more junk in the future. Such a space may already be taken on the computer, filled with such goodies as a tape backup unit, another CD-ROM drive, another hard drive, and a mystery grab-bag assortment of other computer things many folks enthusiastically spend their hard-earned money on.

Buttons and lights: Most of the computer's buttons are on the keyboard. A few of the more important ones are on the console, and on the fancier PCs these buttons are accompanied by many impressive tiny lights. These buttons and lights include the following:

On-off button: This is the PC's main power button, the one you use to turn the darn thing on. It may be on the front of the computer, though older models placed it back on the right side. The on-off button is usually accompanied by a light, though computers make enough racket you can usually hear when they're turned on.

Reset button: This button allows you to restart the computer without going through the bother of turning it off and then on again. Chapter 4 explains why anyone in their right mind would want to do that.

Turbo button: Worthless. This holdover from the early days of the PC lets the computer run in two modes: very slow and as fast as it can. Obviously, most people opt to run their computers fast since that's what they paid for. The slow setting is rarely, if ever, used. A small light accompanies the Turbo button.

Hard drive light: This light flashes when the hard drive is working. Since the hard drive lives inside the console, this light is your reassurance that it's alive, happy, and doing its job.

Sound connectors: Popular on many of today's multimedia computers are connections for adding speakers, headphones, and a microphone to your computer. Sometimes these things are up front, most often they're 'round back.

Keyboard lock: Since 1984 or so, most PCs have come with a tiny key and lock. You use the key to lock up the keyboard; when the keyboard is locked, the computer ignores what you type. Some locks even prevent you from opening the computer's case and getting inside. But mostly these locks are for show. For example, I have several computers in the office from different manufacturers, and the same key works with all the locks. So much for PC security . . .

✔ The console isn't the only part of your computer system that sports an on-off switch. Your PC's monitor, printer, modem (and almost everything else) also has its own on-off switch. See Chapter 4 for more information on turning everything on.

✔ Try not to block the air vents on the front of the console. If you do, the computer may literally suffocate. (Actually, it gets too hot.)

✔ Look in Chapter 11 for information on the horrors that lurk on the console's ugly backside.

✔ Hard drive lights used to be red, but that freaked everyone out since a flashing red light usually means something is wrong (witness your typical police car). The green light is more comforting — reminds me of Christmas.

"So where is my A drive?"

The A drive is your computer's first floppy drive. It's the only floppy drive if you have one, and it's typically the *top* floppy drive if you have two.

Then again, it could be the *bottom* floppy drive.

To find out which floppy drive is which, watch them when your PC starts. The first floppy drive, drive A, will have a light on it that lights up for a few moments after the PC starts. Immediately write "DRIVE A" on that drive using an indelible marker or use a label maker to create a label for the drive.

This book's Cheat Sheet includes space for you to jot down drive A's location. That way you'll always remember.

✔ Your first hard drive is always drive C. If you have a second hard drive, it's drive D.

✔ Chapter 7 describes all this disk drive lettering nonsense in crystal clear detail.

✋♏︎□○♋︎◆◆✗♒︎♓︎□♈︎●⬚♍︎□
(Become a master of hieroglyphics)

Along with all the lights and switches, the typical computer console sports a whole Nile full of symbols. No one ever tells you what they are, since they're supposedly international symbols (and even aliens from space would be able to discern their functions without consulting an intergalactic dictionary). In any event, I've listed them all for you in Figure 1-3 in case you stumble over one you cannot recognize and an alien from space isn't handy.

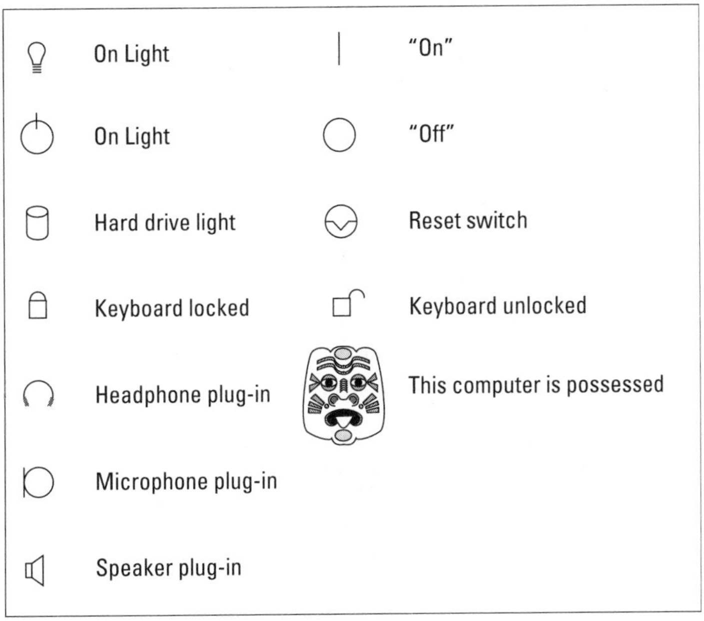

♀	On Light	|	"On"
⏻	On Light	○	"Off"
⛁	Hard drive light	⌣	Reset switch
🔒	Keyboard locked	🔓	Keyboard unlocked
⌒	Headphone plug-in	🗿	This computer is possessed
◖○	Microphone plug-in		
◁))	Speaker plug-in		

Figure 1-3:
Common
computer
hieroglyphics.

- ✔ Forget seeing ON or OFF on a computer switch. To be more politically correct, computers use a bar for ON and a circle for OFF (as shown in Figure 1-3). You can remember this by keeping in mind that a circle is an O and the word OFF stars with the letter O. (Then again, so does ON. Just don't think about it.)

- ✔ Most consoles have a little light that lets you know the computer is on. This little light is accompanied by a special symbol. In Figure 1-3, three "the computer is on" symbols are shown. What? Would it be that difficult to beat the word "ON" into a foreigner's brains? In any event, when the computer is on, it makes noise. That's a definite way to know.

Variations on the typical computer theme

Not all computers are going to look like the image in Figure 1-1. In fact, that's an old IBM PC shown there. Today's models are loosely based on the later IBM AT design, which is now being replaced by anything slab-like that looks sleek and has blinking lights — two of the highest status symbols a personal computer can attain. Here are some other terms used to describe various PC modes and models:

Desktop: A typical PC configuration with a slab-like console and a monitor holding everything down like a $500 paperweight.

Desktop (small footprint): A PC's footprint is the amount of desk space it uses. A small footprint desktop model is just tinier than the full-sized desktop model. Of course, in the end it makes no difference; the amount of clutter you have always expands to fill available desk space.

Laptops: A specialty type of computer that folds into a handy five-pound package, ideal for toting around. Laptop PCs work just like their desktop brethren; any exceptions are noted throughout this book.

Towers: Essentially a console standing on its side making it tall like a tower. These PCs have more room inside for expansion. They typically sit on the floor while the monitor and keyboard are on top of the desk. Preferred by power users.

Mini-towers: A small, squat version of the tower PC designed for people who work near airports where there are height restrictions. Seriously, you can put a mini-tower on top of your desk, typically next to the monitor and keyboard.

Tiffany Towers: This is actually the name of a stripper and has nothing to do with computers at all.

Your Basic Software

Computer software doesn't get the credit it deserves for running your computer. That's probably why it's overpriced. In any event, you need the software to make your hardware go.

The operating system (or "Who's in charge here?")

The most important piece of software is the *operating system*. This is the computer's number one program, the head honcho, big cheese, Mr. In-Charge, Fearless Leader, the King.

The operating system rules the computer's roost, controlling all the individual pieces and making sure that everything gets along well. It's the actual brains of the operation, telling the nitwitted hardware what to do next. The operating system also controls applications software (see the next section). Each of those programs must bend a knee and take a loyalty oath to the operating system.

- ✔ The computer's most important piece of software is the operating system.

- ✔ The operating system typically comes with the computer when you buy it. You never need to add a second operating system, though operating systems do get updated and improved from time to time. See Chapter 20 for information on upgrading the operating system.

- ✔ It used to be, in the olden days (say, 1986), you would buy a program for a specific type of computer. The software store would have sections for IBM, Apple, and Commodore. Today, you buy software for a specific operating system: DOS, Windows, OS/2, and Macintosh.

- ✔ For the PC, the most popular operating system used to be DOS. Presently, DOS is being supplanted by Windows. Other popular operating systems exist, but Windows is pretty much king of the heap.

- ✔ Chapter 5 chitty chats about Windows.

Other types of programs

The operating system is merely in charge of the computer. By itself, it doesn't really do anything for you. Instead, to get work done, you need an application program. Application programs are the programs that do the work. These programs include word processors, spreadsheets, databases, and so on. Whatever it is you do on your computer, it's being done by an application program.

Other types of programs include utilities, games, educational, and programming software. There could be other categories as well, but I'm too tired right now to think of them.

- Part V of this book covers computer software, especially the bizarre arena of communications or online software and the Internet.

- Utilities are programs that carry out special tasks, typically enhancing the abilities of the operating system.

- Games. Well. What more can I say?

- Educational software doesn't mean only programs to teach Tommy to count. I heartily recommend typing-tutor software to teach you to be a better typist at the computer. Personally, I've used musical software to train my ear so I can be a better musician. (Hasn't helped much.)

- You don't have to learn how to program the computer to use it.

  Even so, if you *really* want to tell the computer what to do with itself, consider picking up a programming package. One of the easiest to learn is Microsoft's Visual BASIC. My friend Wallace Wang wrote the book *Visual BASIC For Dummies* (available from IDG Books Worldwide, Inc.), and it's an excellent way to get started.

One, Final, Consoling Word of Advice . . .

The last thing you should be concerned about is that your PC — your personal computer — will blow up. It'll never happen. No sparks. No flash. No boom.

In many science fiction movies, computers blow up and spew fire and rocks. Irwin Allen did this in all his '60s TV shows. Even *Star Trek*'s Mr. Spock would be fond of pointing at some alien computer and uttering, in his calm Vulcan way, "Push this button, and the entire planet will become molten rubble." But in reality, it won't happen. Computers are just too dull.

Chapter 2
Helpful Hints on PC Setup

• •

In This Chapter

▶ Opening the boxes and unpacking everything

▶ Finding a place for your PC

▶ Setting up the console

▶ Setting up the monitor

▶ Connecting cables

▶ Setting up the printer

▶ Examining surge protectors

▶ Dealing with hardware and software

• •

*N*othing can be more satisfying than opening up something new. Computer marketing types even have a name for it: the "out of box" experience. It almost sounds religious.

> *Yes, doctor. I had an out-of-box experience. For a moment, I saw our old toaster. And then the water heater that blew up last year. It told me I had to go back, go back to assemble my PC.*

Sheesh.

Setting up a computer is a task about as endearing as wiring together a VCR and television so you can watch cable and record HBO at the same time. No one looks forward to it. Fortunately, it's something you need to do only once, or just pay someone else to do for you.

Opening the Big Boxes and Unpacking Everything

Setting up a computer starts with opening big boxes — typically, two to three. You should start by locating a packing list, which should be attached to the outside of one of the boxes. Make sure that everything is present and accounted for and that you have everything you paid for.

- ✔ Sometimes packing lists come separately, or you may have an invoice. Either way, make sure that you have all the boxes you need.

- ✔ If you got the computer through the mail, check to be sure that all the pieces have arrived together. The same rule applies if your computer arrived at your office from the computer or MIS department. If not, contact the delivery people and threaten them with babysitting a two-year-old.

- ✔ Always keep the phone numbers of your dealer and computer manufacturer handy. (There is space for those numbers in this book's Cheat Sheet.) Also, look out for special support numbers; some manufacturers offer 24-hour, toll-free support via an 800 number. Write them numbers down!

Where will Mr. Computer live?

Before you unpack anything, find a home for your computer. Clear off your desk or tabletop, allowing enough room to set down the computer and keyboard. Remember, it may have an octopus of cables and *peripherals* around it. Make room for all that stuff, too.

- ✔ Computers need room to breathe. Don't put your computer in a closet, box, recessed vault, grotto, or other cave-like place with poor ventilation.

- ✔ Don't put the computer by a sunny window as this heats the computer up and gives it anxiety.

- ✔ If you can sit on the table, it can support the computer. Don't put the PC on a wobbly table or anything you wouldn't sit on yourself (like the cat).

Open 'em up!

To open your computer boxes, take the same approach any kid takes at a birthday party: The biggest box must contain the best stuff, so start unpacking with the biggest box first.

The big box probably contains the computer console, plus other pieces and parts. The next biggest box may contain the monitor or display. Any other boxes contain the manuals, the keyboard, and extra goodies.

If you bought a printer, it comes in its own box as well.

And, of course, all the software you bought comes in more boxes. (The computer industry is a gold mine for the cardboard box industry.)

- ✔ If a box says "open first," do that.
- ✔ Say, is that the AT&T building or the box it came in?
- ✔ Some boxes have opening instructions. I kid you not! My huge monitor had to be opened on the top and then turned upside down so I could lift the box off of the monitor. Remember, gravity can be your friend.
- ✔ All the boxes have numbers on them, usually product numbers. Add them up! If the total is greater than 10,000, phone your dealer. You've just won a prize!
- ✔ I'm kidding, of course.

Unpacking the console

The console is probably in the largest box, so unpack it first. If the monitor is in the biggest box don't open it first. This is the console section. Unpack your monitor later. For now, open the box the console came in, no matter what size it is, even if it's eensy-teensy tiny and comes in a matchbox.

The console itself is the least mobile of the units you'll unpack, so setting it up first gives you a good starting base.

Box opening etiquette

Be careful opening any box. The "grab and rip" approach can be dangerous, since those massive ugly staples used to close the box can fling off and give you an unwanted body piercing. (It's fashionable in parts of Silicon Valley to have a large staple through the eyebrow.) Same holds true with using a box knife; use a small blade since you don't want to slice through or into anything electronic — or fleshy, for that matter.

Remove any packing material, such as nonbiodegradable foam or polystyrene. Lift the console out of the box and carefully set it on the table top. If it comes in a plastic bag, remove the bag as well.

Watch as the millions of tiny foam peanuts fall all over the floor. If you're lucky, it's a wood floor and static electricity will energize each foam peanut. They're alive! You'll never get rid of them. Note how some scamper off to reside under the credenza.

Hoisting the monitor

The monitor comes in its own box, separate from the console. Remove the packing foam and set it aside. Then carefully lift out the monitor. It's OK to cut the monitor free from its plastic bag; keeping the bag on makes the screen difficult to see.

Set the monitor aside for the meantime. You need to dink with the console before you can proudly set the monitor on top of it.

Is there a separate keyboard box?

Sometimes a third (or fourth) box is included with your computer — in addition to any software and manuals you may get. This box may contain the keyboard, the mouse, other interesting hardware, or just the manuals that attempt to tell you all about your computer.

The printer's massive box

Carefully remove the printer from its box. It has its own manual plus any cables and connectors that are necessary. If you don't feel like setting up the printer just now, that's OK. There's no sense in overwhelming yourself.

- ✔ The section "Setting Up the Printer" later in this chapter goes into detail on setting up your printer for the first time.
- ✔ If you bought any printer paper, cables, and so on, set them aside with the printer.

More miscellaneous material

Various goodies may also be contained in the console box; be sure to look for them! Computers often come with boxes inside of boxes, like the old Chinese magic box. Sometimes the keyboard, manuals, and various cables are lurking inside the console box. Check for them before you toss anything out.

✔ Double-check all your boxes for extra goodies: cables, manuals, power cords, and so on. I once rescued my keyboard from the trash can because it was hidden in a box within the box my console came in.

✔ Chapter 16 provides additional information on setting up your computer printer.

"Should I toss out the boxes?"

Computers are shipped with a lot of packing material, plastic bags, twist ties, rubber bands, nylons, and Hershey bars. You can throw out everything you think is trash if you want. Or, to be good to the environment, you can recycle everything. However, if the computer ends up being a lemon, you may need to ship it back in the original containers or risk losing your warranty.

The best advice is to save all the boxes and packing foam for at least a month, which should give you time to see whether the computer needs to be returned. After that, feel free to toss out the boxes.

I keep all my computer boxes and the packing material (except for the annoying foam peanuts). Heck, I have boxes from 1984. The reason? When I move — although it's not that often — I prefer to pack the computers in their original boxes. Many moving companies won't insure your computers unless they're in the original packing material with the original foam peanuts and Hershey bars, so I never toss out my computer boxes. That's why God invented attics anyway.

Putting It Together

Assembling a computer is something better left to a technical person. Remind your office computer gurus that they should be assembling your office system. At home, invite your computer-knowledgeable friends over to see the new PC. But don't tell them it's sitting on the floor suffocating in a bag. Surprise them. Computer people are often delighted to assemble a PC. It's like delivering a calf but without the slosh.

If you're stuck and have to assemble your own PC, here's what you need:

- ✔ A medium-sized Phillips or standard screwdriver (I don't know which — get both).

- ✔ A tiny, flat-head screwdriver — one designed for teensy, tiny screws.

- ✔ About an hour of your time.

- ✔ Plenty of patience.

- ✔ You probably don't need two screwdrivers but gather up a few anyway. It looks impressive.

- ✔ Keep pets and small children at a distance when you set up your PC. If you keep a cold beverage handy, put it in a safe spot where spilling it won't be a problem (like in another state).

- ✔ You may also need a flashlight to see behind your computer.

Setting up the console (the boxy thing)

Start by setting the console where you want it. The pretty side, usually containing the company label and computer model name and number, goes toward you. Remove the console from its plastic bag, if you haven't already done so.

- ✔ Don't block the front of the console with the keyboard or books or a box of Kleenex. Remember that you still need access to the front of the console to turn it on, swap disks, and stare at the pretty glowing lights when you're bored.

- ✔ The console is the first thing you setup, seeing as how everything else plugs into it.

- ✔ For now, give yourself some working room behind the console. You need to weasel your way back there to attach some wires and cables. After that's done, you can shove the console to its final resting position.

- ✔ If you have a tower-model PC, the console will sit flat on the floor, usually under a desk. Pull it out away from the desk for now so you can connect the cables described later in this section.

- ✔ Note that some manuals refer to the console as the *system unit*.

Where do it go, George?

There should be a picture of your assembled PC somewhere, either in its setup manuals or on the box. That should help. If not, gander back at Figure 1-1, which is an IBM PC circa 1981, but still shows you where everything goes. The figure below shows various cables you plug into the back of a typical PC. These figures show generalities; your computer may be slightly different.

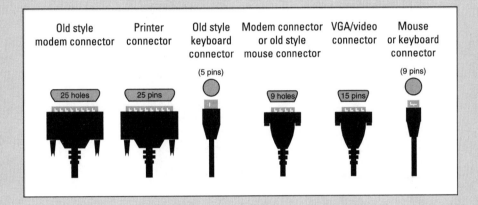

Removing the disk drive tongue depressors

The PC's disk drives may contain paper or plastic doohickeys. Look for the disk drive slots on the front of the console.

For a $3^1/_2$-inch disk, press the button underneath the disk drive slot, and the plastic holder is ejected part way; pinch it and pull it all the way out.

If you have an older $5^1/_4$-inch drive, a square piece of cardboard is stuck in the hole. Gently flip open the latch, pinch the cardboard, and yank it straight out.

You can toss out the disk drive tongue depressors if you want. I keep mine for the same reason I keep the boxes: just in case I need to move the computer. You don't need to stick the depressors in the drive when the PC is turned off. But putting them there whenever you haul the computer long distances prevents something from happening to the disk drives. I don't know what exactly, but I'll bet it's nasty.

Connecting cables to the console

The console is the main computer unit. As such, its duty is to have as many unsightly cables hanging out of it as possible. These cables connect around the back, where they're most inconvenient to access.

You will be connecting several, if not all, of the following cables to the console:

- ✔ The power cord
- ✔ The keyboard cable
- ✔ The mouse cable
- ✔ The monitor cable
- ✔ External speaker cables
- ✔ Microphone cable
- ✔ The printer cable
- ✔ Network cable
- ✔ Transatlantic cable
- ✔ Jumper cables
- ✔ George Washington Cable

General notes on connecting cables

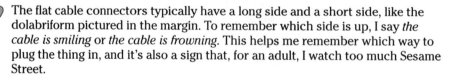

The flat cable connectors typically have a long side and a short side, like the dolabriform pictured in the margin. To remember which side is up, I say *the cable is smiling* or *the cable is frowning*. This helps me remember which way to plug the thing in, and it's also a sign that, for an adult, I watch too much Sesame Street.

The nerds call those things D-shell connectors. The connector does look like a D, a real dorky one.

Before connecting a keyboard cable or similar round connector, look into the hole. Make sure that the pins in the cable are all lined up with the tiny holes inside the hole. The smaller, round connectors have notches on one side of the hole, and the cable needs to be lined up.

Don't plug anything into the console while the computer is turned on. You won't get electrocuted (although I'm not certain), but you may damage either the computer or the thing you're plugging in. And always wait until the computer is turned off before plugging in your keyboard cable.

Some connectors look alike. But there are subtle differences. Refer to the figure in the sidebar "Where do it go, George?" for cable identification tips. Note that some connectors have holes, others have pins. Some computers even have their connectors labeled, either with words or symbols (which means you paid more). Table 2-1 shows what some of the words mean and what could possibly plug into them.

A connector or hole with pins is technically a *male* connector. A connector or hole with tiny holes the pins plug into is a *female* connector. I draw a complete blank as to why this is so.

Table 2-1	Things You May Plug Cables Into
Whatzit	*What Plugs into Whatzit*
COM1	Plug your mouse into this hole if the connector fits, otherwise you can plug a modem in here.
COM2	This hole is typically used for outboard motors, er, modems.
LPT1	Printer plugs in here.
LPT2	If you're greedy, your second printer plugs in here. Only plug a second printer in here; don't plug your first printer into an LPT2, LPT3, or anything else.
MOUSE	Mouse must plug in here.
MONITOR	Plug the monitor into this hole.
KYBD	Keyboard goes here (or any other combination of the letters in KEYBOARD).
MIC	Microphone.
LINE IN	Stereo (not the microphone).
SPEAKERS	Must be the speakers in here.

Setting up the monitor

Set the monitor on top of the console. Or set it to the side, depending on whether you have enough desk space.

Of course, if you have a tower PC, which goes under the desk (or in a nearby tower), the monitor just sits atop your desk. Nothing criminal in that.

You don't want to read this bothersome explanation

Most of today's computers are sold with a VGA graphics system. That's a fancy term describing how the monitor's and computer's insides are trained to produce some of the most impressive computer graphics in the world (Earth). On that system, the video cable has 15 wires in it. Likewise, the connector on the console has 15 holes. To deceive you, another connector of the same size appears on the back of many consoles. But that connector has only 9 holes.

The 9-hole connector is a *serial port*, to which you may connect a mouse, a modem, or some other interesting gizmo. It's not where you plug in the monitor. The monitor plugs into a 15-hole connector.

Older PC graphics systems may have a different number of holes in the connector. You can usually spot them by a single-hole RF jack connector just to the side of the video connector. If you find the RF jack, you're very close to where you plug in the monitor. (RF jack refers to a type of connector; it's not a sandwich you'd get at a Jack-in-the-Box.)

The monitor has two cables. One goes into the console, which is how the computer displays information on-screen. Call that cable the video cable. The second cable is plugged into a wall socket. Call that the power cable. Plug them both in now. Do it simultaneously, using both arms. (Just kidding.)

- ✐ If there isn't enough cable to put the keyboard and monitor to one side of the console, you can buy extension cables at your favorite computer store.

- ✐ Chapter 13 provides more information on monitors, including how to work the various knobs.

- ✐ Some monitors come with a tilt-and-swivel base, which enables you to move the monitor to various orientations, albeit stiffly. This type of base is also an option you can buy for the monitor if it's not already built in.

- ✐ As with the console, the monitor needs to breathe. Don't set anything on top of the monitor or cover its wee tiny air vents in any way.

Setting Up the Printer

The printer is a device separate and unique from the computer. In a way, it's like a separate computer, one designed just to smear ink all over paper.

Setting up a PC printer is a snap. The hard part comes later, when you must force your software to recognize and obey the printer. (I've put that off until Chapter 16, which is buried in the middle of this book where no one can find it.)

You set up the printer similarly to the way you set up everything else. Take it out of the box, unpack it, and then set it where you want it. Put the printer near the computer — the nearer the better — but it doesn't need to be too close.

- ✔ Keeping the printer at arm's length can come in handy.

- ✔ Be sure to look through the printer box for manuals, font cartridges, and other stuff the printer needs.

- ✔ Printers don't come with cables — for a reason. Not every printer will be hooked up to an IBM type of computer. Therefore, you need to buy an IBM printer cable separately.

- ✔ Laser printers require *toner cartridges,* which must be purchased separately. Other types of printers usually come with their own ribbons, inkwells, carbon paper, octopi, and so on.

Printer pieces parts

Printers come in many pieces. There's the printer itself, the ribbon or toner cartridge, and the thing that holds the paper. An instruction sheet that comes with the printer explains what goes where. Find that sheet and heed its instructions.

Basic printer setup requires yanking a few shipping items from the printer's insides, installing the ribbon/toner cartridge, setting up the paper-feeding mechanism or paper tray, adding any font cards, and plugging in the cables.

- ✔ Si la feuille du mode d'emploi a l'air français, c'est peut-être parce que c'est écrit en français. La plupart des modes d'emploi ont des directives en plusieurs langues. Il faut chercher la version en anglais.

- ✔ If the instruction sheet reads like it's written in French, it probably is. Most instruction sheets list instructions in several languages. Look for the English version.

- ✔ Laser printers require a detailed internal setup, which usually requires that you yank out several plastic doohickeys, peel tape, and apply salve to the printer's aching foot pads. Other types of printers may require similar removal of parts. Those parts hold the printer's insides inside during shipment. You don't need to keep them; freely toss them out (even if you plan on moving the printer later).

- ✔ If you have a font cartridge, it goes into the special font slot hidden somewhere on the printer. An instruction sheet should tell you where it goes. Make sure that the printer is turned off when you plug in the font cartridge.

Connecting the printer cables

Printers have two required cables: the power cable, which plugs into a wall socket, and the printer cable, which plugs into the computer. (Congress passed a law ten years ago requiring that every computing device have at minimum two cables.)

The printer cable should already be connected to the PC's console, as described earlier in this chapter. The other end of that cable plugs into the printer. This is the fun part. The connector is big and has two clips on it. There's no way to plug it in wrong, and little guesswork is involved as to where to put it.

- ✔ The majority of printers plug into the computer's printer port. Aren't you glad that makes sense? A few, however, plug into the PC's serial port, which causes a major headache — one that's postponed until Chapter 16 (see the section on using a serial printer).

- ✔ You don't need to use the printer right away. I recommend that you get to know the PC first. Then worry about the printer.

Trivial printer cable information

Your printer can be a maximum of only 20 feet from your PC. That's the longest a printer cable can be before information is lost. Cables longer than 20 feet just can't carry the signal from the computer, and nothing (or random information) is printed.

The typical printer cable is 6 feet long — good enough for setting the printer nearby but not necessarily next to the computer. Longer cables are available, and you can always daisy-chain cables. But keep in mind the 20-foot limit.

What about Those Surge Protectors?

Computers make you realize something about modern living: There aren't enough power sockets to plug everything in.

The standard computer requires two power sockets: one for the console and another for the monitor. Extra devices, modems, scanners, printers, expensive gadgets with impressive lights, and so on, all require their own power sockets. As usual, there are right and wrong ways to deal with this situation.

Oodles of printer tips

Here are some handy computer printer tips you don't have to commit to memory (they're repeated in Chapter 16 anyway, for good measure):

🖛 Printers need paper. Laser printers can print on any copy machine paper, but they also accept letterhead and plain typewriter paper.

🖛 Avoid using bond paper in a laser printer. Bond paper may have dust or powder on it; that stuff clogs up the printer. Also avoid erasable typing paper.

🖛 Non-laser printers can use fanfold paper. This paper comes with dozens (or hundreds) of sheets connected together. Detachable dots on the sides of the paper enable it to be pulled or pushed through the printer. Insert the paper by using the dots and guides. Some printers automatically line up the paper and are ready to print when you turn them on.

🖛 You don't need to have the same printer model as your computer. For example, any model of printer — not just an IBM printer — works with an IBM computer (although IBM salesnoids may claim differently).

🖛 You don't need to have the printer turned on unless you're printing something. Leaving some laser printers turned on wastes up to 1,000 watts of electricity per hour. That makes for a big electrical bill when you're not printing anything.

🖛 Some newer laser printers are "environmentally friendly." They will go quite like a submarine, barely sipping any power until you need them. Then they surface, chow down the power, print, and return to silent mode until you need them again. Sneaky.

🖛 The printer does not print unless it's *online*, or *selected*. A button on the printer somewhere enables you to activate the printer, bringing it online or making it selected. No, it's not enough just to turn on the printer.

The wrong ways follow:

🖛 Never use an extension cord to meet your power needs. People trip over extension cords and unplug them routinely.

🖛 Don't use any power splitters or those octopus-like things that turn one socket into three. Computers need grounded sockets, which must have three prongs in them.

🖛 Don't lick the plug before you stick it into the wall.

The right ways follow:

- ✔ Buy a power strip. This device plugs into a single socket and contains up to six additional sockets. Everything associated with the PC — even the lamp on your desk — can plug into the power strip. You can turn on the whole shebang with your toe through the hole in your sock if that pleases you.

- ✔ Buy one of those PowerMeister things. They usually sit below the monitor and have a row of switches: for the computer, monitor, printer, and other items. A single master switch enables you to turn on everything at once.

- ✔ Always plug a laser printer into its own socket, never into a power strip or an uninterruptible power supply (see the sidebar nearby).

What's Next?

With the computer all set up and ready to roll, you're probably tempted to turn it on. But wait. You should look for a few things before you steamroll ahead:

- ✔ Find any manuals that came with your computer. Look for the ones that contain directions and troubleshooting help. Keep these manuals handy.

- ✔ Always retain the manuals that came with your computer plus any software manuals. Keep any disks and their software manuals together.

Excuse me, I'm an *uninterruptible* power supply

An uninterruptible power supply, or UPS (not the shipping company), is a handy device every PC owner should have. It's not a power strip. Typical UPS units are about the size of a small car battery (hint, hint) and have two, often more, power receptacles on them. Into those receptacles you can plug in your console and monitor.

What the UPS does, in addition to guarding against spikes, surges, and other nasty power things, is keep your PC running when the power goes off. Not for a long time (mine lasts about 10 minutes), but long enough to let you save and

quit Windows and turn off your PC nicely. That way you never lose information due to a power outage.

By the way, you don't need to plug *everything* into a UPS. Printers, no way! You can print when the power comes back on. Same with scanners, modems, and other fancy devices. And destroy those dreams of computing for hours during a blackout, being the envy of the block and so on; when the power goes out, save your work and turn off the PC.

✔ You can throw away most of the little scraps of paper. Don't throw away anything that has a phone number on it until you've written the number down.

✔ Mail in your registration or warranty card. Make a note of the computer's serial number and file it away as well. In an office situation, you should keep track of all your equipment's serial numbers.

✔ Make sure that you have legitimate copies of your software. For example, you should have Windows on your PC's hard disk and a copy of the proper manual. If you don't have a manual, or if you have only photocopied pages, your dealer has sold you a bootlegged version of the software. Do the right thing: Rush to the software store and buy a copy of Windows for your computer. (Don't worry about reporting the dealer; he or she will pay in the long run.)

Dealing with software

You may have purchased some software with your computer. If so, great. However, leave all those boxes alone for now. One of the mistakes many beginners make is overwhelming themselves with computer software. Although it's OK to buy lots of software (and if you haven't, you'll probably buy more later), it's counterproductive to use it all right away.

You may skip this stuff on surge protectors, but only if you're foolish

A special type of power strip is the surge protector, which has protection against power surges and other nasty electrical things that can fry the computer. But *caveat emptor* here: There are varying degrees of surge protectors.

The simplest form of electronic protection is the line filter. It sifts out noise from the power lines, giving you cleaner power. Surge protectors are more expensive. They protect against power surges, which happen when the electricity company puts out a greater amount of juice over a

long period of time. Spike protection is the highest, and most expensive, type of protection. A spike is a single, high-voltage charge — usually caused by a lightning strike. Only special spike protectors can guard against them, sacrificing themselves and saving your computer's life. (It's kind of religious.)

How serious is all this? Not very. Unless the power in your area is highly unstable and lightning strikes often, don't worry. A power strip with a noise filter, however, is a good investment.

✔ Your computer's operating system (Windows) is the most important piece of software you have. Locate those disks and put them on top of the pile.

✔ See Chapter 5 for more information on what an operating system is.

✔ If you have anything you must do — a priority project, for example — set the software you need aside from the rest of the stuff. For example, if learning 1-2-3, Word, or PageMaker is your top priority, set the software aside and get ready to learn and use it first. Everything else can wait.

✔ Remember that no job can be done immediately. No matter how annoying your boss is, you must learn software before you can be productive with it. Give yourself at least two weeks before you squeeze something brilliant from a computer.

✔ Part V of this book covers software in a general sense.

Dealing with other hardware

You may have purchased other hardware goodies, each waiting for setup. Put them on hold for now. Later chapters go into detail on using devices like a mouse, modem, fax, or scanner. The idea here is not to overwhelm you with too much computer stuff right away. Learning what you have set up already will take time enough.

✔ Hardware is added either internally or externally to the computer.

✔ Installing internal hardware requires some type of computer nerd. True, you can do it yourself. Many books and magazine articles go into the details, if you want to bother with installing internal hardware. My advice is force someone else to do it.

✔ OK, if you're bold, you can do it yourself. Check out *Upgrading and Fixing PCs For Dummies,* which is sort of a follow-up to this book.

✔ External hardware requires a power cable and some type of cable to connect it with the PC. A few devices don't use a power cable (they run on your brain waves). Also, you need special software to run the external hardware; a scanner requires scanning software, and a modem requires communications software. These and even more baffling concepts are covered in Part IV of this book.

Chapter 3

Compuspiel
(The PC Jargon Roundup)

• •

• •

*Y*ou know you're a computer owner when . . . you refer to your spouse as a *peripheral*. Or maybe you call your son building a Lincoln Log structure a *child process*. You say your boss has no *CPU*. Or maybe your mother-in-law is all *output* and no *input.*

Computer terms fill the indexes of boring manuals and pop up in the conversations of computer geeks. Now that you have a PC, you'll start using the terms, too — just like sick people speak in medical terms they wouldn't have known weeks ago: lacerated basal phalanx for a severed toe, thrombophlebitis for a blood clot in the leg, spasmodic torticollis for a stiff neck, and on and on. Only now you can do it, too, and have nothing seriously wrong with you.

ASCII

ASCII is an acronym, but that's not important. What is important is how you pronounce it. ASCII is pronounced *ask-ee* (similar to nasty). It is not pronounced *ask-2*.

You'll typically find ASCII used to describe something that's text-only. For example, an ASCII file contains pure text, numbers, and common punctuation symbols. It doesn't contain italics, fancy headlines, or pictures of clowns.

- ✔ Most word processors and other programs permit you to save a file in an ASCII, or plain text, format. Because ASCII means that the text is stripped down to its bare essentials, an ASCII file can be read by most other programs and computers.

- ✔ Windows typically refers to the ASCII format as a "text document" or "text-only."

- ✔ Why not save all data files in ASCII format? Because ASCII is too limiting. Word processors stick their own special codes into ASCII files to simplify formatting and other chores. Plus, ASCII only applies to text and numbers. It's useless for graphics and similar information.

- ✔ ASCII stands for the American Standard Code for Information Interchange. It's a set of numbers (0 through 127), each of which is assigned to a letter of the alphabet (both upper- and lowercase), the numerals 0 through 9, punctuation symbols, other weird characters, and 32 special control codes that represent keys on the keyboard, such as Enter, Backspace, Tab, Esc, and so on, and aren't you bored now?

Default

A horrid word, usually associated with your mortgage, default really means "here's what happens when you don't do anything." In a way, it's what happens when you don't pay your mortgage. On a computer, it's what happens when you don't make any choices and blindly obey the computer's suggestion.

I hate the word *default*. Computer nerds and manuals use it thusly:

```
The Print Very Tiny Text option is on by default.
```

Or:

```
The default colors are red with a green background.
```

Where did ASCII come from?

In the mid-1960s, programmer types created ASCII to be a universal language, like Esperanto, but with a big-business-sized marketing budget. The programmers decided to limit the number of ASCII characters to 128. At the time, this was a good-sized number (huge, in fact); most computers at the time could efficiently handle values of 128. (Today's PCs deal with 256-sized values on up.)

The idea was that any ASCII-compatible computer could exchange files and information with other ASCII-compatible computers, even if the two computers came from different home planets. This idea still works today. You can take an ASCII file from an IBM type of computer and magically beam it into a Macintosh, and the file still looks more or less the same. (Nothing is perfect, however, and the end result always requires additional work; don't get your hopes up.)

This means, if the computer were to have its way, it would make these selections, thinking that everything would be aesthetically pleasing to you.

- ✔ If you ever want to choose the default option, just press the Enter key.

- ✔ Basically, the default option or choice is the option that works best for 99 percent of the people using the program. So, if you just press the Enter key instead of fiddling around, the program automatically makes the right choice. Supposedly.

- ✔ The *default* option is similar to the *any* key in that neither of them appears on the keyboard.

- ✔ Default can also mean *standard option* or *what to select when you don't have a clue*. For example, small children pinch each other by default.

Data

If you need to use the words *information* or *stuff* and you have a computer, you say *data* instead.

The only major cultural crime committed here is pronouncing data incorrectly. It's *DAY-ta*. Say it like someone from the Northeast would say *waiter,* but with a D instead of a W.

Do not pronounce data as DADDA. Your DADDA is married to your MOMMA.

Documents

Documents are special types of files created by word processors. They're written things — stuff you can print and send to people: memos, letters, chapters from a book, reports, essays, mail you'll regret you sent later, and so on. Anything a word processor produces is a document kind of file.

✔ Non-word processing software may refer to the files it creates as documents as well. It just sounds more professional than data file or "that thing I did in CorelDRAW!"

✔ Spreadsheets create worksheets, which might also be called documents.

DOS Prompt

In Windows 95, the DOS Prompt is the name of the program that used to be your PC's operating system. Now it's relegated to being yet another window on the screen, a text-based way to control the computer and run old, decrepit DOS programs.

The DOS prompt itself consists of the strange and confusing characters you see at the beginning of each line while you're working with DOS. It's the computer's way of prompting you to tell it what to do.

The DOS prompt usually looks like this:

```
C:\>
```

✔ You type commands at the DOS prompt to make the computer do something useful.

✔ The letter in the prompt usually tells you what disk drive you're currently raiding.

✔ This book rarely touches the subject of DOS. For that information, I recommend checking out the all-time bestseller *DOS For Dummies,* or if you're using Windows 95, check out *DOS For Dummies, Windows 95 Edition,* both of which are written by me and available from IDG Books Überwelt.

Files

A file is a collection of information (hey: *data*) stored by the computer. There are different types of files, each storing different types of stuff:

Program files contain instructions for the computer to do something useful, like balance a checkbook.

Data files contain the stuff you create, like a letter to Ms. Manners or a picture of your office falling into a bubbling pit of molten lead.

Text (hey: *ASCII*) files contain plain ol' boring text.

- ✔ They didn't have to call them *files*. They could have called them *packets* or *cubbies* or *containers* or *reticules*. But they called them files. (Probably because computers are used mostly in offices.)

- ✔ Files are ethereal. You can't pick up and hold a file. You can hold the disk that contains the file (or files). And you can print a file and then hold the sheaf of papers. But you can't touch a file. In a way, they're like angels.

- ✔ The name given to a file is referred to as the *filename*.

- ✔ You must come up with your own names for the files you create. If the program refuses to accept your creative filename, you're probably in or treading dangerously close to the Forbidden Filenames Zone. Turn to Chapter 9 quickly, before the beating of the drums reaches fever pitch.

Function keys (a.k.a. F-keys)

Your keyboard has various zones and areas, just like various neighborhoods around big cities. There are alphanumeric, numeric, cursor, and function neighborhoods. (And there are empty spaces, too, just like around Indianapolis.)

Some of the keys in the top row on your keyboard are labeled F1 through F12. These are your keyboard's *function keys*. They're called that because they have no standard purpose, not like the P key which produces some sort of P when you press it (unless you're eating potato chips and a crumb lodges under the P key).

IBM's designers left the purpose of each function key open, so whichever program you're using may do something different with these keys. In Windows, however, the F1 key always displays help. But that's the only key that's the same; other programs may use F2 through F12 for something entirely weird.

GUI

GUI is yet another computer acronym. It's pronounced *gooey*, as in *ooey GUI rich and chewy*. GUI stands for Graphical User Interface and means that you control the computer through pictures and symbols on the computer's screen. This process is the opposite of typing in text commands at a DOS prompt. Supposedly it's easier, but the jury's still out.

To use a GUI, you need a pretty powerful PC. Today's models are up to the task, but a few years back PCs lacked the graphics horsepower to display a GUI properly. That, and you need a mouse to make everything work right.

- ✔ Where did the term GUI come from? Who knows. Read the mountains of legal paperwork, or take a software attorney to lunch.

- ✔ After you pronounce GUI as *gooey* a few times, you'll be able to stifle the urge to giggle. That urge will return when you pronounce the plural, *gooeys.*

- ✔ Some popular GUIs are Windows, OS/2, the Macintosh MultiFinder, and NeXTstep.

Hard Copy (Getting Hard Copy)

Hard copy is information printed on a piece of paper; *to get hard copy* means to print information. When someone tells you to get a hard copy of it, that person means for you to print it. The reason is obvious. No one wants to lug around the computer so people can see what's on the screen.

The term hard copy has been commonplace in newspaper offices since the late 1800s. When the Morse code operator heard something juicy coming over the wire, the operator told the editor, who whirled around and barked, "Get me a hard copy of that, Beemis, pronto!" Beemis (not his real name) then handed the editor a printed copy of the information he previously heard as dashes and dots. The term's association with the tabloid journalism of the 1890s gives it a somewhat steamy connotation, leading to irrelevant TV shows of the current period.

✔ Some people make a hard copy of anything they create. That way, when the computer dies unexpectedly, they still have something to show for their efforts.

✔ Hard copy can be anything from a single page to an entire book that spews from the printer.

✔ For more information about hard copies, refer to Chapter 16.

Hardware

A computer's hardware is the part of the PC you can actually touch: the console, printer, floppy disks, and monitor (which shows fingerprints, so don't touch it just to test me out).

Coined in the 1500s by burly blacksmiths, hardware refers to any physical tool. In the '60s, nerd programmers decided to call programs software (the opposite of hardware), since they were out to prove their masculinity or something.

✔ Hardware either lives inside the computer or comes with a cable that plugs into the computer.

✔ By itself, hardware does nothing but drive up the electricity bill. Hardware needs software to tell it what to do.

IBM Compatible

IBM stands for International Business Machines, the huge company that specialized in making huge computers for other huge companies. When IBM saw how much money tiny Apple computer was making with tiny Apple computers in the mid-1970s, IBM wanted a piece of the action.

They were successful. Many copied IBM's success and labeled their computers, components, and software *IBM compatible*. That meant the computer worked just like IBM's; the components could work in an IBM computer, or the software could run just like IBM's stuff.

Today the phrase isn't as popular as it used to be. It's being replaced by DOS compatible or Windows compatible, though that's essentially describing the same thing everyone used to call IBM compatible.

✔ Clone was another term used to describe an IBM-compatible computer. It usually implied a cheaper, non-name compatible. The term is often considered an insult.

✔ IBM dominated the computer market until about 1985. Ever since then, IBM's slice of the pie has been small. However, 80 percent of all computers sold are IBM compatible.

Icon

Father Murphy would certainly freak if you told him you were *clicking on icons,* yet that's just what you do on a computer running a GUI. (See "GUI" earlier in this chapter.)

Computer geeks needed a name for the symbols in a GUI. Those symbols often represent something greater, so they called them icons.

✔ These icons have nothing to do with icons you may see hanging in a Greek Orthodox church. (There's a big difference between Greeks and geeks.)

✔ In case you really don't know: Icons are pictures of the saints. They typically hang in churches, though I have an icon of St. Jude on my computer.

✔ St. Jude is the patron saint of those who believe their situation to be hopeless.

Key Combination

Chapter 15 discusses using your keyboard and includes more on this subject. For now, a key combination is when you press two or more keys at once. You do this all the time when you press Shift+S to get a capital S. With the computer, there are three shift keys: Shift, Alt, and Ctrl. Pressing those keys in combination with other keys is called a key combination.

Pressing your forehead against the keyboard is called exhaustion.

Kilobyte and Megabyte

Bytes are confusing, but they don't have to be. A byte is merely computerspeak for a storage place that holds only one character. The term *kilo* means 1,000, so one *kilobyte* is roughly 1,000 bytes, about 1,000 characters, or a little less than half of a page of text or a statewide Shriners' convention.

The term *mega* means one million or 1,000,000. One *megabyte* is 1,000 kilobytes, so it is about 1,000,000 characters or somewhere close to 500 pages or an Idaho full of Shriners.

- ✔ Kilobyte is commonly abbreviated as K.
- ✔ Megabyte is commonly abbreviated as MB.

Macintosh

The very first computer with personality was the Macintosh. Your PC, it doesn't have personality. It's a serious business machine. Apple, who makes the Macintosh, spends millions each year trying to convince the general public its computer is for business. Yeah. Right.

Seriously, the Macintosh is just a different computer. It has a GUI, like Windows, plus a lot of fun and interesting software. But it's not as popular, and therefore isn't as widely supported, as your PC.

Read this stuff only if you want to be precise

OK, confession time. One kilobyte does not equal 1,000 bytes or characters. It's really 1,024 bytes. The extra 24 bytes are actually a tax levied by Congress. Seriously, 1,024 is the number 2 raised to the 10th power — 2^{10}. Computers just love the number 2, and 1,024 is the closest power of 2 to 1,000. It's OK for us humans to think that 1K = 1,000. The extra change does, however, add up over time.

Likewise, 1MB equals 1,048,576 bytes, not an even million. One megabyte is actually 1,024K, which means that you have 1,024 multiplied by 1,024 to give you one mega of bytes. This stuff, like the concept of a million dollars, is all trivial.

> ✔ Macintosh people call their computers Macs instead of PCs.
>
> ✔ And since Mac people paid a lot more for their computers, they take it really personal when you attack them — even when you're more than justified and the facts stack up like the pancakes at an IHOP.
>
> ✔ News flash! As this book goes to press, Apple computer is up for sale. Will the Macintosh go the way of the Betamax as a standard of days gone by?

Multimedia

Treat *multimedia* as nothing more than a buzzword. Simply put, a multimedia PC is one with sound, a CD-ROM drive, and enough graphics sizzle to play television-like videos on the screen.

Many of today's PCs qualify as multimedia systems, though sound and a CD-ROM drive are still options for most. It's a big deal if you plan on playing games or using any educational software (or if you plan on creating multimedia presentations and fun stuff).

Multitasking

To multitask is to do more than one thing at a time. For example, when you're on the phone, cooking dinner, looking at the TV, and fending off a small child, you're multitasking; you're doing four — or more — things at once. Computers can do that with no problem and without losing track of the conversation, burning dinner, or putting food in baby's ear.

Multitasking is really a job for the computer's *operating system* (see below). All computer hardware can multitask; it takes software to make it do so.

Multitasking doesn't seem obvious or even useful to many first-time PC users. The reason is simple: You're only one person, you have only one set of eyes and hands. Your computer has only one keyboard and one monitor. What's the point of trying to do several things at once?

Ah, the secret: A lot of the time you spend using the computer is spent waiting. You wait for the database to sort. You wait for a graphic image to redraw itself; you wait for the computer to copy a file. But with multitasking, all this stuff can happen *while you're doing something else*. That's the beauty of it.

✔ With a multitasking computer, you can move on and do something else while the computer toils at some task by itself.

✔ When you're not working on a particular program, it's said to be in the *background,* which is similar to putting something on the back burner. It continues to cook, but you don't need to pay attention to it.

✔ Whatever you're working on in a multitasking environment is said to be in the *foreground.* Just like putting something on a front burner, where it can bubble over and melt into your shoe.

✔ Windows is a multitasking operating system. You can find more information about it in Chapter 5.

Network

A network is two or more computers connected by some type of network hose and special network software that allows all the machines to stop working at once.

Seriously, networked computers can share information. They can all use one printer, for example. They can all access files and programs from common hard drives, and employees can send messages back and forth asking each other where to have lunch that day.

Here are three ways to tell whether you're on a network:

1. **Your co-workers and you can share a printer, files, or messages without getting out of your chairs.**

2. **You must log in or log out when using the computer.**

3. **When your computer stops working, *everyone* in the office screams.**

✔ If you don't have a network, forget about them.

✔ If you're in an office where two computers share a single printer and you have this thing called an A-B switch connecting them, what you really need is a network.

✔ See Chapter 10 for more networking information, if you dare.

Opening a Program or File

"Hey, Vern! Give me a can opener and some vice grips. Let's open that Excel file on your PC."

Uh, not exactly. *To open* in compuspiel means to transfer something from disk to the computer's memory; to *run* a program means to open a file on disk to work with it.

✔ You open data files by using special Open commands in your program. For example, in Windows, you open files to load them into memory.

✔ You also open program files to run them. See "Run, Execute, and Launch" later in this chapter.

✔ The old term for opening a file was *load*.

The following expressions mean exactly the same thing as opening a program:

- Executing a program
- Running a program
- Starting a program
- Loading up a program
- Booting up a program
- Launching a program

Operating System

An operating system is software that controls your computer. It's the main piece of software. The head honcho. The big cheese. The software all other software bows to. Major kowtow to the operating system.

Both your PC's hardware and software must be controlled by an operating system. There are three popular flavors: DOS, Windows, and OS/2.

DOS (where the OS stands for Operating System) is the granddaddy of them all. It's old, cryptic, text-oriented, slow, and limited, with the added plus that they don't make it anymore. (Well, Microsoft doesn't make it, but IBM still does. Sorta.)

Windows used to be a DOS program. Presently, however, Microsoft decided Windows should wing it alone as an operating system. It's less cryptic than DOS, tries to be fun to use, and ends up being about as manageable as a 40-pound carry-on bag in a commuter plane (but it's pretty).

Windows 95? See "Windows."

OS/2 (where the OS actually stands for Operating System) was designed by Microsoft and IBM to replace DOS. Then Microsoft got mad at IBM and decided that Windows would replace DOS. Whatever. IBM decided OS/2 was still good, so they push it to this day. It has a lot of virtue but a relatively small following.

 ✔ This book concentrates on Windows, specifically Windows 95. If you haven't yet upgraded, you will! Not that I'm nuts about Windows 95 either, but when an 800-pound gorilla wants you to eat a dirt clod, you eat it (if you gather my drift).

Quit, Exit, and Close

Just as programs can be started up, they can be turned off. But you don't do so by flipping the computer's power switch, no matter how tempting this idea may be. Instead, you must find the way the program meant for you to quit.

The manual helps. If you have one, look in the index for the word *exit*. Or, if you have a computer guru nearby, you can slowly wave the manual high above your head.

 ✔ Nearly all Windows programs quit using the last command in the first menu, which is typically the File⇨Exit command.

 ✔ When the program leaves the screen, it leaves you in Windows.

 ✔ Remember to save your work before exiting a program.

 ✔ Part of the joy of Windows is that you don't really have to quit a program when you're done. You can instead *minimize* it, or shrink it down to unobtrusiveness. That temporarily gets it out of the way so you can do something else. (All this is covered in Chapter 6.)

The following phrases all describe leaving a program:

- Exiting a program
- Quitting a program
- Getting out of a program

- Returning to Windows
- Closing the program's window
- Bag this junk, and let's get a pizza

RAM or Memory

RAM and *memory* are two interchangeable terms. They both refer to temporary storage inside the computer. Regardless of whatever it is technically, you should know that the more RAM or memory you have, the more the computer can do. More RAM is better than less RAM, and a Dodge RAM beats the pants off a Ford truck any day of the week.

- ✔ More memory means that you can do more than with less memory.

- ✔ Replace the word *memory* with *money* in the preceding item and read the sentence again.

- ✔ RAM stands for random-access memory. Specially, it refers to the type of chips inside the computer where information is stored.

Run, Execute, and Launch

Running a program means working with it so you can do something useful. You can run 1-2-3, you can execute 1-2-3, and you can launch 1-2-3. These are three confusing terms for the same thing.

- ✔ You run a program by starting it in Windows. This can be done by double-clicking the mouse on the program's icon or by plucking the program's name from the pop-up Start menu.

- ✔ *Run* is the most common term, but some manual writers say *execute* since the thought of putting 1-2-3 before a firing squad is so emotionally satisfying.

Save

Saving is the process of telling the computer to transfer the information you just created to a disk for storage and safekeeping. Therefore, *save your data* has nothing to do with religious conviction.

✔ When you save something to disk, you can reload it later to work on it again. If you don't save, you'll have to re-create it all over again from scratch.

✔ If you don't tell the computer to save your work, it won't do so automatically.

✔ Actually, Quicken does save your work automatically. It's the only program I know of that does that without any effort on your behalf.

✔ After you learn how to save your work, try to save it every five minutes or so. Some programs even offer an Automatic-save feature that automatically saves your work every few minutes or just after the power goes out.

Send to the Printer

When you send something to the printer, it means you're telling the program to send the results of your work through a cable to a printer, the mechanical thing nearby that always runs out of paper. *Send to the printer* is another confusing term that means the same thing as *get hard copy*.

✔ When you send something to the printer, you don't take it to Kinko's or Insty-Prints. You tell the computer to transfer the information from its screen to its own printer, usually sitting no more than 20 feet away.

✔ Printers never waste paper until you turn them on.

✔ If you send something to the printer and the printer just sits there, wait a few moments. Then try turning the printer on.

✔ Refer to Chapter 16 for more information on printers.

Software

Software is a set of instructions that tells the computer how to do things. It's intangible; you can't see it. You can only see where it's stored or its results.

✔ Software comes on a disk, but the disk itself isn't the software. The software is the information stored on the disk.

✔ The computer's software controls the computer's hardware — physical things (like the printer) that you can actually touch and smell and taste if you have big, sharp teeth.

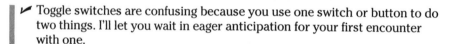

Technical tidbits I'd skip if I were you

Actually, the software is the instructions stored on the disk, the medium is the floppy disk, and the hardware is the floppy disk drive. With a compact disc (CD), the software is the music itself, the medium is the CD, and the hardware is the CD player. With a radio, the software is the sound, the medium is the airwaves, and the hardware is the radio itself. With a VCR, the software is the movie, the medium is the — well, you get the idea.

Toggle

In compuspiel, when something is a toggle, that means it has two settings, one of which is on and the other is off. If you activate the toggle, it switches from one setting to the other, like a toggle switch. I suppose that's where they got the term. Anyway, don't boggle over toggle.

> ✔ Toggle switches are confusing because you use one switch or button to do two things. I'll let you wait in eager anticipation for your first encounter with one.

Version

Software changes. Bugs are ironed out, things are improved, and new features are added. To keep track of the changes, software developers slap version numbers onto their software.

The first version of a program is known as version 1.0, called version one-point-oh. A minor improvement would make version 1.1 (one-point-one). A major improvement would start all over again with 2.0 (two-point-oh).

A version number helps you keep track of how old or recent your software is. It's especially important with your operating system. For example, some programs will not run on the older version of Windows, version 3.0 (three-point-oh). Some programs only run on version 3.1 (three-point-one). Some only run on Windows 95, which is actually a fancy name for Windows 4.0 (four-point-oh).

✔ The software version number is usually listed on the box, though with some programs (such as Windows 95), you have to tell the program to display that information.

✔ Most people avoid the point-oh version of software: 1.0, 2.0, 3.0, and so on. Major release numbers typically have bugs and other problems that aren't fixed until the 1.1, 2.1, or 3.1 release.

Windows

The current and most popular operating system for the PC is Windows, lovingly cobbled together by Microsoft. Windows was designed to replace the ugly and nonintuitive DOS prompt with a beautiful and nonintuitive graphical user interface (see GUI).

It's called Windows because it fills the screen with overlapping windows — boxlike areas containing their own programs or other information. The graphics also represent what you create more accurately than DOS's boring text screen. For example, you can type a document in your word processor and see it on the screen pretty much the same way as it prints.

✔ Windows, with an initial capital letter, refers to the Windows program itself. The lowercase version, windows, refers to the boxlike areas on-screen.

✔ Windows 95 is really Windows version 4.0. It's the current version of Windows around which this book is geared.

✔ A special jumbo version of Windows, Windows NT, works for big companies with big computers and big networks and big dollars.

✔ Windows wasn't inspired by the Macintosh. Nope. No way. And Microsoft has lots of lawyers on retainer who will make you agree.

Part II
Using Your PC (If You Already Own One)

The 5th Wave   By Rich Tennant

"COMPATABILITY? NO PROBLEM. THIS BABY COMES IN OVER A DOZEN DESIGNER COLORS."

In this part...

No one frets over using a TV. There are two knobs (or were at one time): the on-off-volume knob and the channel changer. Push-button phones? No problem: Punch in the number and it rings on the other end. No Enter key. No setup.

No wonder computers can be such a pain in the neck. Too many buttons! No dials! Nothing that says, "Pay attention to me and ignore everything else."

The chapters in this part of the book are designed to familiarize you with the computer — how to turn it on and get it to do something. Truly, that's the only stuff you need to know. Everything else is for show.

Chapter 4

The Big Red Switch

In This Chapter

▶ How to turn the computer on

▶ What happens after you flip the Big Red Switch

▶ How to log in to the network

▶ How to get the Windows tip-of-the-day

▶ How to turn the computer off

▶ Whether or not to leave your PC on all the time

▶ How to reset or reboot your computer

Should turning something on or off be complicated? Of course not. But then again, a computer isn't known for being the most logical of devices. Heck, you'd think the computer would have several on and off switches just to make it tough on you. But no.

The truth is that there's just one Big Red Switch that makes the PC stop or go. Of course, the switch is often neither red nor big, but that's not a big deal. What is a big deal is when and how to throw the switch and all the stuff that happens in between. That's what'll make you pull your hair out in clumps or chant a mantra while clutching your New Age Power Crystal in one hand and flipping the power switch with the other.

Well, fret no more. This chapter covers the basics of turning a computer on, covers what happens just after that, and then doesn't neglect the important stuff about turning the computer off. A lot happens as Mr. PC begins his sunshiny day. Oh — and this is definitely worth $6 of the cover price — this chapter tells you the lowdown on whether or not you can let your computer run all day and all night without ever turning it off. (Yes, it can be done.)

Turning the Computer On

Turning a computer on is as easy as reaching for that big red switch and flipping it to the ON position. Some computers may have their big red switch in front, and some have the switch on the side. Still other computers may even paint their big red switch brown or fawn-white, or it may be one of those push-button jobbies.

- ✔ In keeping with the international flavor of computing, computer companies have done away with the illogical, Western-culture-dominated habit of putting the words *ON* and *OFF* on their on/off switches. To be more politically correct, the PC's switch uses a bar for ON and a circle for OFF (go back and see Figure 1-3 to refresh your own memory banks).

- ✔ If you can't see the screen, wait awhile. If nothing appears, turn the monitor on.

- ✔ If the computer won't turn on, check to see whether it's plugged in. If it still doesn't come on, refer to Chapter 24, "When to Scream for Help."

- ✔ Two nerdy terms for turning on a computer: Power-on and power-up.

- ✔ If the computer does something unexpected or if you notice that it's being especially unfriendly, first panic. Then turn to Part VI of this book to figure out what went wrong.

- ✔ Make sure that a disk isn't in drive A when you start the computer. If a disk is in floppy disk drive A, the computer won't start from the hard drive like it's supposed to. Keep drive A empty. (Some people keep a disk in drive A because it looks cool; don't be a fool. Just say no to disks in drive A when you boot the computer.)

- ✔ See Chapter 7 for more information about drive A.

Technical stuff to ignore

Your computer has many plug-inable items attached to it. Each one of them has its own on/off switch. There is no specific order to follow when turning any equipment on or off, though an old adage was "Turn the computer box on last." Or was it first? I don't remember. But one way to save the hassle is to buy a power strip or one of the fancier computer power-control-center devices. You plug everything into it and then turn on the whole shebang with one switch.

"The manual tells me to boot my computer: Where do I kick it?"

Oh, don't be silly. Booting a computer has nothing to do with kicking it. Instead, booting simply refers to turning on a computer. *To boot a computer* means to turn it on. Rebooting a computer is the same as pressing the Reset button. It's all weird nerd talk.

Look! Up on the screen!

Heavenly choirs rejoice! Windows 95 is here!

Of course, you don't see Windows 95 right away. First comes some text. Then a few fragments and whatnot, a copyright notice, and maybe you'll catch the following — Windows 95's only text screen message, bidding farewell to the way PCs used to work:

```
Starting Windows 95 . . .
```

After that, the PC goes graphical. You may see more bits of text fly by, like the closing credits of a movie (but don't bother looking for the Dolly Grip or Best Boy).

✔ Starting the computer with the Big Red Switch is the mechanical part. What you're starting is the computer hardware, which is really nothing but a lot of heavy, cold, and calculating electronic junk that the cat likes to sleep on. Eventually, your computer's software actually brings the computer to life, allowing it to do something. With Windows 95, you see the "Windows in the clouds" scene, which is only meant to entertain you while Windows seemingly takes several weeks to get out of bed.

"My computer says 'Non-system disk.' What gives?"

This happens a lot, even to Bill Gates!

```
Non-system disk or disk error
Replace and strike any key when ready
```

Remove the floppy disk from drive A and press the Enter key. Your computer will then start normally.

The reason you see the message is that you or someone else has left a floppy disk in your PC's A drive. The computer has tried to start itself using software on that disk and — whaddya know? — no software is on that disk! The software (your PC's operating system) is really on your PC's hard drive, which can't be loaded until you remove that dern floppy disk from drive A and whack the Enter key.

And just who the heck are you?

Windows seems pretty easy to get into; it's doing all the work! But if your PC is shackled to a network, you'll be forced to show some ID before getting into the good stuff. Apparently, you can't buy liquor or drive a computer without proper identification.

The Enter Network Password dialog box, as shown in Figure 4-1, is Windows' way of gently asking, "Just who the heck are you?" You type in your special user name, press the Tab key, and then type your password. Click the OK button, and Windows lets you in.

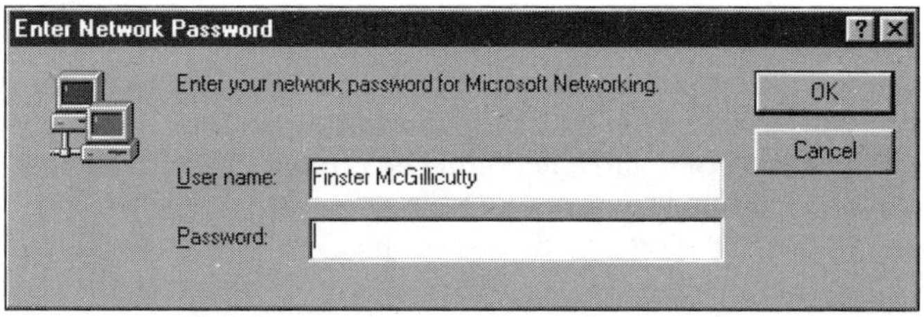

Figure 4-1:
Windows
meekly asks
for a
password.

> **Enter Network Password**   [? X]
>
> Enter your network password for Microsoft Networking.   [OK]
>
> [Cancel]
>
> User name: [Finster McGillicutty   ]
>
> Password: [   ]

If you type the wrong password, the security alarms sound, a metal gate drops over you and the PC, the hounds are released, and Windows dutifully erases the hard drive lest security be breached.

Just kidding! If you goof up, you get a second shot. If you goof up again, Windows lets you in anyway.

✔ Windows probably already knows your user name and displays it proudly for you, as in Figure 4-1. Your job is merely to enter the proper password.

✔ Press the Tab key to move between the User Name and Password text boxes.

- Telling the network who you are is technically called *logging in*. It has nothing to do with timber.

- Chapter 10 discusses computer networking if you want to go nuts about it.

- If this whole password/login stuff annoys you, just press the Esc key on the keyboard to bypass the feeble security.

- If they guarded the Crown Jewels as feebly as Windows guards its network, we'd all be wearing funny expensive hats.

Here's your tip of the day: Click the Close button and get to work

Microsoft must have felt they didn't make Windows easy enough. Every time you start, you'll see the cheesy Welcome to Windows dialog box. Ugh! Time for another valuable and heretofore unknown tip.

Click the Close button to rid the screen of that annoying dialog box.

- If you don't know how to work a computer mouse or figure that *point-and-click* is what you do with a gun, refer to Chapter 14 (the latter half).

- If you really never want to see the Welcome to Windows dialog box ever again, click the mouse in the box by Show this Welcome Screen next time you start Windows (see Figure 4-2). This action removes the little check mark from the box, and you'll never be bothered by it again.

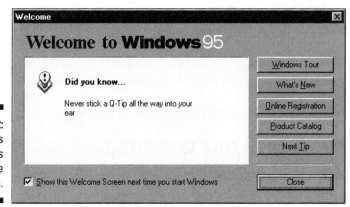

Figure 4-2:
Windows
imparts
some
wisdom.

Some "Did you know . . ." things you won't find in the Welcome dialog box

Did you know . . .   Elvis used to take a .22 and shoot flashbulbs floating in his pool while he ate watermelon hearts.

Did you know . . . $10,000 of Microsoft stock purchased in 1986 would be worth over a quarter of a million dollars today?

Did you know . . .   a chigger bite can itch like the devil.

Did you know . . .   sausage was invented by the ancient Babylonians.

Did you know . . .   the cheapest palmtop computer is a pad and pencil.

Did you know . . .   steamed skim milk with two shots of espresso in a 16-ounce cup is a "double-tall-skinny latté."

Did you know . . .   St. Nicholas is the patron saint of pawnbrokers.

Did you know . . .   in 558 Chlotar, the son of Clovis, reunited the kingdom of France.

Did you know . . .   West Quoddy Head, Maine, is the farthest eastern point in the continental United States.

Did you know . . .   a whop bop a loo bop a bop bam boom.

Did you know . . .   a porterhouse is a T-bone steak with a larger tenderloin side.

Did you know . . .   *Mad Magazine*'s Alfred E. Neuman was originally named Melvin Kosnowski.

Did you know . . .   the tomato was legally declared a vegetable by the U.S. Supreme Court. (It's actually a fruit.)

    ✔ Don't bother clicking on any button in the Welcome to Windows dialog box other than Close. If you do, you're on your own. (And you've been warned!)

It's about time this operating system showed up

After a time, and then times and half a time, Windows 95 presents itself on the screen in all its graphical goodness and glory (Figure 4-3). Windows is finally ready for you to use. Time to get to work.

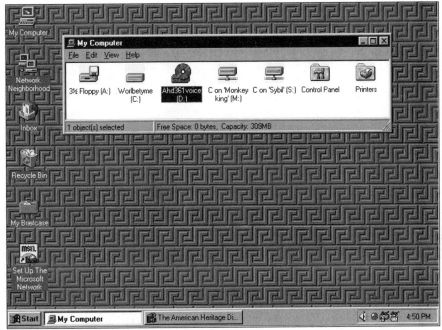

Figure 4-3:
This isn't
your father's
operating
system.

✔ Chapters 5 and 6 offer more information on Windows and getting to work.

✔ Windows really does take a while to show up on the screen, so don't be discouraged; rumor has it Samuel Beckett was working on *Waiting for Windot* before he died.[1]

[1]This is a literary reference. Beckett wrote *Waiting for Godot* (Gah-do), who never shows up.

Getting Your Work Done

Between turning your computer on and off, you should do something. Get work done.

Alas, that's the subject of the next two chapters. This is just the starting and stopping your PC chapter.

Turning the Computer Off

Sure, turning the computer off is easy: Just flip the big red switch. The power goes DINK, the fan softly warbles away, and the hard drive spins to a low hum and then stops. Unfortunately, that's just not polite enough for your computer. It's rude. Windows insists that you shut down properly, or it gets really, really sore.

Before you can feel the satisfaction of flipping that big red switch, heed these steps to properly furl Windows' sails:

1. Pop up the Start menu.

If you can see the Start button on the taskbar (look in the bottom-left corner of Figure 4-3), click on that button using your mouse.

The best and most reliable way to make the Start menu appear is to press the Ctrl+Esc key combination. This works every time, whether you can see the Start button or not.

2. Choose the Sh<u>u</u>t Down menu item.

Click on it with the mouse or press the U key, since you can't yodel without the U sound.

The Shut Down Windows dialog box appears (see Figure 4-4), filled with even more options for shutting down your PC.

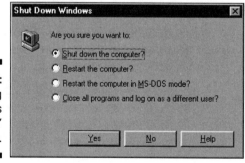

Figure 4-4:
This dialog box is Windows' exit door.

3. Click the <u>Y</u>es button.

Ignore the options! The proper one you want, `Shut down the computer`, is already selected for you.

4. Windows is outta here!

Bye-bye.

✔ If you haven't saved any information in any programs, you'll be told about it. Go ahead and save everything.

✔ If you've been running some older DOS programs, the whole operation stops. You must quit your DOS programs *before* you shut down Windows. (It's a sibling-rivalry thing.) Refer to your DOS program's manual or a proper...*For Dummies* book near you.

Eventually, after more disk commotion than seems necessary, you see a screen that tells you, and I quote, "It's now safe to turn off your computer." Look Ma, no sparks!

5. **Flip the big red switch off.**

Click. You're done.

✔ Yes, you shut down by first pressing the Start button. Such logic.

✔ Keyboard shortcut to shutting down Windows 95: Ctrl+Esc, U, Enter. Ah, such lovely little keystrokes to quell the beast. But remember, Windows merely sleeps. It comes back to life again when you restart the computer.

✔ Never turn off the computer when you're in the middle of something. Always quit your programs, and then shut down Windows properly. The only time you can safely turn off your PC is when the screen tells you that it's *safe* to do so. An exception to this is when your computer has gone totally AWOL. When that happens, refer to Part VI of this book.

✔ If you are used to DOS (where you could shut down the computer any-time), be wary of seeing that friendly C:\> on the screen and thinking "Golly, it's OK to shut down the computer now." Not so with Windows 95! You must first *quit* DOS, which you do by typing the EXIT command:

```
C> EXIT
```

This makes your DOS prompt vanish, and, lo, you're back in Windows.

✔ If Windows detects any unsaved programs as it quits, it will ask you to save them. For DOS programs, Windows will beg you to save them and actually refuse to quit: Go ahead and save your DOS stuff; then quit your DOS programs; then repeat the steps in this section before you flip the big red switch.

✔ It's a good idea to wait at least 30 to 40 seconds before turning the com-puter on again. This gives the computer's hard drives time to slow down and stop. (Basically, it's just a bad idea to flip the PC's power switch rapidly from on to off to on again.)

✔ If possible, try not to turn the computer off more than three times a day. My advice is to leave the machine on all day and, if you really want to turn it off, turn it off only at night. However, there is a school of thought that recommends leaving the computer on all the time. If that's your cup of java, refer to the next section.

"I want to leave my computer on all the time"

The great debate rages: Should you leave your computer on all the time? Well, anyone who knows anything will tell you "Yes." Leave your computer on all the time, 24 hours a day, 7 days a week, 14 days a week on the planet Mars. The only time you should really turn a system off is when it will be unused for longer than a weekend.

Computers like being on all the time. You leave your refrigerator on all night or when you're away on trips, so why not the PC? It won't raise your electrical bill much, either.

The only thing you should be careful about is turning the monitor off when you're away from the computer. Switching the monitor off avoids the perils of phosphor burn-in, or what happens when a computer is left on too long and retains an image of Lotus 1-2-3 (or whatever you use a lot) on the screen — even when the system is off. Turning off the monitor while you're away solves this problem.

✔ Screen-dimming programs (screen savers) can *blank out* your monitor after the PC has been idle for a given amount of time. Windows has one located in the Control Panel. From the Start menu, choose Settings⇨Control Panel and then open the Display icon by double-clicking on it with the mouse. Click on the Screen Saver tab and do whatever is necessary there, which I don't have time to explain all here.

✔ If you do leave your computer on all the time, don't put it under a dust cover. The dust cover will give the computer its very own greenhouse effect and bring the temperatures inside the system way past the sweltering point and annoy Al Gore.

Resetting Your PC

Resetting your computer is a way to turn it off and on again without having to actually do that (and it's healthier for the PC than kicking the power cord out of the wall, despite the satisfying feeling that gives you). When you reset, you're restarting the computer while it's on.

You can reset in two ways: If your computer has a reset switch, you can push it. Ka-chinka! The computer stops whatever it's doing (or not doing) and starts all over again.

The reason for leaving your computer on, if you care to know

There are lots of interesting reasons why you should leave a computer on all the time. One is that the initial process of turning a computer on is a tremendous jolt to the system. It's often said that you subtract one day from the computer's life each time you switch the system off and then on. But who knows?

The truth is, leaving the computer on all the time keeps the temperature inside the box even. When you turn the system off, the electrical components cool. Turn the PC on again, and the components heat right back up. (The system's fan will keep them from getting too hot.) It's that temperature change from turning the system off

and on that causes the damage. After a time, the solder joints become brittle, and they crack. That's when the real problems occur. By leaving your PC on all the time — or just by minimizing the times you turn it off and on — you can prolong its life.

An opposing school of thought claims that, although the preceding is true, leaving the computer on all the time wears down the bearings in your hard drive and causes the cooling fan to poop out prematurely. So be nice to your hard drive's packed bearings and turn the PC off once a day. Ack! You just can't win. (I leave all my computers on all the time, if you care to know.)

The second way to reset is to press the Ctrl, Alt, and Delete keys at the same time. You need to do this twice in a row in Windows, since Windows doesn't like you to press Ctrl+Alt+Delete, reasons for which I'll get into in the next section.

- Ctrl+Alt+Delete is known as the three-finger salute, or *control-alt-delete*.

- A reset is often called a *warm boot*. This is like a cold boot that has been sitting in front of the furnace all night.

- As with turning a computer off, you shouldn't reset while the disk drive light is on or while you are in an application (except when the program has flown south). Above all, do not reset to quit an application. Always quit your programs properly and wait until Windows tells you it's safe before you turn off the computer.

- Remember to remove any floppy disks from drive A before resetting. If you leave a disk in, the computer will try to start itself from that disk.

The proper way to reset in Windows 95

Windows 95 just won't let you press Ctrl+Alt+Delete to reset. The reason is probably because it's a bad idea to reset in the middle of something — and Windows is always in the middle of something. So instead of being a reset command, Windows uses Ctrl+Alt+Delete to kill off programs that run amok.

If you press Ctrl+Alt+Delete in Windows 95, you'll see a Close Program dialog box, like the one shown in Figure 4-5. It's best not to mess with this dialog box, so click on the Cancel button or press the Esc key.

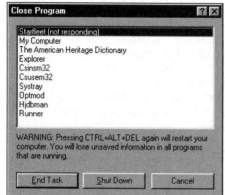

Figure 4-5:
Windows
95's Close
Window
dialog box.

✔ Don't press Ctrl+Alt+Delete in Windows unless you want to kill off a program. And if you want to kill off a program, see Chapter 25, the section "Killing Off a Program Run Amok."

✔ If you really want to reset in Windows 95, you need to use the Sh<u>u</u>t Down command, as described in the section "Turning the Computer Off," earlier in this chapter. In the Shut Down dialog box, step 2, choose the second option, <u>R</u>estart the computer.

✔ In the old version of Windows, Ctrl+Alt+Delete also killed off a program, but only the program you were currently using. This process was confusing for everyone, which is a good reason not to use Ctrl+Alt+Delete in the older version of Windows.

When to reset

Now the question arises: When should you reset? Obviously, anytime you're panicked. Personally, I only reset if the keyboard is totally locked up, and the program appears to have gone to the mall for some Mrs. Field's cookies and a soda. (Sometimes Ctrl+Alt+Delete doesn't work in these situations, so if you don't have a big reset button, you have to turn the computer off, wait, and then turn it on again.)

The only other time you really need to reset is just to start over. For example, I was experimenting with a program that made my keyboard click every time I pressed a key. There was no obvious way to turn off this annoying pestilence, so I reset.

Chapter 5

The Operating System
(Or "It Does Windows!")

. . . .

In This Chapter

▶ Exploring the reasons why there are operating systems

▶ Understanding Windows

▶ Using the taskbar

▶ Manipulating windows on the screen

▶ Working a dialog box

▶ Getting help

. . . .

*T*he PC's original operating system was DOS. But DOS was ugly, and everyone complained about it. So Microsoft gave us Windows, which is pretty, and everyone complains about it. Still, your PC needs an operating system, and Windows is probably the one you're stuck with. I know this because I've seen Bill Gate's planner and it says, in the section on taking over the world, step 9, "Get everyone to use Windows 95."

This book specifically covers Windows 95. The following tidbits of text will help get you oriented with your PC's operating system, whether you have it or not, whether you like it or not.

> ✔ The emphasis of this book is on using your PC and not really Windows 95. If you want more information or specifics, get *Windows 95 For Dummies* by my pal Andy Rathbone, available from IDG Books Komputerweltindasüberomerschwietsenkobberomff.

"Why the Heck Do I Need an Operating System?"

I've always figured operating systems were unnecessary. In fact, the first thing I did when I got my very first DOS computer was type `ERASE DOS`, just to see what would happen.

Nothing happened.

Well, I got a `File not found` error. Lucky for me, DOS didn't get erased.

DOS, like Windows, is an operating system. It's necessary to run your computer. It's the software that controls everything, all the hardware. Additionally, your PC's operating system is what dishes up applications programs for you — serving them to you like a waiter in a restaurant. You choose Word Processing from a menu, and the operating system runs that program. Simple. Maybe even fun.

- ✔ Your primary duty with Windows is to tell it to run your software. This task is covered in the next chapter.

- ✔ As a secondary duty, you use Windows to manage the many files and documents you create. That's another aspect of an operating system: organizing all your computer junk and storing it properly on the hard drive. This subject is covered in Chapter 9.

- ✔ The tertiary (meaning *third*) duty of Windows is to run your computer. This is the geeky aspect, the thing that drives too many people over the edge. Might be covered in this book. Might not. I haven't made up my mind.

Windows, Your PC's Real Brain

The main program in charge of your PC is Windows. Ideally (which means this could never happen in real life), a computer's operating system should be quiet and efficient, never getting in the way, and carrying out your instructions like a dutiful and grateful servant.

In reality, Windows is a rude little kid. It behaves like an arrogant teenager who's handsome and fun but won't tell you where he's hidden your car keys or your wallet unless you play poker with him. In other words, with Windows in charge of your PC, you must play the game by Windows' rules.

Where is the desktop?

Windows works graphically. It shows you graphical images, or *icons,* representing everything inside your computer. These graphics are all pasted down on a background called the *desktop*. In Figure 5-1, the desktop has the famous Windows Clouds background.

You control everything using your computer's mouse. The mouse controls the pointer on the desktop, which looks like an arrow-shaped UFO in Figure 5-1. You use the mouse and its pointer to point at things, grab them, drag them around, punch 'em, scratch 'em 'till they bleed, and mousey things like that.

Oh, you can also use the keyboard, but graphical operating systems like Windows love mice more than keyboards.

✔ The desktop is merely the background on which Windows shows you its stuff — like an old sheet you hang from the wall to bore your neighbors with your Cayman Islands vacation slide show.

✔ The little pictures are called *icons.*

✔ Figure 5-1 shows what Windows may look like. On your computer it will look different (probably because your computer doesn't like you).

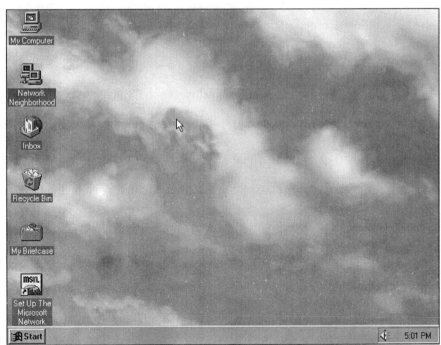

Figure 5-1:
The
Windows
desktop.

✔ Refer to the end of Chapter 14 for more information on using a mouse, including all those mouse activities and the terms associated.

✔ Using your keyboard is covered somewhat in Chapter 15.

Between labors, Hercules did not go to the taskbar

That gunboat gray strip along the bottom of the desktop is called the *taskbar.* It's the Windows main control center.

On the left end of the taskbar is the Start button. Yes, that's where you start programs in Windows. But you also shut Windows down using the Start button. Start. Stop. Microsoft can't make up its mind.

On the right end of the taskbar is the *system tray.* I like to call it the loud time because it typically looks like a speaker shouting out the current time of day. Other items may show up in the system tray (see Figure 4-3, for example). If you don't have a sound system in your PC, the speaker doesn't show up. And if you're computing on the International Date Line, the time doesn't show up either.

From time to time, buttons appear in the middle of the taskbar. Each button represents a window or program you have floating open on the desktop. Or it could represent a program you've put away or *minimized,* which is covered in the next chapter. This all means something, which I'll probably get into later.

✔ You can point the mouse at the various items in the system tray to get more information or to control them. Clicking on the items usually does something, depending on what and how you click. For example, double-click on the time and you can set the computer's clock (covered in Chapter 11).

✔ The taskbar can float on any edge of the desktop; use your mouse to drag it to the top, left, or right sides of the screen. (Point the mouse on a blank part of the taskbar to drag it.) Most folks leave it on the bottom, which is where this book assumes it lies.

The almighty Start button

Everything in Windows starts with the Start button, conveniently located on the left side of the taskbar. The Start button itself controls a pop-up menu (and sub-menus galore!), on which you'll find various commands and programs.

To pop up the Start menu, click on its button by using your mouse. Click.

If you'd rather use your keyboard, press the Ctrl+Esc key combination. This action is guaranteed to work, popping up the Start button's menu even when you can't otherwise see the Start button.

There. That's it for the Start button discussion in this chapter. For more information, see "Starting a Program in Windows 95" in the next chapter.

The My Computer and Explorer programs

The second chore of an operating system is to work with the files, documents, and other junk you have stored on your computer. Two programs tackle this job: My Computer and the Explorer.

"My taskbar is gone!"

The taskbar tends to wander. Not only can it go up, down, left, and right, but it can get fatter and skinnier, too. Sometimes it can get so skinny you can't see it anymore. All you find is a thin gray line at the bottom of the screen. This can drive you batty.

That thin gray line is still the taskbar. It's just that someone has shrunk it down to Lilliputian size. To make it thicker, hover the mouse pointer over the taskbar's edge. The mouse pointer changes to a this-way-or-that-way arrow. Then drag the taskbar to a nicer, plumper size. You can even use this trick to make the taskbar fatter when it's crowded with too many buttons.

Another way the taskbar can disappear is if you tell it to hide. This task is done in the Taskbar Properties dialog box: Right-click the mouse on the taskbar and choose Properties from the pop-up shortcut menu. In the Taskbar Properties dialog box, make sure the Auto hide option doesn't have a check mark by it (click on the box by Auto hide to remove the check mark). Click the OK button to go on your merry way.

Remember: You can always get at the Start button by pressing Ctrl+Esc. This works whether or not the taskbar is visible or sent by Houdini to some other realm.

My Computer has Macintosh written all over it. It's a program that displays information in your computer as pretty little icons, each of them grouped into folders.

You start My Computer by double-clicking on the little My Computer icon in the upper-left corner of the desktop. This effort displays a list of goodies inside your computer, primarily your disk drives. (See Figure 5-2.)

Figure 5-2:
Open My
Computer
and see
what lurks
inside
your PC.

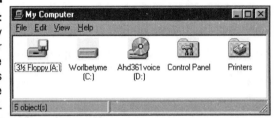

If you point at and double-click one of your system's disk drives, such as drive C:, it opens to reveal a window full of folders and icons (Figure 5-3). The icons represent files on your system. Folders can be opened (by double-clicking) to display another window chock-full of more files and folders. It can get insane!

Figure 5-3:
This window
shows you
files and
folders.

✔ You double-click on an icon to activate it. Double-clicking on some icons runs programs. For folders, the double-click opens the folder, revealing its contents.

✔ Icons represent files on your computer, which can be files you create, program files, or other files no one knows anything about.

✔ Folders are simply storage places for more icons and files.

✔ See the section "Closing a window" later in this chapter for information on closing windows opened in My Computer.

The Explorer works just like My Computer, though it displays information in a different way. (Microsoft just couldn't make up its mind, here; "Which way do we have people see files on their computers? Hey! Why not two utterly different ways!")

Start the Explorer by clicking on the Start button and choosing Programs➪ Windows Explorer from the menu.

Unlike My Computer, the Explorer has only one window (see Figure 5-4). The disk drives and folders on your computer appear on the left side of the window; files and folders appear on the right.

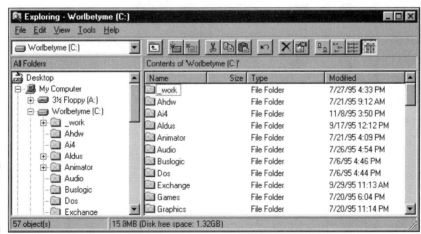

Figure 5-4:
The Explorer
in action.

OK. Enough of the Explorer. Choose File➪Close to quit the program since there's no use wasting screen real estate with something so ugly.

✔ Computer nerds prefer the Explorer. I'd recommend using My Computer first until you get used to it. Then use the Explorer, which can be quicker.

✔ My Computer and the Explorer programs will be discussed in more detail in Part III of this book.

The geeks tweak at the Control Panel

The third chore Windows accomplishes is serving as kindergarten teacher for all your computer's innards and peripherals. Those devices are controlled, coddled, and contained using the Control Panel.

The Control Panel is a folder that appears all over Windows 95. You can start it from the Start menu by choosing Settings⇨Control Panel. Or you can double-click the folder that appears in the main My Computer window (see the previous section). Either way, the Control Panel window with all its pretty icons appears, similar to what's shown in Figure 5-5.

Figure 5-5:
The Control
Panel.

Each of the icons in the Control Panel represents some aspect of your computer, something to control. By double-clicking on an icon, you see a window with more information, more controls, more chaos.

My advice: Leave this one to the experts.

Close the Control Panel's window by choosing File⇨Close from the menu.

> ✔ Various chapters in Part IV of this book will have you messing with parts of the Control Panel. Mostly, you'll leave it alone.

✔ The number of items you find in the Control Panel varies. In Figure 5-5, some extras include Accessibility Options, Find Fast, HiJaak Catalog Setup, and Tweak UI. I have no idea what most of these do. In fact, they frighten me.

Using Windows' Gizmos

Windows is a virtual F.A.O. Schwarz of fun things to play with, stuff to drive you crazy, and interesting toys over which you'll waste colossal amounts of time. There are tiny buttons you push with the mouse, graphics that slide and stretch, things to poke, and stuff that drops down. In other words, *gizmos* are on the screen, most of which control the way the windows look and how programs in Windows operate.

Changing a window's size

Your windows can be just about any size, from filling the entire screen to too small to be useful, and everything in between.

To make a window fill the entire screen — which is where it's the most useful — click the maximize button in the window's upper-right corner. (This step changes the button's full window image thing to an overlapping window image thing. Click that button again to restore the window to its original size.)

To turn a window into a mere button on the taskbar, click the *minimize* button in the upper-right corner of a window. This action shoves the window out of the way, shrinking it down into a button on the taskbar — but isn't the same as quitting. To restore the taskbar button back into a window, click on it.

When a window isn't full-screen or an icon, you can change its size by grabbing an edge with the mouse: Hover the mouse over one side of the window or a corner, press and hold the mouse button, and drag the window in or out to a new size. Release the mouse button to snap the window into place.

✔ Enlarging a window to full-screen size is called *maximizing.*

✔ Shrinking a window down into an icon is called *minimizing.*

✔ Positioning a window just so on the screen and then having Windows move it for no reason is called *frustrating.*

✔ If you use your imagination, the maximize button looks like a full-screen window and the minimize button looks like a button on the taskbar. Then again, if you use your imagination, Windows looks like a bright sunny day with green grass and birds chirping in the meadow.

Moving a window around

Windows puts its windows wherever Windows wants. To move a window to a new position, drag the window about by its title bar (the top-most strip on the window, typically above the menu bar). This is akin to the cliché of a caveman dragging his woman around by her hair. That never really happened, of course, not after the women started carrying their own clubs, anyway.

Scrolling about

Often, what you're looking at in a window is larger than the window. For example, if a tanned, svelte, and bikini-clad Claudia Schiffer (or Mel Gibson for the ladies) walked by a very tiny window in your wall, you would only be able to see a small part of her bronzed form. If you could move the window up and down the wall, you could see more of her, but only the same size as the window at a time. This is how scrolling works.

To facilitate scrolling a window around, one or two scroll bars are used. The scroll bar is a long skinny thing, with an arrow at either end and an elevator-like box in the middle, as shown here in the left margin. You use the arrows and elevator to move the window's image up or down or left or right, revealing more of the total picture.

Accessing a menu

All the commands and whatnot of the Windows application are included on a handy — and always visible — menu bar. It's usually at the top of a window, right below the title bar and down the street from Larry's Bar.

Each word on the menu bar — File, Edit, and so on — is a menu title. It represents a drop-down menu, which contains commands related to the title. For example, the File menu contains Save, Open, New, Close, and other commands related to files.

To access these commands, click the menu title with the mouse. The menu drops down. Then select a menu item or command. If you don't like what you see, click the menu title again to make the menu go away or select another menu.

    ✔ You can access the menus using your keyboard, if you like. Press the Alt or F10 key. This highlights the first menu on the menu bar. To select a menu or item in a menu, type the underlined letter, such as F for <u>F</u>ile. The letters to press are underlined in this book, just as they are in Windows.

✔ In this book, you'll see the format <u>F</u>ile⇨<u>C</u>lose used to represent menu selections. To access that command on the menu, you would press Alt,F,C.

✔ To access the <u>F</u>ile⇨<u>C</u>lose command, you could also press Alt+F (the Alt and F keys together, and then release both keys) and then C.

✔ Oh, bother. Just use your mouse. Point. Click. Click. Sheesh.

Closing a window

 Closing a program's window is the same thing as quitting the program; you make it disappear. The most common way to close a window is to click the X button in the upper-right corner of the window.

Another striking way to close a window — striking because it's obvious — is to select the E<u>x</u>it or <u>C</u>lose command from the <u>F</u>ile menu. This action also quits the program you're running.

✔ You can't quit Windows 95 by closing a window, which is how it worked in the old version of Windows. Instead, use the Sh<u>u</u>tdown command on the main Start menu. See "Turning the Computer Off" in Chapter 4 for more information.

Gizmos in a Dialog Box

A dialog box is yet another way Windows has for showing you information. In this case, the window contains gadgets and gizmos you use to control something. You use your mouse to make settings, adjust, and fine-tune, and then you click an OK button to send your choices off to Windows for proper digestion.

If all that sounds complicated, consider the old DOS prompt way of doing things:

```
C> FORMAT A: /S /U /F:144 /V:DOODYDISK
```

That's a real, honest-to-goodness, DOS command. In Windows, a dialog box lets you do something similar but in a graphical way. Figure 5-6, in fact, shows you how the same command looks.

All the doojobbies in Figure 5-6 are manipulated with the mouse. What they do isn't important right now. What the doojobbies are called is important. All the following definitions refer to Figure 5-6.

Drop-down list

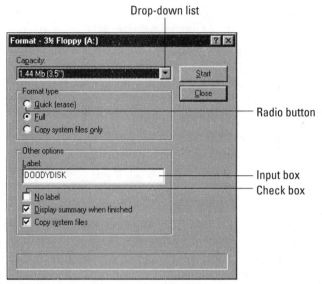

Radio button

Input box

Check box

Figure 5-6:
The Format
dialog box.

Drop-down list: Under the word `Capacity` you find a drop-down list. You drop down the list using the down-pointing arrow button to the right side of the list. This displays a list of choices, one of which you point at and click with the mouse. If the list is long, it will have a scrollbar to one side, which you can use to scroll through the long list.

Radio button: The round buttons in a dialog box are called radio buttons. They're grouped together into families, such as the three shown in Figure 5-6. Like an old car radio, only one of the buttons can be punched at a time. To punch a button, click on it once with the mouse. A round dot fills the one button that is *on*.

Input box: Any box or area you can type into is called an input box. In Figure 5-6, it's the box under the word `Label`.

Check box: The square buttons in a dialog box are called check boxes. Unlike radio buttons, you can click the mouse in as many or all of the check boxes as necessary. A check mark appears in the box if an option is on. To remove the check mark and turn the option off, click the mouse in the box again.

After you've made your selections, you typically click on an OK button. (In Figure 5-6, the OK button is called `Start`.) If you don't like your choices, click `Close`.

To get help, click on the question mark button in the dialog box's upper-right corner. This action changes the mouse pointer into the combo arrow pointer-question mark thing. When that happens, point and click on any part of the dialog box to see a pop-up cartoon bubble supposedly offering help. Click the mouse to make the cartoon bubble go away.

- Pressing the Enter key in a dialog box is the same as clicking the OK button with your mouse.

- Pressing the Esc (escape) key on your keyboard is the same as clicking the Cancel button in a dialog box.

- Some dialog boxes feature an *Apply* button. It works like an OK button, but it allows you to see your changes without closing the dialog box. If you like the changes, you can then click OK. Or if the changes stink, you can reset them or click the Cancel button. See? Microsoft is being nice here. Make a note of it on your calendar.

- If more than one input box are in a dialog box, use the Tab key to move between them. Don't press the Enter key, since that's the same as clicking the OK button and telling Windows you're done with the dialog box.

- Another type of list, similar to the drop-down list but not shown in Figure 5-6, is a *scrolling list.* It works the same as the drop-down list, but the list is always visible inside the dialog box.

- If you like a mental challenge, you can use your keyboard to work a dialog box. Look for the underlined letter in each part of the dialog box (such as *p* in Capacity in Figure 5-6). Press the Alt key plus that key, and it's the same as clicking on that command with a mouse.

How to Properly Beg for Help

Windows has an incredible help system, and all Windows-specific programs share it. You always activate Help by pressing the F1 key. From there you're shown the help *engine* that enables you to look up topics, search for topics, or see related items of interest, all by properly using your mouse. The help engine is divided into three panels: Contents, Index, and Find. Here are some hints:

- The Contents panel shows you information just like the yechy manual, with chapters and pages and text written by Ph.D.s for Ph.D.s.

- The Index panel is the most useful. Click on the word Index to see that panel, and then type your topic into the box at the top of the panel, such as **Bold text**. In the bottom part of the panel, click on the subtopic that interests you, and then click on the Display button to read all about it.

- Ignore the Find panel.

- Most of the helpful information is displayed as a list of steps or tips.

- You can click on the gray squares to see more information about related topics.

- To get general help on Windows, choose Help from the main Start menu.

- You can click green underlined text (with a dotted underline) to see a pop-up window defining the term.

The help engine is its own program. When you're done using help, remember to quit: Click on the X close button in the upper-left corner of the window.

General Windows Advice

Use your mouse. If you don't have a mouse, you can still use Windows — but not as elegantly. Ack, who am I kidding? You need a mouse to use Windows!

Have someone organize your Start menu items for you. Also ask this person to put your most popular programs on the desktop as *shortcut icons.* Offer a jar of mixed nuts (less than 50 percent peanuts, lightly salted) as a bribe.

Keep in mind that Windows can run several programs at once. Look at the buttons on the taskbar to see whether a program is already running before starting a second copy. (Yes, you can run several copies of a program under Windows, but you probably only need to run one.)

Chapter 6

Getting Your Work Done

● ●

● ●

*E*ver notice that people in soap operas don't do any work. Sure, they all have jobs. You may see them "at work." But no one really works. They talk. They whisper about James breaking up with Linda since Eva is leaving the convent. They wonder if Alex really has an evil twin. They fear Harry, who walks around with an egg carton and is under investigation for stealing tissue samples from the eye clinic. And they giggle about Wilma, who claims to be pregnant with an alien space baby and keeps complaining that the grocery store doesn't stock any size 9 Huggies.

For you, life is more routine (save for the reading of Uncle Cedric's will, which even "America's Funniest Home Videos" believed to be staged). Eventually, the time comes to get something done. This is what you bought all that software for: to get your work done.

Starting a Program in Windows 95

Oh, you can sit and spin in Windows all day without getting anything of value done. To get working, you need to start a program. That's done by using the Start button and the annoying menu that pops (actually *slips*) up. Here are the steps:

1. Pop up the Start menu.

Click the mouse on the taskbar's Start button. Up pops the menu.

Pressing the Ctrl+Esc key combination does the same thing.

2. Choose <u>P</u>rograms.

Click on the word <u>P</u>rograms, and you'll see the slippery Programs sub-menu appear, such as the one shown in Figure 6-1.

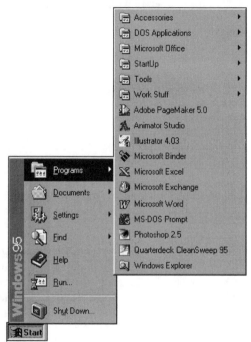

Figure 6-1:
The
Programs
sub-menu.

3. Pluck out your program from those listed in the sub-menu.

For example, in Figure 6-1 you would point and click on Adobe PageMaker 5.0 to start that program.

If your program doesn't appear on the list, then try one of the other sub-menus listed; Accessories, DOS Applications, Microsoft Office, and others contain even more programs.

Yes, and there are even sub-sub-sub-menus (and on and on) with even more programs.

You gots programs comin' outta yer ears!

4. Your program starts; the Start menu goes away.

✔ There may be times the program you want to start appears right on top of the main Start menu. If so, point, click, and the program starts.

✔ The menus are rather slippery. They pop up and disappear as your mouse roves over them. So be careful! It can be aggravating if you're sloppy.

Starting your program from an icon on the desktop

A quick way to start a program without playing slip-and-slide with the Start menu is to find its icon floating on the desktop. This works for any icon on the desktop, whether it represents a program or a file you created, such as your database listing the times weird Harry shows up at the eyeball clinic.

To place an icon of your favorite program on the desktop, fire up the Explorer or My Computer program. Locate your program (this is the technical part) in its proper folder or wherever it's stashed. (You can refer to "Finding

Wayward Files (and Programs)" in Chapter 9 if you need help.)

Now the cinchy part: Using the *right* mouse button, drag the icon from the Explorer or My Computer window out onto the desktop. Remember to use the right button, not the button you'd normally press. When you release the right button (pointing at the desktop), you'll see a pop-up shortcut menu appear. Choose the item Create Shortcut(s) Here. Lo, the shortcut will be created on the desktop, available for easy access.

✔ Quickly start any recently worked-on stuff by using the Documents submenu: Pop up the Start menu and click on Documents. Look for your document on the list. If it's there, click on it to start. If it's not there, you can take the day off and watch your favorite soap.

Maximizing Your Work

This section has nothing to do with self-help. Instead, you might find it useful to maximize your program's window after it starts. Some programs, they start full-screen right off. Other programs start as only a measly window on the screen. Blech! Who needs that?

 To make your program's window fill the screen — and get every dollar per pixel you paid for that monitor — click on the window's maximize button. (The middle button in the upper-left corner, or just look at the image in the margin.)

✔ Some windows can't be maximized. Some games, for example, have a fixed window size you can't change. Don't be greedy.

✔ If you have a humongous monitor, you may opt to run your programs without switching them to full-screen.

> ✓ If you're working with several programs, you may want to arrange their windows on-screen so that each is visible. To do that, right-click the mouse on a blank part of the taskbar, or right-click on the time (on the right side of the taskbar). From the menu that pops up, choose either `Tile Horizontally` or `Tile Vertically` to arrange your windows on the screen.

Switching from One Program to Another (without Quitting)

In Windows you can run several programs at once. Imagine the productivity boost! Dream of getting two things done at once! Then realize the chaos. Fortunately, you don't really run several programs at once as much as you can switch between two or more at a time without having to stop and restart, stop and restart, over and over.

Although Windows can run more than one program at a time, as a human — and I assume that you are — you can only work on the program whose window is up in front or top o' the pile or filling the entire screen. To switch to another program, you have several options.

The Quick Way: The quickest way to switch programs is to grab the mouse and click in another program's window, providing that window is visible. Clicking in a window brings that window to the top of the pile.

The Quick Way if You Can't See the Window: Look for a button on the taskbar corresponding to the window you want. Click that button. Thwooop! The window stands before you, eager to please.

 The Shove-Aside Way: Minimize the current window, shrinking it down to a button on the taskbar. This doesn't quit the program; it just shoves it aside, enabling you to access whatever other windows lie behind it. You accomplish the minimization process by clicking the minimize button in the upper-right corner of the window (see the image in the margin).

Non-Mousey Ways: If you run out of mouse methods for switching programs, try one of the two keyboard methods. These are awful to remember, though I'm personally fond of the Alt +Tab key combination approach.

> ✓ **Alt +Tab:** Press the Alt and Tab keys at the same time — but hold down the Alt key and release the Tab key. This displays a little picture box in the center of the screen displaying icons for all your windows and programs. Keep holding down the Alt key and tap the Tab key until the icon representing your program or window is in the box. Release the Alt key.

- **Alt + Esc:** Press the Alt and Esc keys at the same time. This switches you to the next program you have active (in the order in which you use the programs). You may have to press Alt + Esc a few times to find the program or window you want.

- To switch to another window, click it.

- You can use two key combinations to switch to another window or program: Alt + Esc or Alt + Tab.

 Minimizing a window by clicking the minimize button in the upper-right-hand corner of the window does not quit that application. Instead, the program is shrunk down to icon size at the bottom of the screen. Double-click that icon if you want to access the program's window.

General Commands for All Reasons

Windows programs all do things in similar ways. One of those ways is to use common commands. This enables you to easily learn new Windows applications since everything is done kind of the same. Another advantage is that you can cut or copy and paste information between two different applications. Ah, yes, more productivity boosting, thanks to Chairman Bill.

Copy

To copy something in Windows, select it with the mouse: Drag the mouse over text, click a picture or icon with the mouse, or drag the mouse around the object. This action highlights the text, picture, or icon, which means it has been *selected* and is ready for copying.

After selecting the whatever, choose Edit⇨Copy. This puts a copy of the whatever into Windows' secret storage place, the clipboard, from whence it can be pasted (see "Paste" later in this chapter).

The quick-key shortcut for this is Ctrl+C. That's easy to remember since C means Copy.

- After your text or picture is copied, it can then be pasted. You can paste into the same program or switch to another program for pasting.

- When you copy something, it's put into Windows' clipboard. Unfortunately, the clipboard holds only one thing at a time. Whenever you copy or cut, the new item replaces whatever was already in the clipboard. (Such a clipboard doesn't seem very handy, but Microsoft would like me to remind you here of all the time you're saving in Windows.)

Cut

Cutting something in Windows is just like copying: You select a picture or text or icon and then choose the Edit⇨Cut menu command. Unlike with Copy, however, the picture or text you cut is copied to the clipboard and then deleted from your application.

The quick-key shortcut for this is Ctrl+X. You can remember this because when you cut something you X-it-out. (I know, I'm pushing it here, but the Ctrl+C key combination is already taken.)

> ✔ You can paste, cut text or a picture from the clipboard back into the current application, or you can switch to another application for pasting.

Paste

The Paste command is used to take text, a picture, or icon stored in the clipboard and slap it down into the current application. You can paste a picture into text or text into a picture, and icons can go just about anywhere. Ah, the miracle of Windows.

To paste, choose the Edit⇨Paste command. Or you can press Ctrl+V, the Paste key, from the keyboard. The V must stand for Vwapp! Or Voom! Or Vomica or something.

> ✔ You can paste material cut or copied from any Windows application into another Windows application.
>
> ✔ You might be thinking, why didn't they just make Ctrl+P the Paste shortcut key. Alas, Ctrl+P is the Print command's shortcut key.

Undo

The powers at Microsoft have graced sloppy Windows users (meaning all of us) with the blessed Undo command. This command undoes whatever stupid thing you just did.

To undo, choose Edit⇨Undo from the menu. Undo just happens to be the first item on the list. How convenient. The key command is Ctrl+Z, the Z meaning, "Zap that mistake back to Seattle!"

> ✔ Undo undoes just about anything you can do: unchange edits, replace cut graphics, fix up a bad marriage, and so on.
>
> ✔ If you look at your keyboard (and you shouldn't if you're a touch-typist), you'll see that the Z, X, C, and V keys are all together on the left side, bottom row. Hey! Those are Windows' common shortcut keys. That may explain why the letters don't make much sense.

Save

After you've etched your brilliance into silicon, and the phosphor on the screen glows warmly in your eyes, you need to save your work to disk. Not only will the computer keep your stuff nice and tidy on disk, but you can open it up later to work on it again.

Saving is done using the File⇨Save command. This summons the Save dialog box, which you then use to save your work to disk. (The Save dialog box is presented officially in Chapter 8.)

The Save shortcut key is the logical Ctrl+S key combination.

- ✔ Always save your work. I save my stuff every five minutes or so.
- ✔ Save! Save! Save! Remember that.
- ✔ Jesus saves.
- ✔ The first time you save something to disk, you must give it a name and tell Windows where to put it (which you'll read about in Chapter 8, so don't think I'm being crude here). After that, you just use the Save command to continue to save the file to disk; you don't have to give it a name again. Just save!
- ✔ A variation of the Save command is Save As. This command works like Save, though it allows you to give the file a new name when you save it. This keeps the original version intact.

Open

After something has been saved on disk, you retrieve it using the Open command. This command lets you find your stuff on disk and open it up like a present on your birthday. Your stuff then appears in the program's window, ready for you to do something with it.

To open something on disk, choose the File⇨Open command, or use the handy Ctrl+O keyboard shortcut. This displays the Open dialog box, where you use the various controls and whatnots to grab your file from disk.

- ✔ The Open dialog box is covered in depth in Chapter 8.
- ✔ Some programs may use the Load command instead of Open. This is typically the earmark of an outdated DOS program, souped up to run on Windows.

Print

The Print command takes your lovely work that you see on the screen and causes something similar-looking to spew forth from the printer.

To print, use the File⇨Print command. This displays the Print dialog box, which has a lot of hocus-pocus in it, so you usually click on the OK button and your something then prints.

The keyboard shortcut for the Print command is Ctrl+P. Easy 'nuff.

> ✔ Make sure the printer is on, has paper, and is ready to print before you try to print something.

> ✔ The actual details of printing something are covered in Chapter 16.

Quit (or Exit)

When you're done working, you quit your program and wander off to do something else. This is perhaps the best command of any Windows program.

To quit, choose the File⇨Exit command. Alas, some programs may not have a File menu, let alone an Exit command. If so, then typically the last command (at the bottom) of the first menu will do the trick.

The keyboard combination to quit any Windows program, and to close any window, is bizarre: Alt+F4. This is just too strange to think up anything clever about it.

> ✔ If your application doesn't have a File⇨Exit command, you can quit by clicking on the program window's X button in the upper-right corner.

> ✔ You don't have to quit. If you're working on something and want to put it aside for later, you can minimize the program. See the section "Switching from One Program to Another (without Quitting)" earlier in this chapter for the details.

Part III
Disks, Drives, Files, and Whatnot

The 5th Wave   By Rich Tennant

BOB WAS ONE OF THE MANY SUFFERERS OF PC OBSOLESCENCE SYNDROME.

OH GREAT! NOW THE "X3's" BEEN UPGRADED!

In this part...

Little did they know in 776 BC, when the first Olympic games were held, that the sport of tossing the discus was a portent of mankind's future. Soon, respectable people in business clothing would be tossing various disks around, some in joy, most in frustration. Even though today's disks are used to store information, there are a lot of similarities to the ancient Greek games.

The chapters in this part of the book deal with disks. Actually, the true topic is information as it's stored on computer disks. That disk could be a floppy disk, hard disk, CD, or some network disk on an alien computer. It really shouldn't be that frustrating, but if you do throw a tantrum and toss a few heavy objects, you're bound to please the Olympian gods.

Chapter 7
All about Disks and Drives

Computer disks, like cookies, come in several shapes and flavors. The floppy disk is the Oreo of computer disks. The hard drive is the monster peanut butter cookie. Disk drives are like human mouths; though in a rather emetic twist of events, the computer merely "chews" on the disk and then spits it out. It's best when the computer *doesn't* eat your disk.

This chapter is about disks and drives and all the madness that comes with them. Here you cut through the heavy mylar mist that enshrouds this ugly and obscure topic. It's a hefty chapter, so grab yourself a cookie and a glass of milk before you start reading.

"Why Are There Disk Drives?"

Computers use disks for storage. Computers can store small amounts of information on little floppy disks and large amounts of information on massive hard disks. The disks are necessary since your PC can handle only as much information as it can fit into its memory at one time. Not only that, the computer's memory (or *RAM*) is temporary. Turn off Mr. Computer, and everything in memory goes *poof!*

- ✔ You use disks to store information long-term. The information, or *files*, can then be opened up later for another peek, a re-edit, to show to friends, or just because.

- ✔ Chapter 12 discusses computer memory or *RAM*.

- ✔ Some bozos refer to disk storage as *memory*. Forget that they said so! Disk "memory" is long-term storage. Don't confuse it with computer memory.

- ✔ Like memory (RAM), disk storage is measured in *kilobytes* and *megabytes*. Refer to Chapter 12 for more information on what these terms measure.

Are Disks Software or Hardware?

A common misconception among computer users is that a floppy disk is actually software. This is not so. Floppy disks are hardware. Keep in mind that hardware is something you can touch or drop on your foot. (Though a floppy disk doesn't hurt as much as a monitor that's been dropped on your foot, it is still hardware.) See Figure 7-1 for a peek at what floppy disks look like.

The confusion comes about because floppy disks store software. The software is on the disk, magnetically encoded. So just as you wouldn't call a compact disc "music," don't confuse the floppy disk with the software that's recorded on it.

Who really cares how a disk works?

Computer disks store information electronically, just like you record images on video tape or music on a cassette. It's the same technology, only a lot more expensive since computer information can't have drop-outs or missing bits and pieces or the whole shebang is lost. Music or video can afford the loss since it wouldn't be detectable by a human being. Computers are fussier.

The disk itself is composed of mylar coated with a magnetic oxide compound, similar to the substance that makes Burger King burgers brown on top. A device called a read/write head literally floats over the disk surface writing magnetic information to the disk or reading the magnetic pulses already stored there. A device called the *disk controller* translates those magnetic pulses into 1s and 0s for digestion by the computer, which somehow makes sense of it all.

Your task: Assemble a disk drive using basic materials you find lying around your house. Completion time: 45 minutes. Good luck!

Floppy Disk Cavalcade!

Almost all floppy disks come in two sizes: 3¹/₂-inch and the older 5¹/₄-inch format. The antique 8-inch format is only used by specialized computers owned by stubborn people who refuse to sell their old junk.

The 3¹/₂-inch disk size is the most popular. These disks come in a rainbow of colors. Older 5¹/₄-inch disks came in such creative colors as black, black, and dark black.

Each size of floppy disk has two types or storage capacities. There's *high capacity* and *low capacity*. The 3¹/₂-inch disks even have a *higher* capacity, leaving the consumer (you and me) with several varieties to be confused with.

Figure 7-1 shows what typical 3¹/₂-inch and 5¹/₄-inch disks look like.

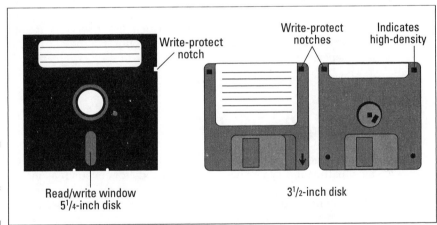

Write-protect
notch

Write-protect
notches

Indicates
high-density

Figure 7-1:
The two
sizes of
floppy disks.

Read/write window
5¹/₄-inch disk

3¹/₂-inch disk

3¹/₂-inch disks

The Macintosh, in keeping with its foolproof and fun look on life, popularized the hardy 3¹/₂-inch disks. They don't have gaping holes in them like the older 5¹/₄-inch models, effectively heading off the temptation to touch the sacred disk inside. They're made of much thicker plastic, so they're much harder to damage.

The typical 3¹/₂-inch disk holds 1.44MB (about a million and a half bytes) of data. But that's only typical, since there are older 720K 3¹/₂-inch disks and newer 2.8MB disks. But don't worry about going crazy. The 1.44MB disk has an HD printed on its case; the 2.8 megabyte disk has an ED, and the old 720K disk, like the littlest pig, has none.

- ✔ Most PCs have one 3¹/₂-inch disk drive, designed to eat 3¹/₂-inch disks of the 1.44MB capacity. You can also use the older 720K disks but, eh, why bother?

- ✔ Your computer must have special, expensive drives to read the ED, so-called extended density 2.8M disks. Because these disks aren't as popular as the other types, most software doesn't come on them.

- ✔ It's tempting to use these disks as beverage coasters. Don't. Moisture can seep underneath the sliding metal thing and freak out the disk inside.

- ✔ Australia: Best scuba diving in the world!

5¹/₄-inch disks

These disks are going out of style faster than black-and-white TV sets. Some computers may still sport a 5¹/₄-inch disk drive, primarily for use if you have a lot of old 5¹/₄-inch disks lying around. If not, you don't need the drive.

- ✔ There are actually two types of 5¹/₄-inch disk: *high capacity* and *low capacity*. The low-capacity disks store only 360K of information; the high-capacity disks hold 1.2M.

- ✔ Both types of disks look virtually identical.

Buying floppy disks

Everyone needs floppy disks for their PC. Though you'll be using the hard drive most of the time, floppy disks come in handy for several reasons:

They can be used as backup safety copies for valuable information on the hard drive. They can be used to transport files from one PC to another. They can be flung across the room in a graceful arc to whack the unwitting dork playing a game on his PC.

If you don't have a stack of floppy disks handy, buy them. You should always buy disks that match the size and capacity of your floppy drives.

Size: There are two sizes of disks: 3¹/₂-inch and 5¹/₄-inch. These values refer to the length of the disk's edge (because all disks are square).

Capacity: The capacity of the disk refers to how much information it can hold. There are two capacities: low capacity and high capacity. A very high or extended capacity also exists for 3¹/₂-inch disks, but no one uses it.

The object is to buy disks to match the size and capacity of your floppy drive. See Table 7-1 for details on what disks to buy.

- ✔ If you're in doubt as to which size and capacity floppy disks you need to buy, you probably need to buy 1.44MB or high-capacity 3¹/₂-inch disks.

- ✔ Only if you have a low-capacity drive do you need to buy the low-capacity disks.

- ✔ There is nothing wrong with buying discount disks in bulk.

- ✔ Pay a little extra and buy preformatted IBM disks. This will save you some time later since unformatted disks must be formatted before you can use them. (The subject of formatting is covered later in this chapter.)

- ✔ Most 3¹/₂-inch disks come in little plastic sleeves. You can throw these away.

- ✔ The 5¹/₄-inch disks come in Tyvek envelopes. Don't throw these away as they protect the naked and exposed surface of the disk.

Table 7-1	Floppy Disk Sizes and Capacities
Floppy Drive Size and Capacity	*Buy These Disks*
5¹/₄-inch, Low	Low-capacity, 360K, or DS/DD
5¹/₄-inch, High	High-capacity, high-density, 1.2MB, or DS/HD
3¹/₂-inch, Low	Low-capacity, 720K, or DS/DD
3¹/₂-inch, High	High-capacity, high-density (HD), 1.44MB, or DS/HD
3¹/₂-inch, Extended	Extended-capacity, 2.8MB, or DS/ED

"Hmmm. I wonder what's on this disk?"

Ever pick up a disk and wonder silently to yourself, "Where the heck did this disk come from?" If you do that a lot, I have one maxim for you:

Label your floppy disks!

Every box of disks — even the cheapies — comes with several sticky labels. Here's how you use them:

1. Write information on the sticky label using a pen.

Describe the disk's contents or give it a general name: *Files for home* or *Backup stuff* or *Emergency disk* or . . . you get the idea.

Why can't I *notch* a disk to make it high capacity?

One of the worst tricks you can pull with disks is to format a low-capacity disk to a higher capacity. It sounds simple, and it even works . . . for a time. But will you trust your valuable data to it, especially when you're only saving a few cents on the dollar?

It goes like this: When the high-capacity 3½-inch disks came out, most people noticed that the disks were identical in every way to the low-capacity disks, save for two things. First, the high-capacity disks had an extra hole in them. And second, the high-capacity disks cost more than the low capacities. This led many misguided souls to believe that you could magically make a low-capacity disk into a high-capacity one simply by punching a hole in it. They even justified

this by saying that both the disks "looked alike." This is as silly as it sounds.

True, if you mutilate a low-capacity disk, you can format the disk at the higher capacity. You can even use the disk for a time with no ill effects. This is how the charlatans were able to dupe so many people; their demonstration disks worked flawlessly back at the store. But once you tried to use those disks two or three times, they became riddled with errors.

Eventually, the modified disks became worthless. Forget about getting your data back! In fact, you couldn't even reformat the disks to a lower capacity. By punching a hole in a 3½-inch disk, you're taking a losing gamble. Don't do it no matter what you hear.

---

2. Peel the label off and gently apply it to the disk.

(Make your own sound effects noises here.)

There. That's easy. With all your floppy disks labeled, you'll never worry about wondering what's on them. And you'll be able to find commonly used disks more quickly.

- ✔ You can always tell what's on a disk by opening it up and looking. No — put that screwdriver away! Instead, use the My Computer program: Open My Computer, and then double-click on the floppy drive containing the disk in question, such as floppy drive A. That displays the disk's contents in a window on the screen.

- ✔ Label disks right after you format them. That way, all formatted disks will have labels. If you find a disk without a label, that tells you it's probably unformatted.

- ✔ You may also want to write the capacity of the disk, say 1.2MB or 720K, on the label. This will help out in situations where you have many computers with different kinds of drives in them.

- ✔ Don't use Post-its as disk labels. They fall off when you're not looking and can sometimes get stuck inside your disk drives.

How low-density disks are different from high-density disks

Though all disks look alike, the magnetic recording material on the disk has differences the eye cannot see. I like to make the comparison between a disk's surface and a sandbox (minus the kids and Tonka trucks).

A low-density disk is like a sandbox filled with coarse sand. Using a rake, you can draw lines in that sand. This works because the lines the rake makes are fairly far apart. If they aren't, the sand will fall back in on itself; it won't hold the grooves made by the rake because the sand is so coarse.

If the sandbox is filled with fine sand, you can use a finer rake and make many more grooves in it. Because of the fine sand, the grooves hold

their pattern. This is essentially the difference between a low-capacity and high-capacity disk. A high-capacity disk has finer magnetic material and can hold many more tracks (where information on the disk is stored) than a low-capacity disk.

When you format a low-capacity disk to a high-capacity, typically by fooling it with a hole punch, it's like making fine grooves in coarse sand. This may hold for a while. But because the sand isn't fine, eventually the grooves (tracks on a disk) disappear. The same thing happens on the disk. Because the information you write to the disk clings to these tracks, when they go, so does your data.

"Which type of disk is this?"

Even if a disk is labeled, sometimes it's hard to tell if it's a low-capacity or high-capacity model. The following tips should clue you in to which disk is which:

If the disk is a 360K 5¹/₄-inch floppy:

The disk label contains one of the following: DS/DD, double sided/double density, 40 TPI, or 40 Tracks Per Inch.

As a visual clue, if you remove the disk and look at its center hole, you see a reinforcing hub ring. The 1.2MB disks typically lack this feature.

If the disk is a 1.2MB 5¹/₄-inch floppy:

Look for the letters HD or the term high-density, double sided/high-density, Double Track, 96 TPI, or 96 Tracks Per Inch.

The visual clue is the absence of a reinforcing hub ring typically found on most 360K floppies.

If the disk is a 720K 3¹/₂-inch floppy:

Visual clues: DS/DD, double sided/double density, DD, Double Track, 135 TPI, or 135 Tracks Per Inch.

The primary visual clue is that the disk is missing a hole in the lower-right corner. (This hole is opposite from the write-protect hole.)

If the disk is a 1.44MB 3¹/₂-inch floppy:

Clues on the label: DS/HD, double sided/high-density, or the interesting graphic (double line) letters HD. (The HD is usually your best clue; all the manufacturers use it.)

The key visual clue is the extra, see-through hole in the lower-right corner of the disk. The lower-capacity disks lack this hole.

If the disk is a 2.8MB 3¹/₂-inch floppy:

These disks have one of the following clues on their label: DS/ED; double sided/extended density; or the best clue, a large graphic "ED" on the disk.

The key visual clue is the extra, see-through hole on the corner of the disk, which the 720K disks lack. Note that this hole is not even (horizontally) with the write-protect hole; it's a bit lower, which is how you can tell the difference between a 2.8MB disk and a 1.44MB disk.

Write-protecting a disk

You can protect floppy disks in such a way as to prevent yourself or anyone else from modifying or deleting anything on the disk.

To write-protect a 3¹/₂-inch disk, locate the little sliding tile on the lower-left side of the disk as you slide it into the drive. If the tile covers the hole, the disk can be written to. If you slide the tile off the hole (so you can see through it), the disk is write-protected (see Figure 7-1).

To write-protect a 5¹/₄-inch disk, go grab one of those tiny, Velamint-size tabs that came with the disk in the box. Peel the tab and place it over the notch in the disk, which should be on the lower-left side as you insert the disk into the drive (see Figure 7-1). With that notch covered, the disk is write-protected.

When a disk is write-protected, you cannot alter, modify, change, or delete anything on that disk. And you cannot accidentally reformat it. You can read from the disk and copy files from it. But changing the disk — forget it!

To un-write-protect a 5¹/₄-inch disk, peel off the little tab. This renders the disk sticky, but it's a livable problem. You can un-write-protect 3¹/₂-inch disks by sliding the tile over the hole.

Floppy disk do's and donuts

Disks store information in the form of magnetic impulses. That means that if you bring a disk close to a magnet, you copy new, random magnetic impulses over your important data. Don't use the water man's refrigerator magnet to stick a floppy to the refrigerator!

- ✔ Keep your floppy disks away from magnets. These include: telephone handsets, speakers on radios and TV sets, executive-style paper clip holders, desk fans, photocopiers, 1.21 gigawatt power amplifiers, and the planet Jupiter.

- ✔ Don't set books or heavy items on top of disks. The pressure can push dust granules into the disk.

- ✔ Avoid extreme temperatures. Don't leave a disk sitting on the dash of your car or even on a window sill. And, even if the novel thought occurs to you, don't store your disks in the freezer.

- ✔ At least make an effort to put each disk back in its protective jacket after use. This is much more important for 5¹/₄-inch disks than the smaller ones.

- ✔ Don't touch the disk surface itself; only touch the protective cover. Don't spray WD-40 inside, even if the disk makes a noise as it spins. (Your disk drive is probably making the noise, anyway. Keep the WD-40 out of there, too.)

- ✔ When mailing a 5¹/₄-inch disk, don't use a floppy-disk mailer from the drug store. Don't fold the disk in half and mail it in a standard-size envelope. Instead, buy a photo mailer, which is the same as a floppy disk mailer but doesn't cost as much.

- ✔ Never use a ball-point pen to write on a disk's label. The hard pen point can damage the disk inside. Use a felt-tipped pen or, better yet, write on the label before you affix it to the disk.

Hard Drive Mania!

Floppy disks can be cumbersome for day-to-day computing. Your computer takes a long time to read and write their information, and they can't hold very much information in the first place.

So the Dorito-breathed geeks who invented floppy disks came up with the ultimate floppy disk: a large, spinning plate that lives inside your computer. The computer reads and writes to this large, spinning plate as if it were a floppy in a disk drive. But unlike floppies, hard drives stay sealed up inside your computer, away from dust, magnets, and carbonated-beverage spray. (In fact, the people who build these hard drives have to wear special suits and work in sterile, spaceship-like rooms to keep any contaminants out. One sneeze, and it's all over for that batch of disk drives.)

Because the large, spinning plate, or platter, is so big and thick, it can hold more information than hundreds of floppy disks. It's also much speedier.

✔ The hard disk is the disk on which information is stored. The hard drive is the mechanism that holds the hard disk. The terms are, however, interchangeable (though incorrectly so).

✔ IBM, always proving that it's different, calls the hard drive a *fixed disk*. No, this does not mean that the disk was once broken. (It's fixed as in unmovable.)

✔ Like their floppy drive counterparts, hard drives have lights on the outside that turn on when the computer is accessing data. If your computer is taking a particularly long time to load a program, look at the hard drive light. It should be blinking in a somewhat random series of flashes. If it's not on at all or it's on all the time, that may mean that something bad is happening (see Part VI for troubleshooting tips).

CD-ROM Drives (or When a Disk Is a Disc)

Another type of disk drive is the CD-ROM drive. Personally, I can't figure out if a CD-ROM is the disc you put in the drive or the name of the drive. Whatever, the CD-ROM drive is yet another type of disk drive your PC may sport.

CD-ROM drives eat special CD-ROM discs. These discs, looking a lot like CD music discs, store megabytes and megabytes of computer information. The drive can access that information, making it available to you just like it was on a hard disk or floppy.

Discs go into CD-ROM drives in one of two ways. The first way is to put the disc into a sliding tray that pops out of the CD-ROM drive like a little kid sticking out his tongue. Put the disc into the tray label up, and then gently nudge the tray back into the computer. The tray should slide back in the rest of the way on its own.

The second way is to slip the CD-ROM into a *caddy* or container. The disc goes into the container label up, so you can see the label through the container's clear cover. Close the container shut and then shove it into the drive.

When the disc is in the drive, you use it just like any other disk in your computer.

To eject the disc, follow these steps:

1. **Locate the CD-ROM drive icon using the My Computer program.**

   Open the My Computer icon on Windows' desktop by double-clicking it with the mouse. A window appears showing you all the disk drives in your computer, plus a few token folders.

Wambooli
(D:)

2. **Point the mouse at the CD-ROM drive icon.**

   A sample of what the icon looks like appears in the margin.

3. **Click the mouse's right button.**

   This displays the shortcut menu for the CD-ROM drive, shown in Figure 7-2.

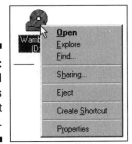

Figure 7-2:
A CD-ROM
drive's
shortcut
menu.

4. **Choose** `Eject` **from the menu.**

   Point at the word Eject with your mouse and click.

   The disc spits out of the CD-ROM drive.

   ✔ The RO in CD-ROM means *read-only.* You can only read information from a CD-ROM disc. You cannot add new information to the disc, erase, or change information already on the disc.

   ✔ CD-ROM discs contain mainly multimedia information or games. I have a CD-ROM disc full of graphical images or clip art. One contains fonts. Another has a game. Another has a game. Even more games. And so on.

   ✔ Unlike floppy drives and hard drives, CD-ROM drives have no specific letter of the alphabet assigned to them. Their drive letter can be anything. See the section "Know Your Disk Drives" next.

Know Your Disk Drives

Unlike parents who buy books when trying to name baby, computers save time and money by referring to disk drives as letters of the alphabet, A through Z.

Every computer has a drive A, which is your first (and the computer's favorite) floppy drive.

If you have a second floppy drive, your computer refers to it as drive B.

The first hard drive in your PC is always drive C — whether or not you have a drive B. Additional hard drives are given letters D, E, F, and so on, all the way up to Z.

- ✔ If you have a CD-ROM drive, it has a drive letter, too. Which letter it is depends on how many other drives are in your computer and the phase of the moon.

- ✔ Windows refers to your disk drives by letter as well. But the letter is followed by a colon. So drive A is A:, and C: is used to identify the first hard drive.

- ✔ Fill in this book's Cheat Sheet with the names and locations of your computer's disk drives and their letters. If you have a punch-tape thing, label your floppy drives A: and B: (if you have a second floppy drive).

- ✔ People pronounce A: as *A-colon,* as in

  Alex Trebek: People use this to digest food.

  You: A colon.

  Alex: I'm sorry, you must phrase that in the form of a question.

Using disk drives

The computer reads information stored on its disk drives. Before it can do that, you must point the PC's nose in the direction of that drive. Yes, you must twist the computer's arm and tell it exactly which drive — A, C, D, or whatever — you want it to use. This is known in computer jargon as *logging*.

For example, to use the disk in drive A, you must tell the computer to *log* to drive A. Actually, you merely open the icon for drive A in My Computer or the Explorer. But some doofus manual somewhere may say "Log to drive A." In that case, you merely open up drive A in My Computer.

- *Logging* is computer lingo for *using*.
- Before you can use a disk drive, you must log to it. This is as simple as opening up that disk drive in the My Computer or Explorer programs.
- Before your computer can read information from a floppy disk, you must insert the disk into a disk drive. This task is covered in the next section.

- Your computer can't use the information right on a disk. Instead, it copies the information to its memory. From there, the computer can manipulate the data, send it to the printer, or occasionally lose it. Because the computer is only working with a copy of the data, the original data is still safe on the disk.
- Never worry if the file on disk is larger than your PC's memory. For example, you may have a 15MB graphics image but only 8MB of RAM in your computer. Don't sweat it! If the computer can't open the file, it will let you know. Most of the time, however, it will surprise you by reading it anyway. Amazing devices, those computers.

Changing floppy disks

Steps: Inserting a 3¹/₂-inch floppy disk into a disk drive

Step 1. Point the disk at the drive, label up with the sliding metal door pointing in toward the drive.

Step 2. Push it in. The drive mechanism will grab the disk and suck it all the way in for you.

- The 3¹/₂-inch disks only go in one way. If the disk doesn't seem to want to go in, don't force it! Just reorient the disk and try again.
- If the disk still doesn't want to go in, there may already be a disk in the drive. Eject it (see the next set of steps).

Steps: Removing a 3¹/₂-inch floppy disk from a disk drive

Step 1. Punch the little button right below the disk drive slot. The disk pops out.

Step 2. Grab the disk. Remove it. Smile.

- Never remove a disk from a floppy drive when the drive light is on. Wait.
- Never remove a disk from a floppy drive while you're using (or "logged to") that drive. Wait until you've saved all your files before removing the floppy disk. Also close the floppy disk's window before you yank it out.

Steps: Inserting a 5¹/₄-inch disk into a disk drive

Step 1. Point the disk label-side up with the gaping hole toward the disk drive.

Step 2. Slide the disk into the drive.

Step 3. Close the drive door or latch.

> ✔ Check to make sure there isn't a disk already in the drive. If so, remove it before you stick a new disk into the drive.

> ✔ Gently close the door latch. If it won't close, the disk is improperly inserted. Try again.

> ✔ There are eight possible orientations for a 5 ¹/₄-inch disk. Don't try them all! Always stick the disk in label-side up, gaping hole into the drive first.

Steps: Removing a 5¹/₄-inch disk from a disk drive

Step 1. Open the drive door or latch.

Step 2. Pinch the disk inside the drive.

Step 3. Slide the disk out of the drive.

Step 4. Place the disk back into its sleeve and store it in a proper place.

> ✔ Keep your disk drive doors open when there isn't a disk in the drive.

> ✔ Refer to the list of warnings for removing a 3¹/₂-inch disk from a drive; the same no-no's apply to removing a 5¹/₄-inch disk.

Formatting a Floppy Disk

All floppy disks must be formatted. Unless you were smart enough to buy pre-formatted floppy disks, you'll have to format them at some point in time. A disk must be formatted before you can use it.

If the disk isn't formatted and you try to access it, Windows spits up an ugly error message, similar to the one in Figure 7-3. If so, click the Yes button and get ready for formatting.

Figure 7-3:
Windows'
"disk is
unformatted"
error
message.

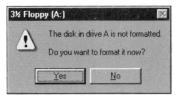

If you know better, stick an unformatted disk in drive A (or B). Make sure the disk is the proper size and such for that floppy drive. Then follow these steps:

1. Open the My Computer icon.

Double-click on the My Computer icon, sitting all by itself in the upper-left corner of the screen. This displays a list of disk drives in your computer, plus two oddball folders (see Figure 7-4).

Figure 7-4.
My
Computer
displays
your PC's
disk drives.

2. Stick an unformatted disk into drive A.

Or use drive B. Or the disk can already be in the drive.

Make sure the disk is unformatted or an older disk you don't mind utterly erasing. The process of formatting a disk removes any information already on that disk. This is something you don't want to accidentally find out later.

3. Select drive A.

Point the mouse at drive A's icon and click once. This highlights that disk drive, selecting it for action. (Or you can select drive B if you're using it.)

4. Choose File⇨Format from the menu.

The Format dialog box appears (see Figure 7-5).

5. Click the Start button.

Ignore those dialog box options! Point at the Start button and click the mouse.

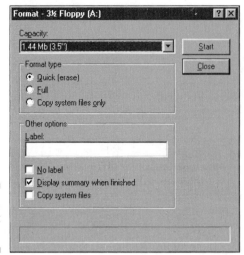

Figure 7-5.
The Format
dialog box.

The formatting process takes a minute or longer, so count the holes in the ceiling tiles for a while. When Windows finishes formatting . . . nothing happens. Well, you may see a summary screen. Press Esc to close the dialog box, and you're ready to use the disk.

- ✔ The floppy drives in the My Computer window have little floppy disks on their shoulders. Don't mess with any other type of drive.

- ✔ Be sure to format a new disk or one that doesn't contain anything you want to keep. Reformatting completely erases a disk, so be careful what you stick in the drive.

- ✔ After the disk is formatted, slap a label on it. You can use one of the sticky labels that came with the disk. Be sure to write on the label before you slap it onto the disk.

- ✔ Never under any circumstances format a hard drive. This is next-to-impossible to do in Windows, but don't even make the attempt. Formatting a hard drive is something they do at the factory. Trained technicians, often wearing white lab coats and caps and carrying clipboards and wearing laminated badges that have bad photos on them, do the formatting.

Chapter 8

Storing Stuff on Your Hard Drive (The Forgotten Art of Using Folders)

*T*he old West. Wild. Untamed. A vast territory empty and ugly. And all of a sudden — here come the settlers! Hundreds of them, dotting the countryside like boils on a sinner. What's needed is a sheriff. A marshal. A lawman. Someone to tame the wilderness and organize the settlers into camps. Nice and convenient. Like John Wayne: polite, gentlemanly, but one you'd never cross. No sirree.

Your PC's hard drive is a lot like the old West. Without a good lawman in charge, things can get unruly and out of hand. Files, like settlers, need to be organized. The good ones need an easy-to-find, logical place to dwell. The bad ones need to be killed off. You can do that, providing you understand folders and how they store and organize your PC's files. It's a tough job, but they're counting on you to do a dang good job, Marshal.

"Why Should I Bother Organizing My Hard Drive?"

The truth is, you don't have to organize your hard drive. Heck, you could use your computer for months and never create or bother with a folder. But problems would crop up quickly:

- Without folders, files just go anywhere. You may be able to find them, you probably won't.

- Different programs stick their files in different folders. Who knows where your stuff is?

- Ever pull your hair out over finding a lost file? It's probably because you didn't mind about folders when you created and saved it.

- With folders, your files can be neatly tucked into areas with similar files. You can organize your stuff by project, by type of file, or however you see fit.

The true problem is that Windows, honestly, doesn't give a hoot whether you use folders or not. If you do, you'll be organized and can always find your stuff. If you don't, working on the computer will take longer, but everything will still work.

Personally, I'd rather be organized and keep those clumps of hair that look *great* on my head.

Building Towns on the Wild Hard Disk Frontier (or "What Is a Folder?")

A folder is a storage place for files in your computer, on the hard drive specifically. Folders keep files together — like a little disk within a disk. All the files in that one folder are all in one, handy place.

In addition to files, folders can also hold more folders. This is just another level of organization. So, for example, you can have a folder named Finances and in that folder have other folders, one for 1996, one for 1997, and on up until the day you die.

- Whether you use your files or not, Windows always puts them in folders on disk. So when you save something in Windows, you're really placing it in a specific folder somewhere on your hard drive.

- Folders contain files, just like folders in a filing cabinet contain files. Golly, what an analogy.

Folders and subdirectories

In the olden days, folders were known as *directories* or often the prepositional *subdirectories*. There is no need to bring this up, though you'll always find some dorky program (including Windows itself) that refers to a directory-this or that-subdirectory. Directory, folder, same thing.

Names and places

A folder is a folder is a folder. But some folders have special names. To witness this and get familiar with Windows' oddball naming methods, take a gander at your PC's monitor. (Turn your computer on since this demonstration works only when the thing is on.)

 The desktop: The thing you stare at when Windows is up and running is called the *desktop.* You may have to close some windows and minimize some programs to see the whole thing. That's the top-most level of organization on your computer. What does it mean? Absolutely nothing.

- The desktop is merely the screen you see when you use Windows.

- Any icons pasted to the desktop, such as the Network Neighborhood, The Microsoft Network, Briefcase, or whatever you've put there yourself, are considered part of the desktop.

- The desktop level is just the top-most level of organization for Windows. It has nothing to do with whether you're a good person or not.

 My Computer: The next level of organization is your computer itself, represented by the My Computer icon in the upper-left corner of the desktop.

Open the My Computer icon by double-clicking on it with your mouse. A window appears, showing you all the disk drives in your computer, plus two guest folders, the Control Panel, and Printers.

- The My Computer icon shows you what's "in" your computer. Since this chapter deals with disk storage, what it shows you is primarily your disk drives: floppy drives, hard drives, CD-ROMs, and whatever else you have available for storing files.

✔ The Control Panel folder is a gizmo that allows you to tweak and fiddle with various parts of your computer. It has nothing to do with disk storage or organizing files.

✔ Ditto for the Printers folder. That's a container for all the printers attached to your computer. (See Chapter 16.)

The root folder: Every disk has at least one folder. That one folder — the main folder — is called the *root folder.* Like a tree (and this isn't a dog joke), all other folders on your hard drive branch out from that main, root folder.

✔ The root folder does not have a cutesy icon associated with it. In fact, if the root folder looks like anything, it looks like the disk drive itself. At least that's how My Computer and the Explorer programs dish it up.

✔ When you open up a disk drive in My Computer or in the Explorer, the files and folders you see are all stored in the root folder.

✔ The root folder might also be called the *root directory.* This is merely a throwback to the old days of DOS (which is a throwback to the days of UNIX, which King Herod used).

Games

Regular old folders: These are merely folders on your hard drive that contain files and maybe even other folders.

✔ Ideally, the folder's name should give you some hint as to its contents.

✔ A few special folders, such as the Control Panel and Printers, don't truly contain files and stuff you store on a hard drive. You can spot these folders easily since they don't look like the plain yellow folder shown in the margin. Don't mess with 'em.

The tree structure

The whole mess of folders and files is all organized into something the computer nerds call the *tree structure.* The folders all start at the root, branching out to more folders and folders, and eventually you end up with files, kind of like the leaves on a tree. There are no aphids in this simile.

Why bother with the tree structure? Because it keeps your files organized. To see how it all works, follow this brief tutorial (which isn't really a tutorial since *...For Dummies* books traditionally shouldn't have tutorials in them, *Q.E.D.*).

1. Fire up the Explorer program.

The Explorer is much better suited for hopping between folders than is My Computer. To start the Explorer from the Start menu, choose Programs⇨Windows Explorer.

The Explorer appears on the screen, looking something like Figure 8-1.

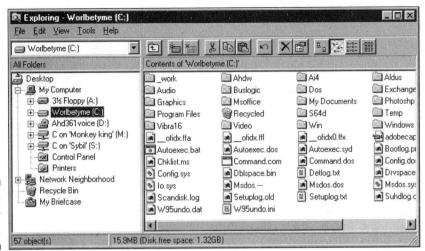

Figure 8-1:
The Explorer
in action.

> ✔ If you don't see the Explorer's toolbar, choose View⇨Toolbar from the menu. Adjust the size of the Explorer's window, if necessary, to see all of the toolbar.

> ✔ The Explorer's window is divided into two parts or panels. On the left is the tree structure — the way your hard drive is organized from the desktop on down to the lowliest folder. On the right is displayed the contents of whatever you have highlighted on the left.

2. Scroll up to the top of the left panel.

If you can't see the Desktop displayed in the left panel, use the scrollbar (the up-and-down one in the middle) to scroll up to the top of the window. The very first thing you should see is the Desktop item.

Beneath the desktop, you find My Computer.

Beneath My Computer, you find all the disk drives in your computer, plus the two weirdo folders.

3. Look in drive C.

In the left panel, click on your computer's drive C.

Drive C may have a name and then a drive letter, such as

```
MICRON (C:)
```

Or it may just have the drive letter and colon in parenthesis:

```
(C:)
```

Either way, click on the drive's name to display its contents in the Explorer's right panel.

✔ What you're looking at in the right panel, the contents of drive C, is actually the root folder. This concept is explained earlier in this chapter.

✔ The four buttons on the far right of the Explorer's toolbar let you see files and icons displayed in four different ways. If you have oodles of time to waste, click on each one to see the different views.

 ✔ My favorite Explorer view is the Small Icons view, as shown in Figure 8-1.

✔ Some folks like the Large Icons view. It's similar to what My Computer shows you.

 ✔ Nerds just love the Details view (last button).

✔ Don't ask me why they put the drive letter (and colon) in parentheses. I would have figured that the colon was confusing enough. But, no, not for Microsoft, I suppose.

✔ Drive C is your computer's first hard drive. Refer to Chapter 7 to discover why that's not drive A and other miscellaneous hard drive trivia.

4. Open up your drive C.

Click on the little plus by that drive. (If you see a minus by the drive, there's no need to click; the drive is already open.)

Opening up drive C by clicking on the plus shows all drive C's folders in the panel on the left side of the Explorer.

✔ The Explorer's left panel shows you your computer's tree structure: the disks and folders. The right panel shows you the contents.

✔ A plus sign appears by a drive or folder when it's closed. You click on the plus to open the drive or folder.

✔ A minus sign appears by a drive or folder when it's already open.

✔ If you're familiar with working an outline program on a computer, the Explorer's tree structure works in a similar way. If you're not familiar with an outline program, just nod your head in silent agreement.

5. Look in the Windows folder.

Scroll down through the left panel until you see the Windows folder. Click the folder's name to see its contents displayed in the right panel.

You may have to use the middle scrollbar to scroll the left panel down far enough to find the Windows folder.

6. Look in the Media folder.

Using the *right* panel only, locate the Media folder. You may have to use the scrollbar(s) to find the folder. When you do, double-click it with the mouse. This opens it up and displays its contents in the right panel.

✔ Opening a folder in the right panel works just like it does in My Computer. It's a very un-Explorer thing to do, so don't let your computer guru know you've tried it.

✔ You may not have a Media folder in your Windows folder. If not, open some other folder that looks interesting. Don't take all day.

✔ Notice how the Media folder in the Explorer's *left* panel is open a bit? That's how you can tell which folder you're looking in. Also, there may be a caption visible above the right panel that says Contents of 'Media'. Big hint, there.

7. Use the `Go to a different folder` drop-down thing to return to the root folder.

Click the mouse on the arrow by the `Go to a different folder` drop-down thing, dropping down the list. Use the scrollbar (if necessary) to scroll up and find the root level, which is listed as drive C (see step 3). Click on that item. Figure 8-2 shows an example.

Figure 8-2: Zooming back up to the root with the Go to a different folder drop-down thing.

This action takes you directly to the root folder — or to any other folder above the one you're currently in. It's a speedy way to move from one folder to another (which is the point of this whole exercise).

If you just want to hop up one folder, use the Up One Level button on the toolbar.

Crawling down through the depths of your system's tree structure is involved but not that painful. This becomes necessary when you create lots of important folders for your stuff.

No, this isn't like spelunking.

Folder Calisthenics

Folders aren't mold. They don't happen with the proper moisture, heat conditions, or proximity to Seattle.

You must make an effort to create folders on your hard drive!

You must make an effort to use folders on your hard drive!

You must believe me when I tell you it isn't that hard!

Enough finger wagging.

Where to put your folders

Folders can live anywhere on your hard drive. Therefore, you can put them anywhere. There are no rules and no speed limit, kind of like it is driving in Montana in the daytime.

- ✔ Sure, you can create all your folders in the root folder (or root directory), the first list of files and folders you see on a hard drive. But that isn't being very organized. Besides, Windows places a limit on the number of folders you can have in the root. Better create 'em somewhere else.

- ✔ By putting folders into categories, you can arrange your work nicely. For example, I have a folder called Graphics. In that folder are folders organized into various image categories. This is one example of how a well-named and organized folder can help you quickly find your stuff.

- ✔ My personal folder organization strategy is to create folders like categories. I have general folders called Graphics, Video, Work, Finances, and one called Stuff.

  My Finances folder has folders for various years. So, for example, inside the 1993 folder you would find everything in that year about my finances in case you ever want to sue me.

  The beauty of this scheme is that whenever I need a financial file, I know to look in the Finances folder, and then in the proper year. Then I'll be able to find the file I need.

  I organize my correspondence the same way: The My Documents folder contains the Letters folder that contains folders for personal, work, and miscellaneous stuff. (Those folders are named Personal, Work, and Misc.) Inside each folder are other folders that further organize things.

- ✔ See? Aren't I organized? You can be, too, providing you create and organize your folders in Windows.

✔ If you have Microsoft Office (the new version), it created a folder called My Documents when it was first installed. This is where Office's programs — Excel, Word, and so on — try to first save their files. If you want to be cool, create your new folders in that folder for further organization.

A brief exercise in creating a folder

Creating a folder is easy. Where to create it is the hard part. As an example, the following steps create a folder named Stuff in the root folder of your drive C.

1. Open My Computer.

Double-click on the My Computer icon nestled in the upper-left corner of the Windows desktop. This opens a window detailing all the disk drives your computer possesses, plus two strange folders.

2. Open your drive C.

Locate your drive C icon, which may have a name followed by (C:). Double-click that icon to open another window.

3. Choose File⇨New⇨Folder.

This places a new folder in the window, looking something like the icon in the margin. (It may look different, depending on which view you've chosen from the View menu.)

Ta-da! There's your new folder.

4. Give the folder a name other than the silly New Folder.

Type in a new name. Be clever. Remember that this folder will contain files and possibly other folders, all of which should relate somehow to the folder's name. For this tutorial, type in the nondescript name Stuff.

✔ Use the Backspace key to backup and erase if you make a mistake.

✔ See Chapter 9 for information on naming files. The same rules apply when naming a folder.

5. Do something with the folder. Create more folders; cut and paste some files in there, you get the idea.

Double-click the folder's icon to open it. You'll find a blank window displayed since it's a new folder and will have no contents.

Now you can create more folders or copy and paste files and folders into the new folder.

See? Wasn't that easy?

✔ You can always create a new folder and move files there. Go on an organizational frenzy!

- ✔ Copying and pasting files is covered in the next chapter.

- ✔ If you just created the Stuff folder but have no use for it, kill it off! See "Removing a folder" just a few paragraphs beyond this very spot.

Making a shortcut to your folder on the desktop

Some folders are just so darn handy you want to keep them on the desktop where you can always get at them. To do so, you shouldn't copy the folder; that would eat up too much disk space. Instead, just create a shortcut — like the shortcut path Peter Rabbit used to get into Mr. MacGregor's garden.

To create a shortcut folder on the desktop, first locate the folder you want to use. You can do this in the Explorer or My Computer programs. Make it a popular folder, such as My Documents or your Work folder or a folder full of stuff you want to impress yourself with when you're feeling down.

Click the mouse once on the folder to select it. The folder appears in a darker color, telling the world it's selected.

Choose the Edit➪Copy command from the menu. The folder is copied, sorta.

Figure 8-3:
The
desktop's
pop-up
menu.

Point the mouse at the desktop and click the *right* mouse button — a right-click. Up pops a shortcut menu, similar to the one you see in Figure 8-3. Choose the Paste Shortcut command from the list. *Voilà,* a shortcut to your folder lives on the desktop.

- ✔ Shortcuts are used just like the real McCoy. Double-click them to open and see the files and folders inside.

- ✔ The advantage of a shortcut is that you can put them anywhere, giving you easy access to your files without copying them all over blazes.

- ✔ See Chapter 9 for more information on shortcuts if the subject is driving you bonkers.

Removing a folder

Find the folder you want to trash by using either the Explorer or My Computer programs. Drag that folder across the desktop and drop it into the Recycle Bin icon.

Fwoosh!

It's gone.

- ✔ Death to the folder!

- ✔ A warning box may appear, telling you that you're about to delete a folder and only bad people do that and don't you want to change your mind? Click Yes to trash it.

 ✔ If you can see the toolbar, you can click on the delete button to zap a folder.

 ✔ You can also use the Undo command to immediately undelete a folder. This only works *right after* the folder is deleted, so be timely. Choose Edit⇨Undo Delete, press Ctrl+Z, or click on the Undo button on the toolbar.

 ✔ Deleting a folder kills off everything in that folder — files, folders, and all the files and folders in those folders. Egads! It's mass carnage! So be careful with this one, lest you have to confess to some hard drive war crimes tribunal.

- ✔ Well, it's possible to rescue anything Windows deletes. This topic is covered in Chapter 9.

Using the Open Dialog Box

One time that folders come into play is when you use the Open command to go out to a disk and fetch up a file. You must know in which folder you put something, plus how to find that folder on the disk. This is all done by working the Open dialog box, which is a pretty standard feature of all Windows programs.

Figure 8-4 shows a typical Open dialog box. Here is how you would work it to find a file for opening on disk:

Figure 8-4:
The typical
Open dialog
box.

1. **Look for your file. If it's there, open it.**

   In the big list in the center of the dialog box is a buncha file icons. If you find your file there, double-click on it to open. That file will then appear, ready for tweaking in your favorite program.

   You may need to use the left-right scrollbar at the bottom of the list to see more files.

2. **If your file can't be found, switch disk drives.**

   Use the Look in drop-down list at the top of the dialog box. Click on the down arrow on the right of the list to display it. Then pluck out a disk drive from the list, such as drive C, to start looking there.

   The contents of the big list in the center of the dialog box change to show you the files on drive C (in the *root folder*).

   If you find your file, open it!

3. **Open up a folder for further looking.**

   If you can't find your file, look for a folder in the big list. Double-click on the folder to open it and look in there for the file.

   Keep opening folders to find the one you want. (If your hard drive is organized and your folders cleverly named, this should be a snap.)

   If you find your file, open it!

    If you want to go back up to the previous folder, click the handy Up One Level button (shown in the margin).

   ✔ At the bottom of the dialog box is a drop-down list titled Files of type. This can help you narrow down the types of files displayed in the Open dialog box's big list. For example, in Figure 8-4, only files of the Word for Windows 6.0 (*.doc) type are displayed in the big list. Another option is All files, which displays every type of file available.

✔ Some Open dialog boxes are more complex than the one shown in Figure 8-4. For example, the Open dialog box in Microsoft Word is really a doozy. It still works the same; there are just more annoying options to ignore.

✔ The Browse dialog box is similar to the Open dialog box. It appears whenever you click a Browse button to go hunt down a file for Windows.

✔ If you're nerdy, you can type the file's full pathname (if you know it) into the File name box. This is a very DOSy thing to do. Cover your mouse's eyes if you try it (you don't want to shame him).

Using the Save Dialog Box

The Save dialog box is the most important dialog box you'll ever use in Windows. It's the key to organization. If you use it properly and take advantage of the unique folders you've created, you'll *always* be able to find your stuff on disk. Misuse the Save dialog box and, heck, the bad guys will take over the Wild West and Miss Millie and the orphans will go hungry, maybe even die. You wouldn't want that on your conscience, would ya?

You summon the Save dialog box by using the File⇨Save command. (I know it says "Save As" in Figure 8-5, but it's still what you see when you first save a file, so there.) Here's how you go about working it:

Figure 8-5:
The typical
Save dialog
box.

1. **Most important: Make sure you're in the proper folder.**

   The Save dialog box initially puts your document someplace strange, like in the Windows folder, or maybe even in the root folder on drive C. Not what you want!

The folder's name is listed in the Save in drop-down list. In Figure 8-5, it's Windows. (Yech!) If that isn't what you want, move on to step 2.

If the folder is OK, skip up to step 4.

2. **Hunt for the folder in which you want to save your stuff.**

Click on the down arrow on the right of the Save in drop-down list (at the top of the dialog box). This displays a drop-down list. In the list, click on the proper disk drive on which you want to save your file, for example drive C.

You'll notice that the contents of the big list in the center of the dialog box change to show you the files in the root folder on drive C.

I don't recommend saving your file in the root folder; it's not kosher.

3. **Open a folder.**

Locate the folder in which you want to save your stuff, or the folder that contains the folder (and so on). For example, open your Work folder or your My Documents folder.

As you open various folders, the contents of the file list in the center of the dialog box change.

When you find the folder you want — the perfect folder for your stuff — move on to the next step. Otherwise, keep opening folders.

4. **Type in a name for the saved file.**

Into the File name input box, type a name. This is the name for your saved file, the name you should be able to recognize later and say (out loud) "Say! That's my file. The one I want. I am so happy I saved it with a short, clever name that tells me exactly what's in the file. Oh, joy."

See Chapter 9 for more information on naming files. Basically you can name a file anything you want, but being brief and sticking to letters and numbers are best.

If you give the file an unacceptable name, you won't be able to save it. Windows is fussy about this.

5. **Click the Save button.**

Click! This last, official act saves the file to disk, with a proper name, in a proper folder.

If the Save button appears to be broken, you probably typed in an improper filename. Try giving the file a new name (step 4).

After you save your stuff once, the File⇨Save command simply re-saves it to disk without you having to give it another name and work the Save dialog box.

You can choose the Save As command again to see the Save As dialog box (again). This allows you to save something you're working on with a new name, in a new location, or as a different type of file.

As with the Open dialog box, some Save dialog boxes are more complex than the one shown in Figure 8-5. Same business goes on, just more things to get in the way.

"What the Heck Is a Pathname?"

A pathname is geek-speak for the longest possible filename you can imagine. It's actually used to pinpoint a file's location on a certain disk drive and in a certain folder. Long. Technical. Complex. It's a wonder anyone has to deal with these things.

As an example, consider the file named Red Blocks.bmp. This file typically lives in the Windows folder on drive C. Therefore, its full, ugly pathname is as follows:

```
C:\WINDOWS\RED BLOCKS.BMP
```

This reads as follows:

`C:`	It's on drive C.
`\WINDOWS`	It's in the Windows folder.
`RED BLOCKS.BMP`	The filename.

Therefore, the pathname tells you right where the file is. As an example, suppose you were told to go out and hunt down the file represented by the following pathname:

```
C:\MY DOCUMENTS\PERSONAL\LETTERS\FAMILY\JODY.DOC
```

You would look on drive C, open the My Documents folder, open the Personal folder, open Letters, open Family, and then look for the file named Jody.doc.

- ✔ The backslash is used as a separator in a pathname. It separates the drive letter from the first folder, all the folders in between, and the last folder name from the filename.

- ✔ A double-backslash(\\ ) at the start of a pathname means you've discovered something on a network hard drive. Run for cover! (See Chapter 10 for more information on computer networks.)

✔ Don't confuse the backslash (\) with the slash character (/). Windows uses the backslash for some backwards reason.

✔ See Chapter 9 for more information on filenames.

✔ A full pathname usually includes the filename extension — the period and last three characters of the filename. You may have directed Windows to withhold that information from you, not displaying it in My Computer or the Explorer. Even so, you *need* that information for a pathname. See? It is technical.

✔ The terrible thing about a pathname is that you often have to make them up yourself. For example, some program may say "Enter the pathname to your file," in which case it's up to *you* to figure everything out.

Chapter 9
Messin' with Files

. . . .

In This Chapter

▶ Naming a file

▶ Discovering what not to name a file

▶ Renaming a file

▶ Selecting file icons

▶ Moving files (cut and paste)

▶ Copying files (copy and paste)

▶ Making a file shortcut

▶ Deleting files

▶ Undeleting files

▶ Dragging files with the mouse

▶ Finding files

. . . .

*F*iles are chunks of stuff stored on your PC's disk drives. When you create something, you save it to disk as a file. To work on it again, you open that file. Easy enough.

The hard part comes with controlling the files. Like a kindergarten teacher with a room full of unruly five-year-olds, it's your job to make sure the files don't get out of hand. Fortunately, Windows lets you organize the files; just like in kindergarten, you can cut and paste, putting them where they belong. And you can give them new names and even kill them off — all without offending anyone's sense of moral justice.

✔ Windows displays files as *icons*. The icon is really the picture you see, either on the desktop or in the My Computer or Explorer programs. The file is what actually lives on disk.

✔ Everything on disk is a *file*. Some files are *programs*, some files are *documents* or stuff you create.

File Naming Rules & Regulations

If there's one thing mankind is good at, it's giving things names. Find a new bug, you get to name it. Discover a comet, and you can slap it with a new name; scientists exploring the cosmos give stars and features on planets new names every day. Even back when God showed Adam all the animals (Genesis 1:19, 20), he gave them all clever names. Adam didn't say, "There's a dog! There's another dog! That's a dog, too!" This leads me to believe that Adam was definitely more than three years old at the time. But I digress.

When you create something on your PC and save it to disk, you should give it a proper name. That name is attached to the stuff you created as a file. You see the file (as an icon) in the My Computer and Explorer programs and anytime you use an Open or Browse dialog box. That's how computers keep your stuff organized.

- ✔ The file's name reminds you of what's in the file, of what's it all about. Just like naming the dog "Downstoppit" tells everyone what the dog is all about.

- ✔ All the rules for naming files in the following sections also apply to naming folders.

- ✔ See Chapter 8 for more information on the Open dialog box.

- ✔ I realize that not everyone accepts the idea that Adam sat down one spring day to name all the beasts that creepeth and crawleth. But you gotta figure someone did it sometime.

- ✔ The rules and regulations offered in the sections that follow apply strictly to Windows 95. Just in case you don't use that operating system and — somehow — get this book, *don't try it!* The filenames won't work. Get the third edition of *PCs For Dummies* or an older DOS or Windows book, instead.

File naming tips

Keep the following notions in mind when you name any file:

Be brief. Keep the filename brief, yet descriptive. The following are good examples:

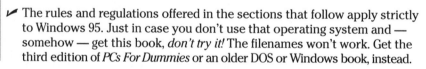

```
Stocks
Outline
House plans
Vacation Itinerary
Plot to overthrow Finland
```

Use only letters, numbers, and spaces. Filenames can contain just about any key you press on the keyboard. Even so, it's best to stick with letters, numbers, and spaces.

- Technically, you can give a file a 255-character-long name. Don't.

- If you give a file too long of a name, it's easier to make a single typo and confuse Windows when you try to open the file.

- Uppercase or lowercase doesn't matter to your computer. Though it's proper to capitalize, say, Finland, your computer will match that to `finland`, `Finland`, `FINLAND`, or any combination of upper- or lowercase letters.

Don't name a file this way

Windows gets mad if you use any of the following characters to name a file:

> `* / : < > ? \ |`

Nothing bad happens if you attempt to use these characters; Windows just refuses to save the file or change its name. (A warning dialog box may glow in your face if you make the attempt.)

- Though you can use any number of periods in a filename, you cannot name a file with all periods. I know this is strange and I'm probably the only one on the planet to have tried it, but it still won't work.

What the heck is a filename *extension*?

The last part of a filename is typically a period followed by one to three characters. This is known as the filename extension. It's used by Windows to identify the type of file. For example, an extension `.BMP` tags a Paint graphics image and `.DOC` indicates a document created by WordPad.

You never need to type in these extensions when you name or rename a file. In fact, you shouldn't. Windows *needs* that information — that filename extension — or it screws up when you try to open the file for editing.

A way around the filename extension dilemma is to choose View⇨Options from the Explorer or My Computer program's menu. This displays the Options dialog box. Make sure two options there are switched on: `Hide files of these types` and `Hide MS-DOS file extensions for file types that are registered`. Click on either of these items to put a dot or check mark by them. This effectively turns off the display of filename extensions so you never have to bother with them again.

Click OK to exit the Options dialog box.

Renaming a file

If you think the name you just gave a file is stupid, it can easily be changed. Here's how:

1. **Locate the file.**

   Use the My Computer or Explorer programs to find your program, or it may be stuck right on the desktop.

2. **Select the file.**

   When you found the file, click on it once with the mouse. This selects the file, highlighting it on the screen.

3. **Press the F2 key.**

   This is the shortcut key for the Rename command. You can also choose File➪Rename from the menu.

4. **Type in a new name.**

   Type in the name. Use the Backspace key to backup and erase if you need to.

   You'll notice that the text for the old name is selected. If you're familiar with using Windows text editing keys, you can use them to edit the old name if you like. (See "Common Windows Editing Keys" in Chapter 15 for more information.)

5. **Press the Enter key.**

   This locks in the new name.

   ✓ You can press the Esc key at any time before pressing Enter to undo the damage and return to the file's original name.

   ✓ Windows won't let you rename a file with the name of a file that already exists.

   ✓ You must give a file a name. You cannot name a file nothing.

   ✓ You cannot rename a group of files at once. Rename files only one at a time.

Files Hither, Thither, and Yon

Files just don't stand still. You'll always find yourself moving them, copying them, killing them off, and so on. If you don't do this, your hard drive gets all junky and, out of embarrassment, you'll be forced to turn off the computer when friends come over.

Messing with files is done primarily in the My Computer or Explorer programs. My Computer is friendlier and makes more sense if you're just starting out. After a time, you may prefer the Explorer since it doesn't litter the screen with windows, one for every folder.

Selecting one or more files

Before you can mess with any file, it must be selected. Like log rolling, this can be done individually or in groups.

To select a single file, locate it in My Computer or the Explorer. When you find the file, click on it once with the mouse. This selects the file, which appears highlighted (blue, possibly) on the screen. The file is now ready for action.

Selecting a group of files can be done in a number of ways. The easiest way is to press and hold down the Ctrl (control) key on your keyboard. Then click all the files you want selected as a group, one after the other. This is known as *control-clicking* files.

If you're looking at files using the icon view, you can lasso a group of them by using the mouse. Drag the mouse over the files: Start in the upper-left corner above the files; then drag down and to the right to create a rectangle surrounding the file icons you want to select (see Figure 9-1). Release the mouse button, and all the files you've lassoed are selected as a group.

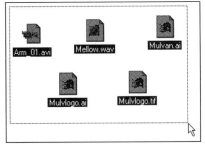

Figure 9-1:
A group of
files is
selected.

> ✔ To select a group of files, press and hold the Ctrl key as you click each one.
>
> ✔ To select all the files in a folder, choose Edit⇨Select All. The handy keyboard shortcut key for this is Ctrl+A.
>
> ✔ To unselect a file from a group, just Ctrl-click it again.

Cutting and pasting files

In the old days, you didn't cut and paste a file, you *moved* it. With Windows, where everything is like kindergarten anyway, you cut and paste.

To cut and paste (move) a file, follow these steps:

1. **Locate the file you want to move.**

   Hunker down in the Explorer or My Computer program, looking for the file or files you want to move.

2. **Select it.**

   Click the file once to select it. Or you can select a group of files, using the techniques described earlier in this chapter.

3. **Choose Edit⇨Cut.**

   The file appears dimmed in the window. This means it's been *cut* and is ready to be pasted. Nothing is wrong; keep moving on with the next step.

4. **Open the folder where you want the file pasted.**

   Again, use the Explorer or My Computer program to hunt down the proper destination folder.

5. **Choose Edit⇨Paste.**

   The file is deeply moved.

- ✔ Don't eat the paste.
- ✔ You can also cut and paste folders; however, this is a Big Deal because you're also cutting and pasting the folder's contents — which can be massive. Don't do this casually; cut and paste a folder only when you're up for major disk reorganization.

Copying and pasting files

Copying and pasting a file works just like cutting and pasting. There are two differences:

The original file isn't deleted. When you're done copying and pasting, you have two identical copies of the file: the original and the copy.

The second difference is that you use the Edit⇨Copy command instead of Edit⇨Cut. See the preceding section for the steps and details.

- ✔ Oftentimes, you don't really need to copy a file anywhere on your hard drive. Instead, you should create a shortcut to that file. See the section "Creating shortcuts" later in this chapter.

Copying a file to a floppy disk

A simple way to copy one or more files to a floppy disk is to use the Send To command. This is cinchy.

1. **Locate the file you want to copy to your floppy.**

   Use My Computer or the Explorer for this.

2. **Select it.**

   Click on the file to select it, or use the Ctrl key and control-click a group of files.

3. **Make sure there is a formatted floppy disk ready for the file in drive A.**

   See Chapter 7 for more information on floppy disks, formatting them, and sticking one in drive A.

4. **Choose File⇨Send To⇨3¹/₂ Floppy (A)**

   The file is copied.

> ✔ The Send To sub-menu lists the type of floppy drives your PC has. For example, if drive B is your 3¹/₂-inch floppy, the menu item will say 3¹/₂ Floppy (B). If drive A is a 5¹/₄-inch floppy, you see 5¹/₄ Floppy (A) on the menu.

Creating shortcuts

A shortcut is a 99 percent fat free copy of a file. It allows you to see and access the file from anywhere on your system but without the extra baggage required to copy the file all over creation.

For example, you can drop a shortcut to WordPerfect on the desktop, where you can always get to it — a lot quicker than using the Start menu.

Making a shortcut is a cinch: Just follow the same steps for copying a file as detailed in the previous sections on cutting, copying, and pasting files. The only exception is that you choose Edit⇨Paste Shortcut from the menu instead of the standard Paste command.

To paste a shortcut on the desktop, point the mouse at the desktop and click the right mouse button. Up pops a shortcut menu, from which you can choose the Paste Shortcut command.

Shortcut to
Work Folder

- ✔ Shortcut icons have a little arrow in a white box, nestled into their lower-left corner (see the figure in the margin). This icon is what tells you the file is a shortcut and not the real McCoy.

- ✔ You can make shortcuts for popular folders and stick them on the desktop for easy access.

- ✔ You can open shortcuts just like any other icon: Double-click to open that document, run an application, or open a folder.

- ✔ Have no fear when deleting shortcuts; removing that icon does not remove the original file.

- ✔ Windows gives each shortcut a name, starting with `Shortcut to` and ending with the original filename. You can use the techniques described earlier in this chapter to rename the shortcut to something more sane.

Deleting files

Unlike credit cards and driver's licenses, files don't simply expire. You must make an effort to rid yourself of old or temporary files you don't need. Otherwise, files collect like lint balls outside a dryer vent.

To kill a file, select it and choose File⇨Delete. This process doesn't truly remove the file; it merely moves the thing over to the Recycle Bin. From there the file can easily be undeleted at some future point.

If there is a sensitive file you want utterly crushed, click on it once with the mouse and press Shift+Delete. Windows displays a warning dialog box, explaining that the file will be utterly crushed (or something to that effect). Click Yes to zap it off to eternity.

- ✔ You can also delete files by pressing the Delete key.

- ✔ Oh, and there's the Delete button on the toolbar. Choose View⇨Toolbar from My Computer's or the Explorer's menu to see the toolbar.

- ✔ You can delete folders like you do files, though keep in mind that you delete the folder's contents — which could be dozens of icons, files, folders, jewelry, small children, and food for the homeless. Better be careful on that one.

- ✔ Never delete any file in the Windows folder or any of the folders in the Windows folder.

- ✔ Never delete any file in the root folder of a hard drive.

- ✔ In fact, never delete any file unless you created it yourself.

- ✔ Don't delete programs! Instead, you can use a special tool in the Windows Control Panel for removing old applications you no longer need. See Chapter 20 for more information.

Undeleting files

Since you probably want your file back in a hurry, here it goes:

Recycle Bin

1. Open the Recycle Bin on the desktop.

Double-click the Recycle Bin icon. It looks like a little trash can, pictured in the margin.

If you have the Plus! package installed, you may have changed the Recycle Bin icon to resemble something else. I don't know what, so I can't tell you exactly here.

Figure 9-2 shows the Recycle Bin's window open on my computer. I've chosen the View⇨Details command because it allows me to sort the files in a specific order, as well as see other nerdy information.

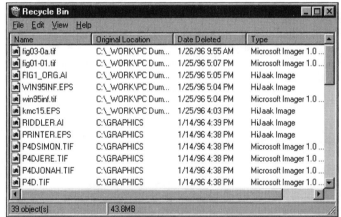

Figure 9-2:
Junk in the
Recycle Bin.

2. Select the file you want recovered.

Click on the file to resurrect it.

An advantage of selecting the View⇨Details command (shown in Figure 9-2) is that you can sort the files in the Recycle Bin according to the date they were deleted. Simply click on the `Date Deleted` column heading, and the files are sorted most-recently-deceased first. (Click that column heading again to sort things in reverse order.) This display helps you scope out recently departed files you may want back.

3. Choose File⇨Restore.

The file is magically removed from the Recycle Bin and restored to the folder and disk from which it was so brutally seized.

4. Close the Recycle Bin window.

Click on the window's X close button in the upper-right corner.

✔ There is no time limit on when you can restore files; they'll be available in the Recycle Bin for quite some time.

✔ Even so: Don't let the convenience of the Recycle Bin lead you down the path of sloppiness. Never delete a file unless you're certain you want it gone, gone, gone.

Flush!

The Recycle Bin can eat up a lot of your PC's disk space, what with storing all those zombie files and whatnot. In fact, my Recycle Bin (shown in Figure 9-2) contains 43.8MB worth of junk! That's four times bigger than my first PC hard drive!

If you need more disk space, you can *empty* the Recycle Bin. Choose File⇨Empty Recycle Bin from the Recycle Bin's menu.

Emptying the Recycle Bin permanently zaps all those files; after doing so you won't be able to recover anything. Be careful!

Working with Files Can Be a Drag

It's possible to cut, copy, and paste your files without having to choose any menu items. You simply grab the files you want to tweak and move or copy them with the mouse.

The only drawback to this approach is that you must have *two* or more folders open on your desktop at once to make it work. As an example, Figure 9-3 shows two windows representing two folders.

Moving files: To move a file from one folder to another, drag it with the mouse from one window to another, which is sort of shown in the figure (envision the dragging action in your head). The mouse is dragging the file UAU!.WAV from the Audio folder into the Video folder.

Copying files: To copy a file from one folder's window to another, press and hold the Ctrl key, and then drag the file. This is known as a *control-drag*.

✔ Files are *moved* when you drag them from one folder to another on the same hard drive.

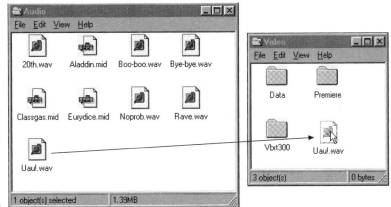

Figure 9-3:
Files fly
between
two folder
windows.

- ✔ Files are *copied* when you drag them from one disk drive to another.

- ✔ To move a file from one disk to another, press and hold the Shift key before you click on the file to drag it.

Finding Wayward Files (and Programs)

Files come and go. You may never find that one file you're looking for — especially if you're an unorganized person. Or maybe you saved your files in a panic during an earthquake. No finger wagging here; instead, follow these steps to locate any wayward file:

The cinchy way to copy and move files (if you can remember it)

Copying. Moving. Dragging. Control-dragging. It's a mess! The way I remember the difference between copying and moving files is not to memorize the techniques at all. Instead, I use the *right* mouse button to drag any file or group of files I want moved, copied, or shortcutted.

When you drag file icons around using the right mouse button and then release the right mouse button, a pop-up menu appears. That menu has four items on it: Move Here, Copy Here, Create Shortcut(s) Here, and Cancel. Choose one of those options to move, copy, or paste a shortcut of the file(s) you're dragging.

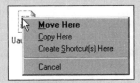

In the Explorer program window, choose Tools⇨Find⇨Files or Folders. In My Computer, choose File⇨Find. This displays the Find dialog box, as shown in Figure 9-4. By working the various controls there, you can hunt down just about any file or folder anywhere in your computer — even if it fell out of a hole in the back and lay tangled in your cable vines.

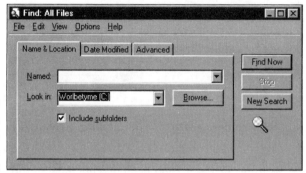

Figure 9-4:
The Find
dialog box.

The following sections tell you how to work the Find dialog box to find whatever files you're looking for. In all cases, when the search is done, you see one of two results:

No dice. If no files are found, you see the message 0 file(s) found at the bottom of the Find dialog box. The file list will be empty. Weep bitterly and gnash your teeth.

Eureka! When files are found, they're listed in the Find dialog box's file list. Figure 9-5 shows files that have been found on the hard drive. Whew!

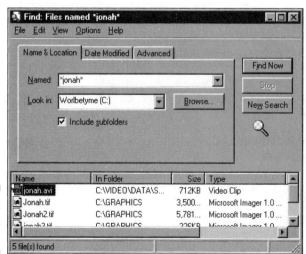

Figure 9-5:
There be
files here!

After the files have been found, you can do one of three things with them:

- Double-click on the file in the file list to open it, to run that program or edit that file.

- Drag the file out onto the desktop, from where you can more easily access it, or drag it into the folder you thought it should be in.

- Simply look in the file list's In Folder column to see which folder holds that file. In Figure 9-5, the second, third, and fourth files are in the Graphics folder on drive C.

✔ You can also get to the Find dialog box from the Start menu. Choose Find➪Files or Folders.

✔ Refer to "What is a pathname" in Chapter 8 for more information on reading the In Folder column in the Find dialog box.

✔ You can mix and match the searching methods described in the following sections. The more you can tell Windows about the file, the easier it can find just the one you're looking for.

"Quick! Hurry! I want to find a lost file!"

Summon the Find dialog box. Click on the Name & Location tab to bring that panel in front (as in Figure 9-4).

1. **Type your file name into the Named input box.**

2. **From the Look in drop-down list, choose your main hard drive, C.**

   Or if you know the file is on another disk drive in your system, choose it instead. (Or just choose one after the other.)

3. **Make sure the box by Include subfolders has a check mark in it.**

   If not, click the mouse in that box.

4. **Click the Find Now button.**

   Any matching files found are displayed in the list at the bottom of the dialog box.

✔ If you don't know the exact name but only know part of a filename, use asterisks to fill in the parts you don't know. For example, I have various graphics files of my son Jonah on disk. To find them all, I had Windows search using this pattern:

```
*JONAH*
```

The results of that search are shown in Figure 9-5. The asterisks match all characters before and after JONAH. If I knew the file started with JONAH, I could type the following:

```
JONAH*
```

The asterisk matches any or all of the characters at the end of the filename. The same holds true for the beginning.

```
*JONAH
```

The asterisk matches all characters that come before JONAH in a filename.

"Where the heck is my program?"

Finding programs works just like finding files. Follow the steps in the preceding section, and type in your program name for the filename.

If you don't know the program name, click the mouse on the Advanced tab in the Find dialog box. That brings the Advanced panel forward.

In the Of type drop-down list, select the Application item.

Click the Find Now button.

The Find dialog box lists all the programs on your computer. All of them. Your program is somewhere in the list. Use the scrollbars to locate it.

"I forgot the name of the file, but I know it contains the word 'execrable!'"

Follow these steps:

1. **Bring up the** Advanced **panel in the Find dialog box.**

   Click the mouse on the Advanced tab to bring the Advanced panel forward if it isn't already.

2. **Make sure** All Files and Folders **is selected in the** Of type **drop-down list.**

   If it isn't, choose that item: Click the mouse on the down arrow to the right of the drop-down list. Pluck out All Files and Folders from the list. (It should be the first item.)

You can save a little time if you know which program created the document you want to find. For example, if you know it's a Word document, you can choose `Microsoft Word document` from the drop-down list.

3. Press the Tab key.

This moves you over to the `Containing text` input box.

4. Type in the text you need to search for.

Enter the smallest tidbit of text you suppose would exactly match text in that one file you're looking for. Such as

`execrable`

Don't add a period at the end.

5. Click the `Find Now` button.

Hopefully, the file list will show you what you want. If not, you can try again with another word.

✔ My wife recently used this method to find our brother-in-law's resumé on the computer. She typed in his last name. Out of the many documents found, one named `Document` turned out to be the right one. Moral: Name your resumé documents `Resumé`, not `Document`.

"I forgot the file's name, but I know it's a spreadsheet!"

Searching by file-type displays a ton of files, but it's a better way to find a wayward file than scouting through *every* file on your hard drive. Here you go:

1. Summon the `Advanced` panel in the Find dialog box.

Click on the `Advanced tab`. This brings the Advanced panel front and center.

2. Choose the file type from the `Of type` drop-down list.

For example, click on `Microsoft Excel Worksheet` in the list. If the file is of another type, choose that proper type from the list.

3. Click the `Find Now` button.

I'll guarantee you that a lot of files will be displayed. Your job is to search through the list to find the exact one you want. Good luck!

If you need to be more precise, you can search for the file better if you know the exact date on which it was created or last saved to disk. This trick is covered in the next section.

"All I know is I created it last Tuesday!"

To find a file created on a specific date, try these steps:

1. **Bring up the** `Date Modified` **panel in the Find dialog box.**

   Click the mouse on the `Date Modified` tab to bring that panel forward in the Find dialog box.

2. **Click on the button by** `Find all files created or modified`.

   This action allows you to choose one of the three options at the bottom of the panel, each depending on how well you can zero in on the date your file was created or last saved to disk.

3a. **If you know the file was created in the last month, click on** `during the previous X month(s)` **button.**

   Use the up or down buttons to change the number of months, 1 for one month, 6 for six months, and so on.

   This process is perhaps the least accurate and most time-consuming way to find a file by its date; lots of files will be listed.

3b. **If you know the file was created just a few days ago, click on** `during the previous X day(s)` **button.**

   Use the up or down buttons to enter the number of days back to search. For example, if today is Thursday and you think you created the file sometime this week, enter 4 into the box.

   This method is more exact than searching by month but not as precise as knowing the exact date.

3c. **If you kind of know the date when the file was created, click on the** `between X and X` **button.**

   Input the proper dates into the boxes, earliest date first. Or if you know the file was created on November 1, 1996, type **11/1/96** into both boxes. Or, better still, type **10/31/96** into the first box and **11/2/96** into the second.

4. **Click the** `Find Now` **button.**

   Windows lists a batch of files for you to scour. Why so many? Because it listed all the files created on the dates you specified. That could potentially be a hoard.

   ✔ Combining this searching technique with the others typically narrows down the file list to the ones you want.

   ✔ Refer to Chapter 8 for excellent methods on storing files in folders so you never lose anything again.

Chapter 10

Ode to the Network Slave

*I*n the beginning, there were these humongous computers called *mainframes*. They lived in air-conditioned glass rooms and sucked up more power than an army of Hoovers. Spindly, tanless men in lab coats ran the computers. They scoffed at and belittled the sorry users of their computers, who were shackled to the mainframe by means of a cable and working on a *dumb terminal* — a computer without a brain. Little did they know that the Personal Computer Revolution was coming. Soon, users would each have their own personal computer. The era of computer independence would be born.

Today, the mainframe computer is all but dead. But filling the space of its vacuum tubes are computer networks. This is where you take a formerly independent computer and wire it together with other personal computers. Two or more computers shackled to each other — with maybe a printer tossed in between them — is a *network*. You can add more computers, printers — even mainframes and orbiting satellites. It boggles the mind.

The concept of a network and how it works is way beyond the realm of *PCs For Dummies*. You'll have to look elsewhere for the techy, plug-this-in stuff. If you're a sole computer user sitting at home in your den, you can read this chapter for extra bonus points, redeemable for valuable cash prizes. Otherwise, everyone at the office or anyone who's heard about *the network* should glance at a few of the sections in this chapter.

🖊 A *node* is a computer on the network. If your computer is on a network, it's a node.

🖊 This chapter covers only the measly peer-to-peer networking that comes with Windows. Novell networking? Banyan vines? Go somewhere else.

Can't We All Get Along?

A lust for sharing information is created on a computer. Not just a lust — a necessity. The screen satisfies this lust by showing you the results of your labors. The printer is another extension, providing you with valuable hard copy. The hard copy — OK, *paper* — can be shared with a number of users, but the information is still locked up electronically inside the PC.

One day, someone noticed how silly it was to make hard copy and then have another computer user retype all that information. After all, the information was in the computer. Why couldn't they just beam it back and forth between computers? And that's what most of them did in two ways: by sharing disks between two computers and by connecting the computers by using special cables.

🖊 Sharing disks is only possible if the two computers read the same disk format. For all PCs, this isn't a hassle. This is the way most information is shared and distributed: You grab it off of a floppy disk and save it on your computer's hard drive.

🖊 Sharing disks between different types of computers, say Macintoshes and PCs, is not easy. Those two systems use different disk formats. A PC cannot read a Macintosh disk, nor can it understand what's on that disk. (Refer to "Exchanging Disks and Files" later in this chapter for more information.)

🖊 Any two computers equipped with serial ports can be connected together with a *null-modem cable* so that they can exchange information. It's also possible for the different systems to talk over phone lines by using a modem. The null-modem cable is simply a more direct route, usually intended for two computers sitting together in the same room.

🖊 Refer to Chapter 17 for additional information on modems. Elaborate elocution on null-modem cables is offered in a technoid sidebar.

Extra boring information about the infamous null-modem cable

Nothing causes more headaches than dealing with the null-modem cable or its evil twin, the null-modem adapter. So stop writing all those cards and letters and listen up.

A null-modem cable is actually a special sort of serial cable. It's also called a *twisted pair*. It's designed so that a cable between two computers' serial ports has the talk-listen wires switched: talk-to-listen, listen-to-talk. Otherwise, the computers would have their talk-to-talk lines and listen-to-listen lines connected, and it would be too much like the United Nations to get anything accomplished. The null-modem adapter is simply a small box that swaps the wires for a standard serial cable.

After both computers are hooked together comes the tricky part. Both systems must run special communications software and require tedious configuring and liters of sweat to get everything right. Even then, you can only exchange basic text files (ASCII) between the two separate systems. This is really something more for bored nerds to tinker with than for real humans such as you and me to worry about.

If you really need to send files between two computers, or a desktop PC and a laptop model, you can buy software to do it. Some software even comes with special cables to make the job easier.

The 29¢ Overview of Everything a Network Is All About

Caution: Do not attempt to drive or operate any heavy machinery while reading the following information.

Computers have networks; so does your television. Computers have programs; so does the television. And computers can use that black cable — with the pokey wire in the middle — just like cable television. In a way, a computer network is very similar to something you'd pick up on your television but far, far more productive.

Up front, I'm happy to tell you that networks, networking, and *connectivity* (a big ugly IBM word meaning "plug this into the cat and watch it jump!") is a job best left up to Those In Charge. No one enjoys working with networks. Sane people pay undernourished compuphiles millions of dollars a year to create and maintain networks. So your knowledge about them need only be minimal. Here's the good stuff:

- Networks are about three things: exchanging files, sharing resources, and running common programs.

- *Exchanging files* means that you can send and receive files from other people on the network without having to leave your computer. Either the files come waddling down the network cable, or you pick them up from a central drop-off point. The idea here is that you can get information from another computer without someone's having to hand you a floppy disk.

- *Sharing resources* refers to common hardware that several computers can use on the network. For example, the printer down the hall may be *on* the network. You can print on it, and so can Bob in accounting or Phyllis or that new person they hired in marketing that everyone assumes is having an affair with the boss. Certain hard drives may be *on* the network. You can copy your files to there or from there.

- *Running common programs* refers to applications kept on other computers. With some types of networks, you can access another computer and run a program on that computer — all through a little wire hanging out the back of your PC. That works, but it slows down the other computer immensely. Instead, a big computer is often dedicated as the file server. Its task is to act as a huge disk drive to hold programs for everyone else to use.

- Networks are often called *LANs*. LAN is an acronym for Local Area Network.

"What is Client-Server Computing?"

I haven't the foggiest idea.

Logging In to the Network

Before you use a network, you must log in. You log in when you first start Windows. You're presented with a dialog box that tells you to log in to the network.

Actually, the box never says "login" or "log in." But that's what it would have said had Microsoft not wanted Windows to be so dern friendly. It says User name instead. Two words. Much friendlier.

You log in by typing in your user name, which is usually some appalling contraction of your first and last names, and then by pressing the Tab key and typing in your secret password, which is probably written on a Sticky Note pasted to your monitor. Figure 10-1 shows the Windows log in dialog box, which you may see every time you start Windows.

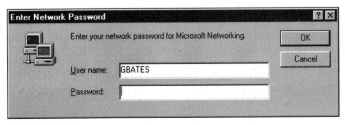

Figure 10-1:
That
annoying
log in dialog
box.

- ✔ After you log in, you can use the network.
- ✔ Even so, if you don't want to log in, press the Esc key when you see the log in dialog box and you can still use the network.
- ✔ If you have a password, don't write it down! Commit it to memory, lest your papers fall into enemy hands.
- ✔ After you've logged in, you can access the network printer and various drives on the network. Using the drives and printers is covered in the following few sections of this chapter.

Doing Net Things

A networked PC means you can do networky things. Primarily you can use other printers and disk drives on the network. And if you find files on those disk drives, you might be able to steal them or run programs. Any folder named Financial Data on any network computer is fair game. It's a Silicon Valley law.

A loverly stroll through the Network Neighborhood

If you have a networked Windows computer, you'll be able to find an icon on the desktop called Network Neighborhood. That's your key to all the computers and printers on the network. The icon is depicted in the margin.

There are two ways to fish for things in the Network Neighborhood. The second way is stupid, so I won't talk about it here at all. The first, and obvious, way is to open the Network Neighborhood icon by double-clicking it. This action displays a window detailing all the computers in your network, similar to Figure 10-2.

Figure 10-2:
Computers
on the
network.

Not every computer on the network shares everything. For example, the computer named Marcia in Figure 10-2 doesn't share anything— no disk drives or printers. The computer named Cindy, however, shares a few things.

You can see what a computer shares by opening up that computer's icon; double-click on it in the Network Neighborhood folder. Figure 10-3 shows how Windows displays the things that Cindy's computer shares.

Figure 10-3:
Items
available for
sharing on a
computer.

✔ Folders in a computer's window are up for grabs.

✔ In Figure 10-3, the folder named Drive C represents all folders on the hard drive C.

✔ You can access files in those folders by opening them up — just as you would on your computer.

✔ Printers in a computer's folder, as in Figure 10-3, indicate that your computer can access and use that network printer for printing. To make it so, double-click on the printer's icon to set things up. (It's a long, technical process you probably want someone else to do.)

✔ The Network Neighborhood is safe enough for you to go outside at night.

✔ You can change the view in the Network Neighborhood window just as you can in any Explorer or My Computer window: Choose a new view from the View menu. Figure 10-2 shows what you see after choosing the View⇨Large Icons command.

Using a network disk drive or folder

The basic job of the network is to keep you from walking somewhere else in your office with a floppy disk. Exchanging disks in that manner is referred to as *sneaker net* by computer wieners. Sneaker net. Get it? The network consists of walking disks back and forth. Ah, such jocularity.

To move a file to another computer on the network, you must access a network drive, which is a hard drive (or a floppy drive) on any computer other than your own. You can fish out the file on that drive using the Network Neighborhood. But a better way is to always have that drive present on your computer. It lives in the My Computer window as a so-called network drive.

Figure 10-4 shows the My Computer window. In it you see two network disk drives, labeled M and S. These are disk drives on other computers on the network; M represents drive C on the computer called Monkey king, and S represents drive C on the computer called Sybil. These hard drives can be used like any other hard drives, though they live elsewhere in the Network Neighborhood.

Figure 10-4:
Check out the networked drives M and S.

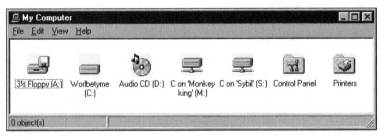

To add a network drive to your My Computer window, follow these steps:

1. **Display the My Computer window on the desktop.**

   Open up the My Computer icon by double-clicking it with your mouse. This displays the main window. Leave it there for a few steps.

2. **Search for the network drive you want to add.**

   Open up the Network Neighborhood icon and search various computers on your network, looking for an available drive. (Refer to the section "A lovely stroll through the Network Neighborhood" earlier in this chapter for more information on probing the Network Neighborhood.)

   For example, you may open Greg's computer and find that his hard drive C is up and available for sharing.

   You can also open up any network drive to look for a specific folder you may want to have handy.

3. Drag the network drive (or folder) into the My Computer window.

Use the mouse to drag the icon from the networked computer's window over to My Computer's window.

When you release the mouse button, you'll see the Map Network Drive dialog box, as shown in Figure 10-5. Don't panic. I've never seen the word *map* used that way either.

Figure 10-5:
The Map
Network
Drive dialog
box.

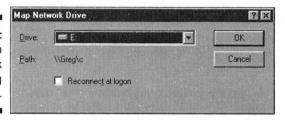

4. Choose a drive letter for the networked drive.

You can give the network drive any available drive letter on your computer (but not letters A, B, or C, which the PC is selfish about). So if you have a hard drive C, and a CD-ROM drive D, you can assign the networked drive any letter from E on up through Z. Whatever's available.

Personally, I would give Greg's hard drive the letter G on my system. G for Greg. Or Gag.

Choose the drive letter from the drop-down list or just press that letter key on your keyboard.

The drive letter you assign is personal to your computer. It does not affect any other computer on the network.

5. Do you always want to use the network drive?

If you want this network connection made every time you start your computer, click in the box by `Reconnect at logon`. This puts a check mark in the box, meaning Windows will always give you that network drive in My Computer's window when your PC starts. Nifty, eh?

6. Click `OK`.

Click. The networked drive is now as easy to use as any disk drive on your PC. Ah, the joys of networking.

✔ Network drives appear as disk drive icons, but with a little pipe beneath them (see Figure 10-4).

> ✔ You can even network with older Windows computers, though it works differently on those systems.
>
> ✔ Novell networks? I haven't a clue. That's why they pay the Novell guys so much money.

Disconnecting a network drive

If you no longer want to connect to a drive on the network, you need to disconnect. This works just like hanging up the phone; the connection isn't there any more, though the other disk drive is still fine and up for grabs on the network. (It doesn't delete the other drive, just like hanging up the phone on your friends doesn't kill them.)

Disconnect any folder by selecting that folder; click on its icon once with the mouse. Choose File⇨Disconnect. The folder is history.

Disconnect a network drive by selecting it and choosing File⇨Sharing from the menu. In the dialog box that appears, click the mouse on the radio button by `Not Shared` (which puts a dot in the circle). Click OK to close the dialog box. The drive is history.

"I Wanna Share My Drives and Folders on the Network!"

Surrendering your vital computer parts to the network is a snap. Of course, you may not want to do this, depending on what you keep on your computer. There is some security involved, but not much.

To make your disk drives or any folder up-for-grabs on the network, follow these steps:

1. **Select the disk drive or folder you want to share.**

   This is done in My Computer or the Explorer. Click once on the disk drive or folder. This action highlights the icon, displaying it in a horrid shade of blue.

2. **Choose File⇨Sharing.**

   The disk drive or folder's Properties dialog box appears, similar to what you see in Figure 10-6. Make sure the Sharing panel is forward; click on that tab if it is not.

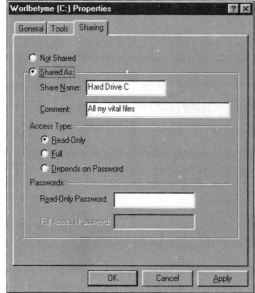

Figure 10-6:
A disk
drive's
Properties
dialog box.

3. Click on the Shared As button.

This puts a dot in that item's radio button, activating the rest of the dialog box. Next comes fill-in-the-blanks.

4. Type in a name for your shared drive.

The input box by Share Name typically contains the disk drive letter or folder name. You can leave it blank or be creative with something a wee bit more descriptive.

Don't press the Enter key yet!

5. Ah, forget typing a comment into the Comment box.

6. Choose an access level.

There are three levels of access for your hard drive, each of them listed under Access Type:

Read Only means that others can only look at the stuff on your hard drive. They can't erase anything, change anything, or add new files.

Full means they can do anything on your hard drive that you can — including erase every file and rename your vital system documents.

Depends on Password allows them either Read-Only or Full Access depending on which password they type. You set the passwords in the two input boxes at the bottom of the dialog box.

My advice: Choose <u>R</u>ead-On1y access. If you trust your co-workers, choose <u>F</u>u11. I don't mess with passwords since I forget them anyway. (All my computers share the same password: *none*.)

7. Click OK.

Your disk drive or folder is now shared. It works the same on your system but is available to others via the Network Neighborhood on their computers.

✔ When you share something, its icon grows a little serving hand.

✔ A *server* is a serving dish, typically silver with a domed lid. A *servant* is a person who serves you something.

✔ Sharing your printer works similarly to sharing a disk drive or folder. The printers attached to your PC are found in the Printers folder, which lurks in My Computer's main window. Aside from sharing the printer, you also need to make sure other computers on the network are properly configured to use that printer before they can print anything. See? Major pain. Let someone else do it.

Down Goes the Network, Glub, Glub, Glub

Networks crash more than little old ladies or teenagers. This doesn't mean that using a network is unstable business. Instead, you run into problems because too many things that barely work don't work well together. Eventually, one puff of air brings the whole house of cards tumbling down.

✔ When you suspect network trouble, yelp for help. Never try to fix the problem on your own (which is a safe assumption).

✔ When a network computer goes down, you can still use your PC; you just can't access any files or printers that were on that dead PC.

✔ Any network difficulty requires professional attention. Always have the network manager or supervisor check out problems before you attempt to do so on your own.

✔ Never unplug the network connections on the back of your PC when the network is on.

✔ *Crash* is the technical term for when a computer stops working. Nothing actually crunches or smashes. In fact, the typical crash is more like an ice age; everything suddenly stops, frozen in its tracks, and when the experts thaw it all out, they'll find a mammoth chewing on buttercups.

✔ General troubleshooting and "Oh Dear Lord, Help Me" advice is offered in Part VI of this book.

Part IV
The Non-Nerd's Guide to Computer Hardware

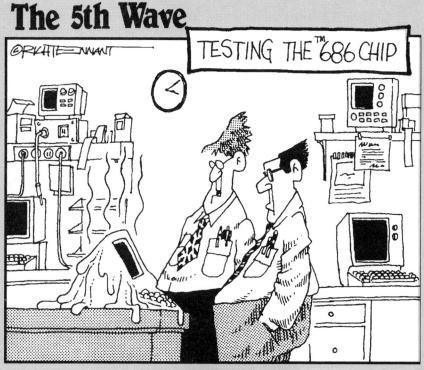

"IT'S FAST ENOUGH FOR ME."

In this part...

This isn't the kind of hardware you find in your neighborhood True Value store. Nope, it's a world of floppy drives, CPUs, EPROMs, cables, and really nerdy stuff. The sad part is you just can't use a computer without encountering hardware. And you need to know the terminology so when the manual says, "Plug this into your mouse port," you know not to take it personally.

There is no need to ever go into a technical description of the hardware in your PC. But as a human being, you very often have to touch that hardware, frequently at the bequest of some manual or loftier human who knows such things. This part of the book describes the various hardware goodies associated with a PC, the terms you encounter, and how everything fits into the Big Picture.

Chapter 11

Just Your Basic Computer Guts

••

In This Chapter

▶ A quick tour of the motherboard

▶ Getting to know the microprocessor

▶ Finding out which microprocessor your PC has

▶ Rumors about the OverDrive chip

▶ Understanding the BIOS

▶ All about printer ports, serial ports, and SCSI ports

▶ Setting the date and time

▶ Understanding expansion slots

▶ The power supply goes *POOF!*

••

*B*eneath its smooth, cream-colored case, your computer is a mess. Yes, it's a veritable sushi bar of interesting pieces, flecks, and chunks of technology. Tossed into this electronics salad are various components whose names you may encounter from time to time. There's the *motherboard, microprocessor, BIOS, ports, power supplies,* and *expansion slots.* This isn't anything you'd see — or even touch — but it's stuff you may want to understand. After all, you paid for it.

⌐ ✔ A major item inside your PC that's not covered in this chapter is memory. See Chapter 12 for a discussion of that.

The Mother of All Boards

The motherboard is the main piece of circuitry inside your PC. Like the downtown of a big city (except for Indianapolis), it's where everything happens.

The motherboard is important because the most important things inside your PC cling to it. In fact, for the most part, the console is simply a housing for the motherboard. (Disk drives used to be separate on some systems.) You'll find the following electronic goodies on the motherboard. There's no need to memorize this list.

- the microprocessor — the computer's main chip
- the computer's memory
- expansion slots and the special expansion cards that plug into them
- special chips called ROM chips
- the BIOS
- other support circuitry
- sharp pointy things

Although the motherboard contains a lot of items, it's essentially one unit and is referred to as such. Just like the mall has many stores but everyone calls it *the mall*.

- IBM calls the motherboard in their computers the *planar* board. Ugh.
- You can add or remove only two things on the motherboard: extra memory and expansion cards (which plug into the expansion slots). This chore, referred to as upgrading, is best left to the gurus.
- Oh, some motherboards allow you to remove and add a microprocessor. I recommend against this, however. I'll probably tell why later.

The Microprocessor

At the core of every computer is the *microprocessor*. That's the computer's main chip. No, it's not the computer's *brain*. (Software is the brain.) Instead, the microprocessor acts like a tiny, fast calculator. It just adds and subtracts (and does the sidestep and the jitterbug).

A more technical description, if you care

The motherboard is a piece of fiberglass, usually dark green in color, because computer scientists are a macho bunch and pink or powder blue is definitely out. Chips and whatnot are soldered to the motherboard and then connected by tiny copper wires, or traces, which look like little roads all over the motherboard. This is how the various chips, resistors, and capacitors chat with each other.

Electricity is supplied to everything via a thin metal sheet sandwiched in the middle of the motherboard itself. Somehow, through the miracle of electronics, everything works and the end result is a working computer. Of course, to make it practical, you need a power supply, monitor, keyboard, disk drives, and so on.

The microprocessor itself deals with other elements in the computer. Primarily these elements provide either *input* or *output,* which compujockeys call *I/O.*

Input is information flowing into the microprocessor.

Output is information the microprocessor generates and spits out.

Pretty much the whole computer obsesses over this input and output stuff.

- ✔ The main chip inside the computer is the *microprocessor,* which is essentially a tiny calculator with a BIG price tag.

- ✔ The microprocessor is also called the CPU, which might stand for Central Processing Unit. Military types like the term.

- ✔ When your lips are tired, you can refer to the microprocessor as the *processor.*

- ✔ Outwardly the microprocessor resembles a large, flat, after-dinner mint — with 200 legs.

- ✔ You measure a computer's power by its microprocessor. So it would be nice if they were given powerful names, like Hercules or Samson or Percival. Unfortunately, microprocessors are named after powerful numbers, like 80386, 486, and Pentium.

- ✔ In addition to the numbers assigned to them, microprocessors are also gauged by how fast they can think. This value is given in *megahertz,* abbreviated MHz. The bigger the MHz number, the faster the microprocessor, which is about all you need to know.

- ✔ Input for the microprocessor comes from several places in the computer: the computer's memory, disk drives, keyboard, mouse, modem, and on and on.

- ✔ The microprocessor sends its output to the computer's memory, disk drives, the screen, the printer, modem, and on and on.

- ✔ Software coordinates all this Input/Output chaos for you. It's like a harried assistant at a day-care center when the kids are all high on Pixie Stix.

"OK, wise guy, so which microprocessor lives in my PC?"

Who knows which microprocessor lurks in the heart of your PC? Better get a big wrench. Better still, right-click the mouse on the My Computer icon in the upper-left corner of the desktop. This action brings up a shortcut menu for your computer.

Choose the last item, P̲roperties. The System Properties dialog box is displayed, looking something like Figure 11-1.

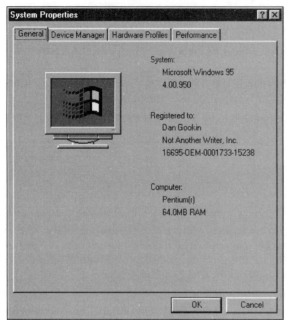

Figure 11-1:
The System
Properties
dialog box.

Details! Details! The first panel of the System Properties dialog box (General) contains information about Windows, you, and your computer. It will say what type of microprocessor lives in your PC and the total amount of memory (RAM) your system has.

✔ In Figure 11-1, the computer has a Pentium microprocessor and 64MB of memory.

✔ Yeah, I paid a lot for all that memory.

✔ The (r) after the word Pentium in the dialog box is supposed to be ®, the registered trademark thingy. It doesn't mean you pronounce the microprocessor's name as *pentiumer.*

✔ Your microprocessor's number appears where you see Pentium(r) in Figure 11-1. For a 486 microprocessor it would just say 80486. This number is the microprocessor you have in your PC, not some secret code.

✔ Refer to Chapter 14 for more information on right-clicking the mouse. You do that a lot in Windows.

Family matters (or "We're all named after famous license plates")

Microprocessors run around in families. The 386 family of microprocessors really started it all. Then came the 486, which was followed by the Pentium. Yeah, it should have been the 586, but they couldn't copyright that number so they made up the word *Pentium* instead. What should be the 686 is then called the *Pentium Pro.* 786? *Pentium Pro Pro* maybe?

The number 80 typically precedes the microprocessor numbers. So:

> ✔ 386 is really an 80386.
>
> ✔ 486 is really an 80486.
>
> ✔ 586 is really an 80-Pentium. (Not!)

Cool people refer to the microprocessor by its shorter, three-digit number.

If you're real cool, you'll call the 486 an i486. I have no idea what the little *i* represents.

Then come the suffixes! All this information is optional reading, though you may be one of those who are really itching to know the difference between an SX and a DX. If so, read on.

The 386DX is a full-power chip. The 386SX is a half-pint chip, having all the smarts of the full-blown 386DX but communicating with the outside world at only half the speed. The 386SX made for a cheaper computer. And the 386SLI was a special version of the 386 designed for laptop and notebook computers.

The 486 family consists of many siblings: The full-on 486DX is the beefy one. Its half-pint brother is the 486SX, which is just as filling but has fewer calories. Actually, the 486SX lacks the advanced math abilities of the 486DX chip.

And then there are the D2 chips, also known as the clock doublers. These chips have two speeds, a slower speed that no one advertises and a faster speed that everyone advertises. There are also D4 chips, which, in a perverse twist of logic only the computer industry can muster, run three times as fast.

Table 11-1 lists the popular numbers assigned to microprocessors, along with other technical drivel associated with them. For your amusement, I've even included the ancient microprocessors of the proto-PCs in the list.

Table 11-1 Microprocessor Number Quiz (Extra Credit Only)

Microprocessor	Relative Power (Bits)	Type of PC and Observations
8088	8/16	Early PCs, the PC XT, and some laptops. This type was a veritable slug.
8086	16/16	The 8086 was faster than the 8088, but more expensive.
80286	16/16	AT types of PCs and compatibles and some laptops. This microprocessor first appeared in the IBM PC AT.
80386	32/32	The father of the 386 family of computers.
80386SX (386SX)	16/32	Laptops and inexpensive systems.
80486	32/32	Also called the i486 or the 486DX.
80486SX	32/32	A cheaper version of the full-blown 80486.
80486DX2	32/32	A slightly cheaper alternative to the normal 486DX.
80486DX4	32/32	An even faster 486DX chip.
586/Pentium	32/64	It's easier to trademark a trendy name than a number.
Pentium Pro	32/64	Super-dooper Pentium.

Pentium jokes

- Pentium. Little. Yellow. Different.

- The doctor said all that bending is hard on your Pentium.

- "And here's another slide of Athens. That's Helen in front of the Pentium."

- Thanks to local industry, our fresh water supply is polluted with Pentium (though the fish have gotten a lot smarter).

- "Where, pray tell, is Deuterium?" "Why, he's gone with Pentium to the Oracle at Delphi."

- You've tried dusting them; you've tried spraying them. Why not try Pentium?

- Did you hear about that new dirty magazine in Latin? Pentium Housium.

- *Whole Wheat Corn Goobers* cereal now comes with 11 vitamins and minerals, including Iron, Zinc, Palladium, and Pentium.

The "and later" syndrome

You may be thrown the following common curve ball: "This software works only with 80386 *and later* microprocessors." It's the "and later" part that gets you. How do you know what is later than an 80386, especially if you don't have a handy *Byte Magazine* PC Microprocessor Time Line in front of you? The following should help:

- Earliest: 8088, 8086, V20, and V30
- Middle ages: 80286
- Latest: 80386, 386SX, and so on
- Extremely tardy: 80486, 486SX
- Absentee: Pentium
- Deceased: Pentium Pro

The latest microprocessors are at the bottom of the list. They can run any and all software written for microprocessors listed above them.

- Some descriptions may say "greater" rather than "later." Later refers to the point in history when the microprocessor was introduced. Greater is like James the Greater in the Bible. He was bigger and more powerful than James the Lesser, who was rumored to be an accountant.
- All microprocessors are said to be *backward compatible*. That means that software written for an earlier microprocessor works on a later model.

Esoteric trivia on the infamous Pentium math bug

About a year after the first Pentium microprocessor came out, a small problem was discovered. Similar to this book's author, the Pentium had a problem doing math, specifically, a division problem. When two particular numbers were divided, the Pentium produced a result that wasn't quite accurate. Oh, for Mrs. Jones's 10th grade geometry class, it would have been OK. But for sending people to Mars, it would have been a tad too big of a boo-boo.

Intel quickly (well, maybe not that quickly) admitted to the mistake and offered replacement Pentiums. Then they fixed the problem, and all the Pentiums that now roll out of the factory do much better in math. And Intel's stock doubled and split, and there was happiness throughout the land. Now there's nothing more to worry about.

Math coprocessors

A computer's microprocessor is really nothing more than a very fast calculator. But for major mathematical calculations, the typical PC microprocessor can be a real slug. A companion chip is available, however, which is the electronic equivalent of giving your microprocessor its own adding machine. The chip is called a *math coprocessor.*

- ✔ The math coprocessor just does math. Figuratively speaking, software can detect the presence of a math coprocessor and send off all the complex mathematics to that chip, relieving the main microprocessor of the tedious arithmetic tasks. The software still works without the math coprocessor, but it runs much slower.

- ✔ Not every application can use a math coprocessor. Typically, spreadsheets and graphics-design packages are the only kinds of programs that run faster with a coprocessor installed. Refer to your software package to see whether it minds a math coprocessor.

- ✔ For the 386 chip, the math coprocessor was extra. You had to buy the 80387 chip and plug it into the motherboard. That 80387 was expensive, and installing it was no joy either.

- ✔ The 486 chip has a built-in math coprocessor. There is no companion 80487 chip.

- ✔ The 486SX chip does not have a built-in math coprocessor. In that case, you need to buy an OverDrive chip that would serve as your math coprocessor (among other things).

- ✔ All Pentium chips have their own math coprocessors built in.

Overdrive things (or more microprocessors to buy)

Overdrive — *Vrrroooommmm!*

Intel, the company that sells the most microprocessors, had a problem. People weren't buying new microprocessors just to give their computers a boost — they were buying whole new computers instead.

So Intel came up with an OverDrive microprocessor. People who plugged this single OverDrive chip into their computers could make their old computer work as much as 70 percent faster.

✔ OverDrive chip: Something else to buy, which indicates you made the wrong microprocessor decision when you first bought your PC.

✔ Most of today's PCs are equipped to handle microprocessor upgrades. The concept sounds nifty: You merely buy a new microprocessor for your PC. You're set back several hundred dollars, but you have a new, leading-technology system. The drawback is that new microprocessors often require new support hardware elsewhere on the motherboard. Simply put, it's better to buy a new computer than to upgrade this way.

✔ I'm being honest with you here even though I own Intel stock.

The BIOS

In addition to a microprocessor and memory, your computer needs some instructions to tell it what to do. Those instructions are written on a special ROM chip called the *BIOS,* which stands for something unimportant but is pronounced *Bye-Oss*.

The job of BIOS is communication. It allows the microprocessor to control — or talk with — other parts of your computer, such as the screen, the printer, the keyboard, and so on. Those instructions were written by the people who built your computer and are permanently etched on the BIOS chip (or chips) soldered onto the motherboard.

✔ Refer to the next chapter for information on what a ROM chip is.

✔ The BIOS is what starts your computer. In fact, you probably see the BIOS copyright message every time your computer warms up.

✔ The operating system (Windows) is the true program that controls your PC. It tells the microprocessor what to do, controls the disk drives, manages your files, organizes information, and communicates with the BIOS to get things done.

✔ In addition to the main BIOS, your computer may have other BIOSs. For example, the video BIOS controls your system's graphics display, the hard drive BIOS controls the hard disk, and so on. Your network adapter may have its own BIOS. Normally, when you see the term BIOS by itself, it refers to the PC's main BIOS.

✔ OK, BIOS stands for Basic Input/Output System. Are you happy now?

What Are Ports?

The term port refers to a hole in the back of the computer, or a festive dessert wine. You can plug in any one of a variety of external devices with which the computer can communicate through a port.

Presently, two popular kinds of ports are in a PC: the printer port and the serial port.

✔ Other external devices, such as the keyboard, mouse, and monitor, are connected via their own special ports. Sometimes external disk drives are added, again, via some form of unique port.

✔ A special type of port is available on some PCs. Technically, this port is the analog-to-digital, or A-to-D, port. A variety of scientific and real-world monitoring devices and such can be plugged into that port. However, most people refer to this port by the device hooked up to it 99 times out of 100: the joystick port.

Printer ports

Mysteriously enough, the printer port is where you plug in your printer. The printer cable has one connector that plugs into the printer and a second that plugs into the computer. Both connectors are different, so it's impossible to plug a printer cable in backward.

✔ For more information on printers, refer to Chapter 16.

✔ Printer ports are also called *parallel ports* or (to old-time nerds) Centronics ports. People who refer to ports in this manner should be slapped.

✔ Other devices can be connected to a printer port, though typically the only one you'll have is the printer. Examples of other devices are voice synthesizers, network connections, external hard drives, extra keyboards, tape backup units, and choo-choo train sets.

Surreal ports

The serial port is far more versatile than the printer port; it supports a variety of interesting items, which is why it's generically called a serial port instead of a this-or-that port.

You'll often plug the following items into a serial port: a modem, a serial printer, a mouse, or just about anything that requires two-way communications. Most computers come with two serial ports.

✔ A serial port can also be called a modem port.

✔ Serial ports are also called RS-232 ports. No, that's not a Radio Shack part number. Instead, it refers to Recommended Standard 232, which I assume is the 232nd standard The Committee came up with that year. Busy guys.

✔ You can plug a computer mouse into a serial port. In that case, the mouse is called a serial mouse. The mouse can also be plugged into its own port, called — shockingly enough — a mouse port. (Refer to your local pet store for more information on mice, or turn to Chapter 14.)

SCSI ports (say "scuzzy")

A special type of serial port is the SCSI port, with the SCSI being pronounced *scuzzy.* I'm not making that up. What does it stand for? Who cares! It's just a special type of fast serial port.

The beauty of a SCSI port is that you can plug a gaggle of things into it. Here are just a few of the items to stick onto a SCSI port:

✔ Hard drives, from one to six of them.

✔ A scanner.

✔ A tape backup drive.

✔ A CD-ROM drive.

Definitely skip over this stuff

Serial ports are complex in that you must configure them. Printer ports are set up to work in a specific manner and require no configuration. But with a serial port, you must configure both the port on your computer as well as the device with which you're communicating.

You need to configure four items on a serial port: the speed at which the port operates; the data word format, or the size of the bytes you're sending; the number of stop bits; and the parity. This is only a real hassle when you need to connect a serial printer — and they don't even make those anymore, so I'm not going to discuss it here.

Your communications software messes with this technical serial port information. That subject is put way off until Chapter 22.

- ✔ A removable hard drive or magneto-optical drive.

- ✔ Oh, I could name more, but that's the basic bones.

- ✔ SCSI ports don't need to be configured like serial ports.

- ✔ Unfortunately, SCSI port devices must be configured. Two annoying items to fuss over are: Each device attached to the SCSI port must have its own unique ID number; also, because each item is plugged one into the other (called a *daisy chain*), the last item must have a special doojobbie on it called a *terminator*.

- ✔ No, that's not an Arnold Schwarzenegger-like Terminator. It's a little switch to throw or a dongle to add that tells the SCSI port, "Hey! I'm the last guy out here!"

- ✔ About half of today's hard drives and CD-ROM drives are SCSI. Betcha didn't know that.

It Knows the Date and Time!

Most computers come with an internal clock. Tic-toc. The clock is battery operated, which enables it to keep track of the time, day or night, whether or not the PC is plugged in.

To check the current time, gander at the far-right side of the Windows taskbar. Living in the system tray is the current time.

- ✔ If you point the mouse at the time, Windows displays the current date and time in a long format. This is shown in Figure 11-2.

- ✔ If you don't see the time, click on the Start button to pop up its menu and choose Settings⇨Taskbar. In the Taskbar Properties dialog box, Taskbar Options panel, look for the check box on the bottom titled Show Clock. Click the mouse on that check box to put a check mark there. Click the OK button, and Windows shows you the time on the taskbar.

Figure 11-2:
The current
date and
time (well,
when I made
the figure).

> Saturday,February 03,1996
>
> 🔊 9:5 PM

- The format for the date and time varies depending on how your computer is set up. Windows displays a date and time format based on your country or region. This book assumes the typical (and I'll agree, backward) U.S. method of listing the date.

- Who cares if the computer knows what day it is? Well, because your files are time — and date — stamped, you can figure things out, like which is a later version of two similar files or two files with the same name on different disks.

"My PC's clock is off"

You'll notice at the Olympics that they don't have PCs sitting at the end of the pool to time the swimmers. Nor are they used in the track and field competitions. Why? Because computers make lousy clocks. Oh, they're OK for a moment or two. But after a week or so, your computer will lose track of the time. Don't fret, this happens to everyone.

To set or change the date and time on your PC, double-click the mouse on the time in the taskbar: Point the mouse at the time on the right end of the taskbar and double-click. Click-click. This displays the Date/Time Properties dialog box, as shown in Figure 11-3.

Manipulate the controls in the Date/Time Properties dialog box to change or set the date or time. Click OK when you're done.

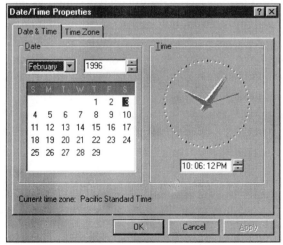

Figure 11-3:
The Date/
Time
Properties
dialog box.

- To set a new month, pluck the proper month from the drop-down list.

- To set a new year, type the year into the year box, or click the up and down arrows with the mouse to change the year.

- Pick a new day of the month by clicking on that number with the mouse.

- Set the clock by typing in a new value for hours, minutes, or seconds. Double-click the mouse on the hours, minutes, or seconds displayed, and then type in a new value.

- To set AM or PM, double-click to select either item and then click on the down or up arrow to change it.

- AM means morning or before noon. PM means afternoon and evening (up to midnight).

- Midnight is 12:00 a.m.

- To set the time, type in the new time. For example, type **10:00** if it's 9:58 or so. Then when the time lady (or whoever) says it's ten o'clock, click on the Apply button in the Date/Time Properties dialog box. That sets the time instantly.

- Few people bother setting the seconds on their PC clocks. I mean, why do it if the thing will be off a few minutes every week anyway?

Expansion Slots

On the back of the motherboard, near the rear of the computer, in the low-rent district, you'll find several long, thin slots. These are *expansion slots,* into which you can plug special *expansion cards.* The idea is that you can expand your system by adding options not included with the basic PC.

- Your PC can have from 3 to 12 expansion slots. The average is 5. Or 8. It depends on how big your console is.

- Although it's possible for anyone to plug in a card and expand a computer system, this is a job best left to those willing to risk both life and machine. (No, it's not life-threatening — at least if the PC is unplugged first — but it is complicated.)

- The salespeople never tell you this one: Most expansion cards come squirming with cables. This makes the seemingly sleek motherboard look more like an electronic pasta dish. Some cables are threaded inside the PC; others are left hanging limply out the back. It's the cables that make the upgrading and installation process so difficult.

- Expansion cards are sometimes referred to as *daughterboards.* Cute, huh? But explain this: The expansion slot is also referred to as the *bus.* Computers. . . .

✔ After you add a new expansion card, you'll need to tell Windows about it. On a good day (sunshine, hot coffee, birds chirping, like that), Windows will recognize and automatically configure the new hardware when you restart your PC. Otherwise, you'll need to open up the Control Panel and start the Add New Hardware icon. The details of this are far too boring to list here.

✔ Adding expansion cards to your computer can be a pain, but it can be done. The book *Upgrading and Fixin' PCs For Dummies* will tell you how.

✔ Some blazingly fast Pentium computers come with blazingly fast PCI slots — a slot like any other, just faster. A regular card works fine in an unused PCI slot, but don't even think about sticking a local-bus card into a PCI slot. Heavens!

The Power Supply (Sometimes It Goes POOF!)

The final mystery item in the box is the *power supply,* which, much to your relief, doesn't go poof! Hardly at all. The power supply does three things: It brings in power from the wall socket, it supplies power to the motherboard and disk drives, and it contains the on/off switch.

✔ The power supply makes most of the noise when your PC runs. It contains a fan that regulates the temperature inside the console, keeping everything nice and cool. (Electronic components get hot when electricity races through them. This heat has the ugly consequence of making them misbehave, which is why cooling is needed.)

I wouldn't read this expansion slot stuff if I were you

There are different systems for expansion slots and cards in a PC. The most common is the ISA, which stands for Industry Standard Architecture. If you have an antique IBM PS/2 system, it's likely that you're using the MCA, or Micro Channel Architecture, expansion slot/card system.

A third standard, used only in very high-end engineering and network server systems, is the EISA. The E must stand for expensive.

Why these different slot systems? Because the ISA isn't as technically advanced as some users require. And it's slow. Today's systems use the fast PCI slots for super-dooper video graphics and slippery-fast hard drives. Everything else plugs into the dopey old ISA slots.

✔ Power supplies are rated in watts. The more stuff your computer has — the more disk drives, memory, expansion cards, and so on — the greater the number of watts the power supply should provide. The typical PC has a power supply rated at 150 or 200 watts. More powerful systems may require a power supply of 220 or 250 watts.

✔ Boom! If lightning strikes or something deleterious comes marching down the power line, your power supply will blow. Don't panic. It's designed to pop and smolder. This effect in no way damages the rest of your computer. You just need to buy a new power supply and have someone replace it. Everything else in your system should survive the disaster (which is how the power supply is designed, fortunately).

Chapter 12

Memory (RAM, the Way We Were)

. . . .

In This Chapter

▶ Understanding PC memory

▶ Memory questions and answers

▶ Adding memory to your computer

▶ The low-down on kilobytes and megabytes

▶ Insane memory terminology

▶ Memory management (Why bother?)

. . . .

*I*n the computer land of Oz, you might find your very own PC sitting alongside the yellow brick road. And, after your introductions, it breaks out into song:

> *I am just a mere computer*
> *Not a fast ex-e-cuter*
> *Of all the big programs.*
> *O the graphics would be flyin'*
> *And the hard drive won't be dyin'*
> *If I only had more RAM!*

Memory, or random access memory (RAM), is a storage place in a computer, just like disk space. Unlike disk storage, memory is the only place inside the computer where the real work gets done. Obviously, the more memory you have, the more work you can do. But not only that, having more memory means the computer is capable of grander tasks, such as working with graphics, animation, sound, and music — and your PC remembers everyone it meets without ever having to look twice at a name tag.

What Is Memory?

All computers need memory. That's where the work gets done. The microprocessor is capable of storing information inside itself, but only so much. It needs extra memory just like humans need notepads and libraries.

For example, when you create a document by using your word processor, each character you type is placed into a specific location in memory. Once there, the microprocessor doesn't need to access it again unless you're editing, searching or replacing, or doing something active to the text.

After something is created in memory — a document, spreadsheet, or graphic — it's saved to disk. Your disk drives provide long-term storage for information. Then, when you need to access the information again, you open it back into memory from disk. Once it's there, the microprocessor can again work over the information.

The only nasty thing about memory is that it's volatile. When you turn off the power, the contents of memory go *poof!* This is OK if you've saved to disk, but if you haven't, everything is lost. Even resetting your computer zaps the contents of memory. So always save (if you can) before you reset or turn off your PC.

- ✔ The more memory you have, the better. With more memory, you can work on larger documents and spreadsheets, enjoy applications that use graphics and sound, and boast about it to your friends.

- ✔ All computers have a limited amount of memory, which means that some day you may run short. When that happens, you'll see an error message shouting, "Out of memory!" Don't panic. The computer can handle the situation. You can add more memory to your system if you like. Consult your favorite computer guru.

- ✔ Turning off the power makes the *contents* of memory go bye-bye. It doesn't destroy the memory chips themselves.

- ✔ When you open something on disk, the computer copies that information from disk into the computer's memory. Only in memory can that information be examined or changed. When you save information back to disk, the computer copies it from memory to the disk.

- ✔ The term RAM is used interchangeably with the word memory. They're the same thing. (In fact, RAM stands for Random-Access Memory in case you've been working any crossword puzzles lately.)

- ✔ Memory is a component of the motherboard, sitting very close to the microprocessor. It exists as a series of tiny chips called RAM chips. The RAM chips typically come as groups soldered together on a thin strip of fiberglass. The whole gang is referred to as a SIMM.

- ✔ You can add more memory to the computer by plugging in more RAM chips (or SIMMs), either on the motherboard itself or via some cutesy memory expansion card. Again, leave this job to the pros.

Common memory questions

How much memory do I need?

Your brain has all the storage you'll need for a lifetime.

No, I mean how much memory does my computer need?

The amount of memory your PC needs depends on two things. The first, and most important, is the memory requirement of your software. Some programs, such as spreadsheets and graphics applications, require lots of memory. For example, Adobe Photoshop (a graphics package) says — right on the box — that it needs 10MB of RAM!

The second and more limiting factor is cost. Memory costs money. It's not as expensive as it was back in the old stone-tablet days of computing, but it still costs a lot. That 10MB of memory that Adobe Photoshop would like could cost you as much as $450. (That's almost $3,450 in dog dollars!)

Generally speaking, all computers should have at least 4MB of RAM. Older models may have less, but to run today's software you need at least 4MB, preferably 8MB or more.

Can I add more memory to my PC?

Yes. This is done typically because your applications need more memory. The programs just won't run (or will run sluggishly) without more memory.

▌ ✔ Refer to "Adding more memory to your PC" later in this chapter.

Can I lose computer memory?

No. Your computer only has a finite amount of memory, but it cannot be "lost" to anything. Programs use memory when you run them. For example, when you run WordPerfect, it eats up a specific amount of memory. But when you quit WordPerfect, all that memory is made available to the next program. So while a program runs, it "grabs" memory for its own uses. When the program is done, it reluctantly lets the memory go.

What about copying programs?

Copying a program or file uses some memory, but don't confuse disk "memory" with computer memory or RAM. You can copy a huge file from one disk to another without worrying about running out of memory. The operating system (Windows) handles the details. (Now, you may run out of disk space, but that's another problem.)

Computer memory can never be "destroyed." Even after a huge program runs or you copy a very large file, your system still has the same amount of RAM it had before.

Disk "memory" is just storage space on disk. It's possible to store a program on your hard drive that's huge in size — hundreds of megabytes — more than could possibly fit in memory. How does that work? Some say it's voodoo. Others say it's because Windows only loads a small portion of the file into memory (RAM) at once. Who knows what the truth really is?

What's EDO RAM?

I have no idea. Most likely it's just faster memory than just plain non-EDO RAM. I'm sure there's a technical description to bore you somewhere, but I'm not up to it now.

By the way, it's pronounced *EE-dough,* as in "Judge Lance EDO RAM." If you say Edo, like "Mr. Ed-O," then you're talking about the capital of feudal Japan.

How much memory is in my PC right now?

This information may be a mystery to you but isn't a secret to your computer. How much memory lives inside the beast can be seen by displaying the System Properties dialog box. The amount of memory (shown as RAM) is displayed right beneath the type of microprocessor that lives in your PC.

  ✔ To display the System Properties dialog box, refer to the section "Okay, wise guy, so which microprocessor lives in my PC?" in Chapter 11.

  ✔ Figure 11-1 shows you what the System Properties dialog box looks like.

  ✔ Refer to the section "Measuring memory" later in this chapter for more information on what a megabyte (MB) is.

Adding more memory to your PC

There is no electronic equivalent of Geritol for your computer. If you think your PC has tired RAM or maybe it didn't have enough memory in the first place, you can always add more.

Adding memory to your computer is Lego-block simple. The only problem is that the typical Lego block set, say the cool Space Station or Rescue Helicopter set, costs under $20. Your computer, on the other hand, may cost one hundred times that much. This is not something to be taken lightly.

Steps: Upgrading memory involves five complex and boring steps

Step 1. Figure out how much memory you need to add. For example, if you have 4MB in your system, you probably need another 8MB to give yourself the full power of Windows. If you have the bucks, you can upgrade to 16MB or even 32MB. More! More! More!

Step 2. Figure out how much memory you can install. This is a technical step. It involves knowing how memory is added to your computer and in what increments. You should simply tell the shop or your favorite technical guru how much you think you need, and he'll tell you how much you can actually have.

Step 3. Buy something. In this case, you buy the memory chips themselves or you buy the expansion card into which the memory chips are installed.

Step 4. Pay someone else to plug in the chips and do the upgrade. Oh, you can do it yourself, but I'd pay someone else to do it.

Step 5. Gloat. Once you have the memory, brag to your friends about it. Heck, it used to be impressive to say you had 640K of RAM. Then came the "I have 4 megabytes of memory in my 386" round of impressiveness. But today? Anything less than 8 megabytes and your kids will roll their eyes at you.

✔ PC memory usually comes in given sizes: 4MB, 8MB, 16MB, and then in multiples of 16MB after that. Yeah, there are oddball sizes, but just about everything can be divided evenly by 2.

✔ Another shocker: You might think that moving from 4MB in your system to 16MB requires that you buy 12MB of memory chips. Wrong! It may mean you have to buy the full 16MB and then toss out your original 4MB. It all has to do with how memory fits in a PC, which is something even the gods themselves don't fully understand.

✔ If you want to try upgrading memory yourself, go ahead. Plenty of easy books on the subject of upgrading memory are available, as well as how-to articles in some of the popular magazines. I still recommend having someone else do it, however.

✔ More information on memory terms is covered throughout the first part of this chapter.

Boring technical details on the differences between RAM and ROM

RAM stands for Random-Access Memory. It refers to memory that the microprocessor can read from and write to. When you create something in memory, it's done in RAM. RAM is memory and vice versa.

ROM stands for Read-Only Memory. The microprocessor can read from ROM, but it cannot write to it or modify it. ROM is permanent. Often, ROM chips contain special instructions for the computer — important stuff that will never change. Because that information is stored on a memory chip, the microprocessor can access it. The instructions will always be there because they are unerasable.

Measuring Memory

Many interesting terms orbit the planet memory. The most basic of these terms refer to the quantity of memory (see Table 12-1).

Table 12-1		Memory Quantities	
Term	*Abbr*	*About*	*Actual*
Byte		1 byte	1 byte
Kilobyte	K or KB	1,000 bytes	1,024 bytes
Megabyte	M or MB	1,000,000 bytes	1,048,576 bytes
Gigabyte	G or GB	1,000,000,000 bytes	1,073,741,824 bytes

Memory is measured by the byte. Think of a byte as a single character, a letter in the middle of a word. For example, the word "spatula" is seven bytes long.

A half page of text is about 1,000 bytes. To make this a handy figure to know, computer nerds refer to 1,000 bytes as a *kilobyte,* or one K or KB.

The term *megabyte* refers to 1,000K, or one million bytes. The abbreviation MB (or M) is used to indicate megabyte, so 8MB means eight megabytes of memory.

Further than the megabyte is the *gigabyte.* As you can guess, this is one billion bytes or about 1,000 megabytes. The *terabyte* is one trillion bytes, or enough RAM to dim the lights when you start the PC.

Other trivia:

- ✔ Bytes are composed of eight bits. The word *bit* is a contraction of binary digit. Binary is base two, or a counting system where only ones and zeros are used. Computers count in binary, and we group their bits into clusters of eight for convenient consumption as bytes.

- ✔ The term *giga* is actually Greek, and it means giant.

- ✔ There is no reason to worry about how much ROM (read-only memory) you have in your computer.

- ✔ A specific location in memory is called an address.

- ✔ Some hardware states that it sits at a specific memory address in your computer. This address is often given as a *hexadecimal* (base 16) number, which often doesn't look like a number at all (i.e., C800 or A400). What does that mean? Who knows? But the numbers are important to the person you pay to install and set up your hardware.

The Only Memory Term You Need to Know

Everyone say this out loud: extended memory.

X tend Ed memo ree.

Memory terms abound, but the substance of all your PC's memory is essentially known as extended memory. If the software package says, "Hail, User! I need 4MB of extended memory." Ignore the "extended." It's just telling you it needs 4MB of memory.

- ✔ Other terms for the PC's memory are covered in sections that follow this.

- ✔ Extended memory is a type of memory in the PC, like they call the front part of your brain the *frontal lobe.* It's just a type of memory. For all systems sold today, however, extended memory means all of memory. Older systems had other types of memory, each suited to a specific purpose. Under Windows 95, however, all memory is extended memory.

Other Memory Terms to Drive You Insane

As the PC evolved, computer users demanded more from it. One thing they wanted right away was more memory. This was tricky stuff because the original PC was designed to hold only 640K of memory — and that was ten times the amount of memory in the best-selling computers of the day. Who knew greedy users would want more?

So various and strange solutions were devised to serve up memory on the platters of hungry PC users. Each time a new memory solution came around, it was given a silly name.

Expanded memory: This was bonus memory given to DOS programs and only DOS programs. Today, a few DOS games may request this type of memory. If so, Windows handles it with little difficulty. Otherwise, this is a great memory term to ignore.

Conventional memory: The basic memory in all PCs is called conventional memory, although some may call it DOS memory and others may even call it low DOS memory. This memory is the first 640K of RAM in your PC. Conventional memory was important because it was where DOS ran its programs. Today, Windows merely swallows this type of memory and calls it extended memory, like all the other memory in your computer.

Upper memory: Right "above" conventional memory in a computer is upper memory. It may also be referred to as reserved memory or high DOS memory. It had a role in the ancient art of DOS memory management — a role that's now stale and hard and should be taken off the day-old shelf and thrown away.

The High Memory Area (HMA): After upper memory came a 64K chunk of memory known as the high memory area. Yet another relic of DOS memory management. DOS users were desperate for the stuff.

✔ Don't confuse extended and expanded memory! They're very similar terms but describe two entirely different things (don't look at me — I didn't make this up). Just remember that you need extended memory. Think of expanded memory as making your head bigger — expanding — which would depress you since you would no longer be able to select from an abundance of stylish hats.

✔ The old DOS conventional memory was limited to 640K. That's all the memory DOS has for running programs. Even if you have megabytes of RAM installed in your computer, you have only 640K in which to run DOS programs. Thus, it was called the "640K DOS barrier."

Managing Memory

There is no longer a need to manage memory with Windows 95.

✔ Only older DOS computers should fuss with memory management. If you're curious or have an older DOS machine and several hours of your time to waste on managing its memory, refer to *DOS For Dummies*, 2nd Edition.

✔ If you run a DOS program in Windows 95, it takes care of the memory management issues for you. But if you need to tweak memory, refer to *DOS For Dummies, Windows 95 Edition*.

Chapter 13

The Bonehead's Guide to PC Monitors

. . . .

In This Chapter

▶ Understanding PC monitors and graphics

▶ PC graphic adapter names and models

▶ Monitor and graphics Q&A

▶ The art of the screen dump

▶ How to clean your screen and monitor

▶ Changing the desktop background (wallpaper)

▶ Adjusting the graphics resolution and colors

▶ Adding a screen saver to Windows

. . . .

*T*he first thing you notice on any computer is the screen, or what a nerd would call the video display monitor or even a CRT (cathode ray tube). In the old days, the wrong kind of display could really fry your eyeballs. I remember riding down the elevator with bug-eyed people desperately searching for Visine. Today's computer screens are easier to look at and can produce much more stunning displays. Visine sales are down considerably.

This chapter is about the video display, computer screen, monitor, or the thing you look at when you use a computer.

Monitors and Graphics 101

While you're staring at the computer's monitor, waiting eternally for Windows, you should know that there really are two things that make up the PC video system: the monitor and the display adapter.

The *monitor* is the physical, television-like thing you see on top of or near the console. Like a TV, it has various knobs for adjustments similar to those on many TV sets. But that's where the similarity ends. Your computer monitor is not a TV set.

The *display adapter* is an expansion card plugged into the motherboard inside your console. The display adapter contains special circuitry that takes information from your computer and tosses it up on the screen. The display adapter tells the monitor what to display, where to display it, and what colors to use — like an electronic interior designer.

Even though it's tucked away inside your PC, the display adapter is more important than the monitor. It determines how many colors you see and how fancy the graphics are that appear on your monitor. Monitors? They just dumb.

- In a way, the PC's monitor is like its mouth. It displays information as a type of visual feedback, enabling you to know what's going on or to see the result of some operation. In that respect, it seems like my PC spends most of its time yawning.

- You need both a monitor and display adapter.

- In some PCs, especially laptops, the display adapter is built into the motherboard.

- Take another look at Chapter 11 for a review of motherboards and expansion cards.

- The term *monitor* refers to the physical device — the monitor that sits on top of or to the side of your console. The terms *screen* and *display* are both used to describe what appears on the monitor's screen — information the computer is showing you.

- The display adapter may also be called the display adapter card, video adapter, video hardware, video system, or Phil.

The yardsticks of PC graphics: color and resolution

Nearly all PCs come with adequate monitors and graphics adapters. For more money you get better stuff, but only a handful of programs bother to use that extra graphics horsepower.

What do you get for your money? More colors and higher resolution, primarily.

More color! Your PC graphics system can only display a certain number of colors on the screen at any given time. For example, most of today's displays can show from 256 on up to 16 million colors, which makes a very vivid — almost photographic — picture.

May monochrome PC video rest in peace

In the olden days, you had more choices for your PC's monitor than color, color, and more color. There were also *monochrome* graphics systems. These worked the same as any PC monitor, but displayed only two colors: green and black, or amber and black, or white and black.

The advantage of monochrome monitors was that they displayed text better than the early color monitors. Those early color monitors could really frazzle your eyeballs — like 12 hours of "Gilligan's Island" crammed into 20 minutes. Monochrome was a good solution. But for Windows and today's graphical applications, monochrome is impractical. You'd probably have to hunt for a monochrome monitor anyway.

Higher resolution! The resolution refers to the number of dots, or *pixels,* on the screen. The more pixels, the higher the resolution and the finer the image.

With resolution and color, there is a trade-off: You can have more of one or the other, not both. A high-resolution display gives you fewer colors. A lot of colors gives you lower resolution. This works, however, because the many colors fool the eye into thinking you have more resolution. (The typical TV has a low resolution but a nearly infinite number of colors.)

Graph-a-bits soup

The world of PC graphics involves a lot of TLAs, three-letter acronyms. These TLAs refer to the history and capabilities of the various kinds of video displays you can have lashed to your PC (see Table 13-1). But let me save you some time.

You probably have some variation of the VGA graphics standard in your PC, most likely SuperVGA.

You see, when IBM's dominance of the PC hardware world ended (c. 476 A.D.), the graphics standards they established faded away. The last standard they devised was dubbed *VGA.* This was improved upon to yield *SuperVGA,* which is what nearly all PCs use today.

Oh, there may be minor improvements here and there. Some high-end graphics adapters expand upon SuperVGA. But only if your software requests it do you have to buy it. Otherwise, SuperVGA is fine for you, me, Bill Gates, everyone.

✔ Yes, there are other unconventional adapters out there. Those listed in Table 13-1 are the most popular, but that doesn't rule out some specific stuff or oddball entries.

✔ Some high-resolution graphics systems are only applicable to certain kinds of software. Computer graphics, CAD, and animation and design are all areas where paying top dollar for your display is worth it. If you're only using basic applications, such as a word processor, you don't need top-dollar displays.

Table 13-1	Video Displays of Prehistory and the Present
MDA	MDA stands for Monochrome Display Adapter. It's the original monochrome display setup used by the first PCs. This type of display offered no graphics, only text.
CGA	CGA stands for color graphics adapter. When the PC first appeared, the CGA was the only way you could see color text or graphics. But the text quality stank.
EGA	EGA stands for enhanced graphics adapter. It was a solution that offered crisper text than the CGA plus many more colors. Its popularity lasted about as long as the Ford Administration.
VGA	In its constant effort to keep everyone off their guard, IBM introduced the VGA standard and told the world that it stands for Video Graphics Array. (Not Video Graphics Adapter, as some are prone to call it.) VGA offers superior colors, high-resolution graphics, and nice, readable text. A variation on VGA is the SuperVGA, which is the graphics standard for all PCs.
OTGA	OK, OTGA stands for Other Types of Graphics Adapters. There's the 8514, which is basically a pricey version of the SuperVGA that has more colors and higher resolution. The XGA standard is yet another Super-DuperVGA card. It never ends.

Ode to the Ugly Text Screen

Your computer monitor is capable of displaying two different things: graphics or text.

Text refers to characters, letters, numbers, and symbols you see on the screen, typically when the computer starts or if you ever bother to use DOS. The text is displayed in neat rows and columns — what you expect to see on a computer display.

Graphics are pictures, images, circles, lines, and squares, and can also include text. Windows uses graphics.

The following information about the PC's text screen is for trivial purposes only:

- ✔ Text is displayed on a PC in rows and columns. Rows march across the screen from right to left, like lines on a page. (In fact, the terms rows and lines are used interchangeably.) Columns are like vertical columns of text, up and down. An A in the upper-left corner of your screen is said to be in the first row and first column.

- ✔ The typical PC's text display has 25 rows and 80 columns — room for about half of a page of single-spaced text.

- ✔ DOS programs can run in Windows either in a window or in the text mode. To switch a DOS program into the text mode, press the Alt+Enter key combination. Press Alt+Enter again to shove the DOS program back into a diminutive window on the screen.

Common Monitor/Graphics Questions and Answers

Since you *see* the monitor, it's often the source of many questions. You would think a device with so few buttons wouldn't cause any problems. *Au contraire!* The following represents some very good monitor questions and answers I've collected over the years. Pay special attention! There will be a quiz at the end of the chapter.

- ✔ *Au contraire* is French for "There are small wood chips in the pâté."

Which display is best?

Simple question, simple answer: SuperVGA. This is most likely the video system you have in your PC already (providing you purchased it in the last six years).

- ✔ Many manufacturers make SuperVGA display adapters. They offer a wide range of features and prices. I can't recommend individual brands, but it's a good strategy to avoid the cheaper, no-name brands.

- ✔ You need a monitor that can handle the output of a SuperVGA adapter. Although some places claim that SuperVGA works with any monitor (and that may be true), the best results are possible only on monitors built to handle SuperVGA.

- ✔ If you're really in this for a pretty picture, try getting a SuperVGA system with two megabytes (2MB) of video memory. It will cost you, but the display will look real good.

What's an accelerated video adapter?

To keep Windows users awake, some savvy manufacturers tossed a special *graphics-stomping* chip onto a special breed of video card. These special *accelerated video adapters* can flicker little windows onto the screen as fast as Windows dishes them out. Those cards really fly out of the deck when you play Solitaire!

    ✔ Accelerated video adapters are typically SuperVGA in nature. They just work faster, that's all.

What's a screen dump?

No, a screen dump is not a pile of old monochrome monitors somewhere in the desert.

Dump is an ungraceful yet popular computer term. It means to transfer a lot of information from one place to another. The information is typically unloaded — like from a dump truck — in one ugly batch, not sorted out or made neat or anything.

A *screen dump* is the process of taking the information on your computer screen and sending it off to the printer. Under DOS, this procedure was done with the magic Print Screen key on the keyboard. In Windows, it does kind of the same thing, but nothing is printed.

In Windows, when you press the Print Screen key, you take a snapshot of the desktop. All that graphical information is saved like a photograph in the clipboard. You can then paste the information into any program that can swallow graphical images. So even though nothing prints, you still get a dump of what was on the screen.

Many of the figures in this book were made by using the Print Screen key. I would then paste the image into the Windows Paint program, where I cleaned it up a tad.

    ✔ If you press Alt+Print Screen, Windows takes a snapshot of the top window on the screen. Yes, this is technically a Window-dump.

    ✔ The Print Screen key might be labeled PrtSc on your keyboard.

    ✔ See Chapter 16 for a demonstration of how the Print Screen key can actually print the screen.

    ✔ Betcha thought I'd put something crude in here, eh Diane?

The graphics looked great in the store . . .

They always do, don't they? Graphics sell computers. To make them look as sweet as possible, the sales people display stunning, 188 bazillion-color graphics images. Or you may see videos displayed on the computer screen, but they've been optimized with special software to run blindingly fast.

In real life, your PC's graphics probably won't stun you. Face it, most applications are boring. You don't see charts forming all the time. Light beams don't shoot out of the microprocessor like on the Intel TV commercials. Nothing much is impressive. This is why you never see a computer running Word or 1-2-3 in the store. Yawn!

Technical Monitor Stuff to Numb Your Brain

Thinking about all the technical issues surrounding a PC monitor will make you shudder. Do it now: Shudder. Egads! Here are some non-layman terms that describe various parts of a PC monitor.

One final warning: You really don't need to read this section. I'd skip it, if I were you.

Analog: This is a type of monitor, as opposed to a digital monitor. VGA adapters must be connected to analog monitors. Some monitors are switchable and can handle both analog and digital signals. My point: Make sure your graphics adapter and monitor sing the same tune.

Bandwidth: This is the speed at which information is sent from the computer (actually the graphics adapter) to the monitor. The bandwidth is a value, measured in *megahertz* (MHz), and the monitor must be capable of accepting the bandwidth of the graphics adapter. The higher the bandwidth value, the better.

Composite: This is a type of monitor that's similar to a TV set. In olden days, PC owners often bought a composite monitor as a cheap alternative to the more expensive RGB monitor. These monitors were used primarily with CGA video systems, and they displayed their images in (fuzzy) green on black.

Digital: A digital monitor must be used by older graphics adapters, such as monochrome, Hercules, CGA, and EGA. These monitors received digital signals from the PC and were limited in the breadth of colors they could display. The most common type of digital monitor was the RGB monitor (more on that in a bit).

Dot pitch: This refers to the distance between each dot, or pixel, on the screen (as measured from the center of each pixel). The closer the dots, the better the image is. A dot pitch of 0.28 mm (millimeters) is really good, with smaller values being even better.

Interlacing: This is a method of tricking the monitor into displaying a picture that is better than it should be able to display. Interlacing takes twice as long to paint the image on-screen by painting only half of it at once. It also makes the picture flicker, which is why a noninterlacing video system is better.

Multiscanning: This is the capability of a single monitor to switch between multiple analog and digital modes. This is the type of monitor you want if your graphics adapter supports several graphics modes and your software often switches between them. (Some manufacturers refer to this as *multisync*.)

Picture tube size: This is the diagonal measurement of your monitor's picture tube, from corner to corner. Bigger monitors mean more display areas and are more expensive. The 14- to 17-inch monitors are common, but you can buy special monitors up to 21 inches and beyond, given the size of your ego or vision problems.

RGB: This is an acronym for Red, Green, and Blue. RGB described the basic digital monitor users preferred with the old CGA. An RGB monitor was a digital monitor.

Scan rate: This is the rate at which a monitor's electron gun paints the image on the screen. It's measured in kilohertz (kHz), and the higher the value, the better.

Thumbprint. Just threw this one in here to see if you were paying attention.

TTL: This is a totally unnecessary term that crops up a lot and confuses the heck out of everyone. Basically, the old monochrome monitors were referred to as TTL monitors by the IBM documentation. TTL monitor equals monochrome monitor. No sweat. But what TTL stood for was a mystery for years. Here's the long-held secret answer: Transistor-to-Transistor Logic. Now, aren't you glad you read that?

Cleaning Your Monitor

Computer monitors grow dust like a five o'clock shadow. And, in addition to the dust, you always find fingerprints and sneeze globs on your screen. Monitors are messy.

To clean your monitor, spray some window cleaner on a soft towel or tissue. Then gently rub the screen. You also can use vinegar if you want your computer to have that tossed salad smell.

Never spray window cleaner directly on the screen. It may dribble down into the monitor itself and wreak electronic terror.

> ✔ For cleaning the monitor's housing (the non-screen part), you can use some Formula 409 or Fantastik. Again, spray it on a cloth and wipe the monitor. This also works for cleaning the PC itself if you're in a nesting mood.
>
> ✔ A fond term for that layer of dust that coats your monitor is *pixel dust.* Ah, computers can be painfully cute at times.

Tweaking Your Monitor

Aside from the knobs on the front (or the back) for adjusting the brightness and contrast, you can do a number of strange things with your PC's monitor. This is all handled by Windows and its Control Panel.

In the Control Panel lives an icon you use to tweak your monitor. The following sections tell you what you can do there. Here's how to open the thing up:

1. Open the Control Panel.

From the Start menu, choose Settings➪Control Panel. This displays the Control Panel's main window.

2. Open the Display icon.

Display

Double-click on the Display icon. This conjures up the Display Properties dialog box, similar to, but prettier than, what's shown in Figure 13-1.

3. Mess with the Display Properties dialog box.

You can change the desktop's background, add a screen saver, and change the system colors or screen resolution using the Display Properties dialog box. The sections that follow outline how this is done.

4. Close the Display Properties dialog box.

When you're done, you can click the OK button to keep your changes, or click Cancel to go back to the way things were.

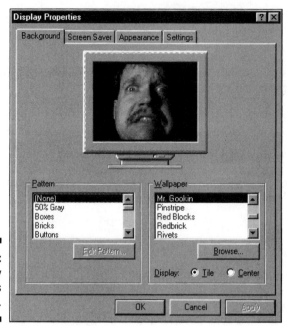

Figure 13-1:
The Display
Properties
dialog box.

The Display Properties dialog box has four panels: Background, Screen Saver, Appearance, and Settings. Each panel displays a different set of controls for manipulating one or more aspects of the display. Click on the proper tab to bring that panel forward.

Changing the background (wallpaper)

The background, or wallpaper, is what you see when you look at the desktop. You can see a pattern or a pretty picture or just about anything other than the dingy gray Windows really wants to display.

Summon the Display Properties dialog box, as described in the previous section. Make sure the Background panel is forward, as shown in Figure 13-1.

There are two ways you can put an image up on the desktop. The first is with a pattern, the second is with a graphical image or wallpaper.

The patterns are listed in the Pattern area of the dialog box. A bunch of them are displayed, each of them equally boring.

The Wallpaper area lists a bunch of graphics files you can apply to the desktop. If the pattern is large enough, it can cover the entire screen. If it's small, you may want to tile them on the screen, in which case you'd click in the radio button by the word Tile.

Anytime you choose a new pattern or wallpaper, it appears in the mini-monitor preview window. It's rather small, so the effect isn't stunning. If you want to see a true preview, click the Apply button.

If you created your own graphics file, you can use it as the wallpaper. First, the graphics must be a bitmapped image or BMP file. So if you have a swimsuit GIF or JPEG file, you must convert it into the BMP format. (You do this on your own.) Then use the Browse button in the dialog box to hunt down your image on disk. After opening the image, you see it displayed in the mini-monitor preview window.

Click OK to keep your new desktop image; click Cancel to forget it.

Adjusting the resolution and colors

Muster the Display Properties dialog box, as foretold earlier in this chapter. Click the mouse on the Settings tab to bring that panel forward. What you see will look something like Figure 13-2.

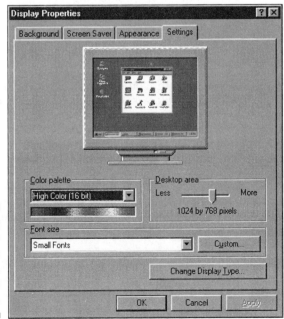

Figure 13-2:
The Display
Properties
dialog box,
Settings
panel.

The Settings panel in the Display Properties dialog box is where you tweak with your monitor's color and resolution. You can have only so much of both, and this part of the dialog box lets you see just how much you can get away with.

I'm not going to go through all the details here. Basically, you choose your colors first, from 256 colors on up to 16 bit or 32 bit or whatever it gives you. *The resolution will change, depending on the number of colors you choose.*

Next, select a resolution. You notice the mini-monitor preview window changes to reflect your choice. And if you choose a higher resolution, don't be surprised if the number of colors decreases. These two things are linked, in case you haven't guessed.

If you're fortunate enough to have a 21-inch or larger monitor, run Windows at the 1024×768 resolution. This displays a ton of information on the screen at once and uses 256 or more colors. You can adjust most of your software (typically through some sort of *Zoom* command) to display text larger on the screen, making it an even trade-off.

✔ The number of colors and resolution depend on your graphics adapter's abilities. Don't blame me if it isn't that high.

Adding a screen saver

Leaving your monitor on all the time leads to something called *phosphor burn-in.* It's insidious. After time, the same image becomes *etched* on your screen. You see 1-2-3 or WordPerfect even with the monitor turned off! This happens because displaying the same image over a long period of time burns up the phosphors lining the inside of your display. Needless to say, this looks tacky.

To avoid phosphor burn-in, you could turn off your monitor when you're not using the PC. Or, better yet, employ Windows built-in screen saver to do the job for you.

Bring up the Display Properties dialog box as discussed earlier in this chapter. Click on the Screen Saver tab to bring that panel forward. The dialog box should look something like Figure 13-3.

Again, this is a messy dialog box, fun to play in, so I'm not going to go into much detail. You choose a screen saver from the Screen Saver drop-down list. Windows offers several.

Click the Settings button to make adjustments for your chosen screen saver.

Click the Preview button to see what the screen saver does. (Move the mouse to turn the screen saver off.)

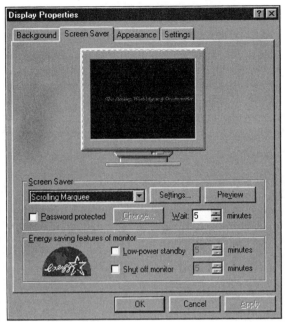

Figure 13-3:
The Display
Properties
dialog box,
Screen
Saver panel.

In the Wait box, enter the number of idle minutes after which you want the screen saver to kick in. For example, in Figure 13-3, the screen is saved after five minutes of no typing or mouse activity; everything goes blank and the computer waits for a key to be pressed or the mouse to move.

Don't bother with a password. If you do, then Windows won't let you back in after the screen saver kicks on. Instead, you have to type a password. Forget the password? You need to reset the computer to get back in.

- A safe key to press for switching off the screen saver is Ctrl. Unlike other keys on your keyboard, this key won't mess with any application that appears after the screen saver vanishes.

- No, that doesn't switch off the screen saver; it merely hides it so you can see the desktop again.

- A cool way to switch off the screen saver is to pound your desk with your fist. That jostles the mouse and deactivates the screen saver.

Chapter 14

The Joys of Having (and Using) a Mouse

· ·

In This Chapter

▶ Getting to know the PC mouse

▶ Reviewing various types of mice

▶ Hooking a mouse up to your PC

▶ Using the mouse

▶ Understanding mouse terminology

▶ Cleaning your mouse

▶ Adjusting the mouse in Windows

▶ Using a left-handed mouse

▶ Dealing with mouse droppings

· ·

*T*he PC wasn't always a mouse-friendly machine. No, the Macintosh was the computer with the mouse. Computer mice were just too much fun to be associated with serious IBM business machines. Mac users? They were a silly lot, anyway.

Today, it's hard to find any PC that isn't sold with its own mouse. Some mice are fun, like the wacky models Logitech sells. Other mice, like the IBM computer mouse (which has the serious IBM letters etched into its case), are meant strictly for business. Regardless, a mouse is a handy thing to have, especially when you're using a graphically drunk operating system like Windows.

▸ Rumor has it that Apple founder Steve Jobs didn't even want the first Macintosh model to have a keyboard. Apparently, he believed everything could be done by using a mouse. (Yeah: "Click 20 times to type an A, 21 times to type a B. . . .")

▸ The plural of computer mouse is *mice*. One computer has a mouse. Two computers, they have mice.

▸ And just why isn't one lice a louse?

A Mouse in Your PC House

A computer mouse is a little plastic rodent running around on your desk. It looks like a bar of soap with a large, rolling ball embedded in its belly. On the top, you find at least two push-buttons. A tail, or cord, runs from the mouse into the back of your PC. Figure 14-1 shows a typical mouse.

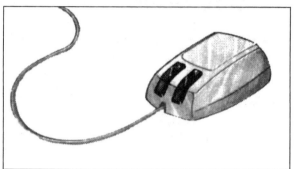

Figure 14-1: One of the first Microsoft mouse models.

✔ Even though your computer may have come with its own mouse, don't think you can't buy another model. Refer to the section "Types of Mice" later in this chapter for some of the varieties.

✔ You need a mouse to use Windows.

✔ You need to designate a special mouse area on your desk and keep it clear of desk debris so that you have room to move the mouse around. An area about the size of this book is typically all you need to roll the mouse around.

✔ A mouse works best when moved across a *mouse pad,* which is a small piece of plastic or rubber that sits on your desk. The mouse pad provides more traction than your slippery desktop, so the mouse's movements are more accurate. (Also, it reminds you to keep that area of your desk clean.)

✔ The best mouse pads have a rough surface, which the mouse can really grip. Poorly designed mouse pads are slick and should be avoided. Also, it's a status symbol to have something cool on your mouse pad: your PC's logo, a photo of your favorite movie star, or a fractal pattern. Uncool mouse pads have the names of computer stores on them or pictures of cats.

Types of Mice

There are many species of computer mice. The most common model looks like a bar of soap with two buttons. Some mice have more buttons. I've seen one model that had 52 buttons so you could actually type with it. (I wonder why the thing never caught on?)

Aside from the standard model, there are a few variations. Some of the most popular are covered in sections that follow.

Rolling the trackball: the upside-down mouse

A trackball mouse looks like a regular mouse turned upside down. Instead of rolling the mouse around, you use your thumb or index finger to roll the ball itself. The whole contraption stays stationary, so it doesn't use up nearly as much room and the cord never gets tangled.

Trackballs aren't for everyone. The only crowd that really loves them are the artist types, who prefer the precise movements the trackball gives you. Are you wearing a beret? If so, you'll probably love a trackball mouse.

- ✔ A trackball has buttons, just like a mouse. In fact, your software won't know whether you're using a mouse or a trackball.

- ✔ The buttons are one reason many normal mouse users hate trackballs: You must press the button with your thumb. Egads!

- ✔ No, you can't just turn your mouse upside down to make it a trackball. You have to buy one.

- ✔ Trackballs are more expensive than regular mice.

Cordless mice

The latest rage seems to be cordless anything, though I can't see a time in the future when we have cordless toasters. A cordless mouse looks like a regular mouse (OK, it's a little fatter) but minus the cord. Instead of a cord, this mouse sends its signals through the air, using either radio waves or infrared technology or mind waves or something. The mouse of the 21st century has arrived!

The cordless mouse sends its signals to a small receiving unit located somewhere on your desk. The receiving unit then relays the signals down a cord that plugs into the back of your computer.

Mickey Niner to base, Mickey Niner to base! Bogey at three o'clock! Prepare to release mouse button.

Kachinka!

✔ A radio-controlled cordless mouse usually costs more than an infrared cordless mouse, and both types cost more than their tailed counterparts.

✔ The receiving unit for a radio-controlled cordless mouse can be anywhere within a six-foot radius of the mouse. The receiving unit for an infrared mouse can be up to six feet away too, but it must be within a direct line of sight. (The radio signal can transmit through objects; the infrared light can't.)

✔ Both types of cordless mice need batteries. Be sure to keep a spare set around so that you can still work when they fail at a crucial moment.

✔ If your infrared cordless mouse starts acting strangely, you've probably set something in front of its receiving unit. It's easy to do because that line of sight area will be the only clean spot on your desk.

✔ This is for J. Fred Niedermeyer of New Brunswick, Rhode Island: No, Fred, you can't use your TV remote control when the infrared mouse fails. And it's not the mouse that keeps changing the channel to "Designing Women." I'd call the cable company if I were you.

Strange mice from planet Claire

I wrote a review of 45 different and strange computer mice for a popular computing magazine. They never published it, and they asked for all the mice back. But I remember using a few of the more bizarre mice. They're listed here for your amusement.

✔ Some mice look like pens. You draw with them on a flat surface. I have no idea why someone would prefer this, since it takes more time to grab and pick up a pen than a mouse.

✔ A pad mouse is like the mouse pad without the mouse. You draw on the pad using your finger (or any blunt object, like a flag pole). Tap the pad to click the *mouse*. This seems OK as an alternative, especially for laptop computers where space is at a minimum.

✔ Some mice are part of the computer keyboard. These keyboard mice usually operate by wiggling a small peg or special key. It sounds silly, but it can be addicting. A keyboard mouse is popular with many laptop models, such as the IBM Thinkpad. Try not to think someone wedged a pencil eraser in the keyboard; avoid the urge to yank it out.

✔ It's a common beginner mistake to pick the mouse up off the desk and hover it in the air. For normal mice, this does nothing. But for 3-D mice, it moves the mouse pointer on the screen. Typically you need special 3-D software to make it all work.

✔ In the early days of the PC mouse, quite a few models were optical. These antique optical mice lacked the mouse ball. Instead, they used infrared light and a special mouse pad to tell which way the mouse was moving. Problem: If you lost the mouse pad, the mouse didn't work. Avoid getting an optical mouse.

Know the differences between a mouse and a mousse!

A mouse is either a furry little rodent — like Mickey — or a handy peripheral for your PC. A mousse, on the other hand, is this stupid French dessert that pretends to be pudding. Or it could be something people put on their hair to make it look messed up. Know which is which before you buy.

Which is best: a bus mouse or a serial mouse?

A bus mouse and a serial mouse look identical, and they both work in the same way: An electronic signal from the mouse flows into your computer through its tail. The difference is the way the tail plugs into the back of your computer.

The tail from a serial mouse plugs into your computer's serial port, typically called COM1.

The tail from a bus mouse plugs into a special mouse port.

Which mouse is better? Well, because they both work the same way, it doesn't really matter.

However, there can be problems with a serial mouse if you have a modem in your computer. Sometimes the mouse and modem get angry with each other, duke it out, and only one ends up working properly.

To ensure that your serial mouse and modem get along, use the Law of Odds and Evens. If your mouse is plugged into an odd-numbered serial port, plug the modem into an even-numbered serial port. For example, plug your mouse into COM1 and your modem into COM2. (Most internal modems are COM2 anyway. That should save you a bottle of aspirin in the future.)

Connecting the Mouse

Plug the mouse into the mouse hole in the back of your computer.

Some PC models, such as those you pay way too much money for, have their own *mouse port*. This port is a tiny, round hole, looking similar to a keyboard connector. (They're identical, in fact.)

If your PC lacks a proper mouse port, you plug the mouse into a serial port, typically COM1 or COM3.

> ✔ It's a good idea to turn your computer off before you connect or disconnect the mouse. See Chapter 5 for shutdown instructions.
>
> ✔ The mouse may come with its own software, which you install by using the Windows handy install program thingy. See Chapter 20.
>
> ✔ The tail points *away* from you when you use the mouse. (Oh, I could tell a story here about a former boss, but I won't.)

Using Your Computer Mouse

The computer's mouse controls a pointer or mouse cursor on the screen. When you move the mouse around, rolling it on your desktop, the pointer on the screen moves in a similar manner. Roll the mouse left and the pointer moves left; roll it in circles and the pointer mimics that action; drop the mouse off the table and your computer yells out, "Ouch!" (Just kidding.)

The mouse should have two or more buttons. Your index and middle finger rest on the buttons while the mouse is cradled in the palm of your hand.

There's no need to squeeze the mouse; a gentle grip is all that's necessary.

You press the left, or main, mouse button by using your index finger. The button is sensitive, so you need only bend your finger a wee bit to press it. The same thing works for the right button; a small bend in your middle finger makes it click.

You use the button(s) to manipulate various items on the computer screen. It goes like this: You move the mouse, which moves the cursor on the screen over to something interesting. You click the mouse button, and something even more interesting happens.

- When holding a live mouse, you keep it in your palm, but with the palm up. A mechanical mouse is held against the desktop with your palm down; its tail extends away from your hand, heading toward the back of your computer.

- Most people hold the mouse in their palm with their thumb against the left edge and their ring finger against the right edge. The index finger and middle finger can then hover over the buttons along the top. (If this were medieval times, the mouse would be a fist weapon, not a finger weapon.)

- Computer nerds grab potato chips with the middle finger and thumb of their right hand. That way their index finger won't get greasy stuff on the mouse button.

- Your mouse can be left-handed or right-handed. The mouse is treated as though you're right-handed unless you tell Windows otherwise. See "I'm a southpaw and the buttons are backwards!" later in this chapter.

- The first time you use a mouse, you want to move it in wild circles on your desk so that you can watch the pointer spiral on the screen. This urge takes a long time to wear off (if it ever does).

- When the mouse cord becomes tangled, raise the mouse in your hand and whip it about violently.

- When the mouse pointer appears to be stuck on the screen, violently slam the mouse down on the mouse pad a few times.

Point the mouse

When you're told to "point the mouse," it means you move the mouse on the desktop, which moves the mouse pointer on the screen to point at something interesting (or not).

Try not to pick the mouse up and point it at something like a TV remote control. It just doesn't work that way.

Buttons on the mouse

The mouse has two (or more) push-button switches on its top, the back side where the tail pokes out. Each button makes a clicking noise when you push it. *Click!*

You use the left button most of the time. That's called the *main* mouse button or sometimes, cleverly, the *left* mouse button. If the instructions say to "click the mouse," you push the left button with your index finger.

The right button is used for special purposes, particularly in Windows 95. Whenever you're directed to use it, the instructions typically say "click the right mouse button," which is also referred to as a right-click.

✓ So as not to confuse you too much, there is no such thing as a *left-click*. It's merely called a *click*.

Click the mouse

A click is a press of the mouse button.

Often you read "click the mouse on the NO button." This instruction means there's a graphic something-or-other on the screen with the word NO on it. Using the mouse, you hover the pointer over the word NO. Then, with your index finger, click the mouse button. This is referred to as *clicking the mouse on something.* (Though you could roll the mouse around on your forehead and click it there if you like — just make sure no one's looking.)

✓ When you push the button on your mouse, it makes a clicking noise. So most programs tell you to "click" your mouse button when they really mean for you to press the mouse button.

✓ When clicking the button, push it down once and release it. Don't hold it down continuously. (Actually, it makes two clicks — one when pushed, and another when released. Is your hearing that good?)

✓ Sometimes you may be asked to press a key combination along with clicking the mouse. A popular combo is Ctrl-click, which means to press and hold down the Ctrl (control) key before you click the mouse.

✓ Watch out! I'm Ctrl-clicking! Stand back!

Double-clicking the mouse

A double-click is two rapid clicks in a row. You do this in Windows to open something.

✓ The time between clicks varies, but it doesn't have to be that quick.

✓ Try not to move the mouse around between the clicks; both clicks have to be on the same spot.

✓ Clicking and double-clicking are two different activities. When the manual says to "click," click the mouse's left button once. Double-clicking is clicking the left button twice.

✔ If you double-click your mouse and nothing happens, you may not be clicking fast enough. Try clicking it as fast as you can. If this speed is too quick for you, it can be adjusted. See the section "Double clicking doesn't work!" later in this chapter.

Right-clicking the mouse

Most of the time you click the mouse's left button, referred to simply as a click. Whenever you need to click the mouse's right button (the not-the-main-button), it's called a right-click.

You do a lot of right-clicking in Windows 95.

Dragging the mouse

To drag something with the mouse, follow these steps:

1. **Point the mouse cursor at the something you want to drag.**

2. **Press and hold the mouse's button.**

   That's the left button. Press and hold the button down — don't click! This action has the effect of picking up whatever the mouse is pointing at on the screen.

   If it's not picking something up, a drag also selects objects by drawing a rubber-band-like rectangle around them.

3. **Move the mouse to a new location.**

   The drag operation is really a *move;* you start at one point on the screen and move (drag) the whatever to another location.

4. **Release the mouse button.**

   Lift your finger off the left mouse button. You're done dragging.

✔ A drag has the effect of grabbing something (pressing the button) and then moving it about on the screen (dragging it). When you release the mouse button, you let go of whatever it was you were dragging.

✔ You can also drag to select a group of items. In this case, dragging draws a rectangle around the items you want to select.

✔ Dragging is used in many drawing and painting programs to create an image on the screen. In this sense, dragging is like pressing a pen tip or paintbrush to paper.

✔ Sometimes you may be asked to press a key while dragging, referred to as a Ctrl-drag (control-drag) or Shift-drag or some other key combination. If so, press that key — Ctrl, Shift, Alt, or whatever — *before* you first click the mouse to drag something.

Right-dragging the mouse

A right-drag is the same as a normal drag. The only difference is you press the *right* mouse button instead of the left one.

Unless you're otherwise told to do so, all drags are left-drags.

Selecting with the mouse

Selecting is the process of highlighting something, making it the target for whatever future plans you have. For example, you select a file you want to copy by first clicking on its icon. You can select text by dragging the mouse pointer over the text you want. Graphics are selected by clicking on them or dragging a rectangle around the area you want selected.

Selecting is the same as clicking. When the manual says to select that doohickey over there, you move the mouse pointer and click on the doohickey. Simple.

Mouse hygiene: cleaning your mouse ball

Your desk constantly collects a layer of dust and hair, especially if you have a cat around or a picture of a cat on your mouse pad. If your mouse isn't behaving the way it used to, you may need to clean its ball. It's easy; there's no need for the repair shop or a guy in a van.

Turn the mouse upside down, and you see a little round plate holding the ball in place. Push or twist the plate in the direction of the arrow that says open. The plate should come off, and the ball will roll out.

Pull out any hair or debris from the mouse-ball hole and brush any stray offal off the ball itself. Put the ball back inside, reattach the plate, and you are on your way.

Try to keep the mouse pad clean as well: Brush it off occasionally to clear away the potato chips, drool, and other detritus that accumulates there.

Tweaking the Mouse

If you ever give your mouse a close examination, you notice it has no knobs or adjustable screws anywhere. Aside from its buttons, there is no way to fine-tune Mr. Mouse's movements or appearance on the screen (that is, unless you use the handy Mouse icon in the Windows Control Panel).

Lurking in the Control Panel is the Mouse icon, which opens up the Mouse Properties dialog box where you can tweak your mouse. The following sections describe a few handy things you can do there. Here are the general steps you take to open the Mouse icon up for business:

1. **Open the Control Panel.**

   From the Start menu, choose Settings⇨Control Panel. The Control Panel's main window appears.

2. **Open the Mouse icon.**

Mouse

   Funny how that mouse icon looks like the type of mouse Microsoft is currently selling. Oh, whatever. Double-click on the Mouse icon. This action brings forth the Mouse Properties dialog box, as shown in Figure 14-2.

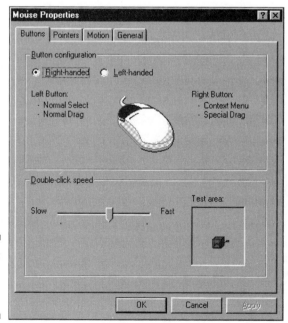

Figure 14-2:
The Mouse
Properties
dialog box.

3. **Goof around in the Mouse Properties dialog box.**

Several subtle things are permissible in the Mouse Properties dialog box. A few of the more popular tasks are discussed in the sections that follow.

4. **Close the dialog box.**

When you're done messing around, you have two choices: click the OK button to keep your changes, or click Cancel to return to the way things were before.

The Mouse Properties dialog box has several panels, each of which controls a different mousey thing: Buttons, Pointers, Motion, and General. To display a particular panel, click on the corresponding tab.

"My mouse pointer moves too slow/fast!"

Especially if you have a large screen monitor, you may want to adjust the mouse's speed, making it more responsive on your large pixel real estate. Or perhaps you notice your mouse pad isn't big enough — or too small. In any case, you can set the mouse's response time and speed by using the Mouse Properties dialog box.

Use the instructions for summoning the Mouse Properties dialog box as presented in the previous section. Click on the Motion tab to bring that panel forward. What you see will look something like Figure 14-3.

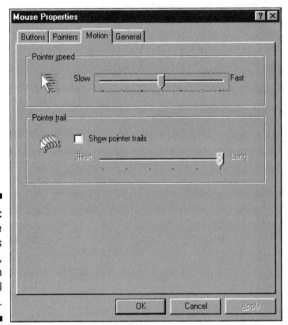

Figure 14-3:
The Mouse
Properties
dialog box,
Motion
panel
forward.

The doojobbie in the Pointer speed area is called a *slider*. Grab it with the mouse, and drag it left to make your mouse slower or less responsive. Drag the slider to the right to make it more responsive.

As a test: Drag the slider to the extreme direction, one side and then the other. Test the mouse along the way by clicking the Apply button. When the pointer gets to a speed/responsiveness that delights you, click OK.

"Double-clicking doesn't work!"

If you can't seem to double-click, one of two things is happening: Either you're moving the mouse pointer a little bit between clicks, or the double-click *rate* is set too fast for mere human fingers to manage.

Bring forth the Mouse Properties dialog box as discussed earlier in this chapter. Click on the Buttons tab to bring that panel forward. (It should look something like Figure 14-2.)

In the Double-click speed area is a slider. Drag the slider to the right to make double-clicking easier. Drag the slider to the left if you keep accidentally moving the mouse between clicks.

To test, first click on the Apply button. This action resets Windows to your new mouse specifications. Then double-click on the jack-in-the-box in the Test area. If you double-click on the box and the stupid clown pops-up, you have a proper double-click speed set.

Click OK to close the Mouse Properties dialog box.

"I'd like to change the mouse pointer to something less dignified"

If you click on the Pointers tab in the Mouse Properties dialog box, you see gizmos for changing the way the mouse pointer looks. I'm not going to go into much detail here, since this is an obnoxious waste of time.

"My buddy has an animated mouse pointer. How do I get one?"

A ton of animated cursors are available in the Microsoft Plus! Package for Windows 95. You might also find some in the same places you pick up shareware software: online or through mail-order houses.

Animated cursors are set up in the Pointers tab in the Mouse Properties dialog box. I'm not going to explain how setting up an animated cursor is done, since those who are willing to try it can usually figure these things out.

If you download animated cursor files or get a disk full of them from a friend, they should be saved in the Cursors folder in the Windows main folder. (The pathname is C:\WINDOWS\CURSORS.) That way they show up in the list when you double-click on a pointer in the dialog box.

"I'm a southpaw and the buttons are backwards!"

Hey, Lefty, if you just can't stand the idea of using a mouse in the right-hand/left-brain dominated world, you can switch things over — even putting the mouse on the nontraditional left-hand side of your PC keyboard. (Oh, brother. . . .)

Summon the Mouse Properties dialog box using the instructions offered earlier in this chapter. In the Buttons panel, click on the `Left-handed` radio button. This action mentally switches the buttons in the Windows head: The right button takes on left button tasks and vice-versa.

✔ This book, and all manuals and computer books, assume that the left mouse button is the main button. Right-clicks are clicks of the right mouse button. If you tell Windows to use the left-handed mouse, these buttons are reversed. Keep in mind that your documentation will not reflect that.

✔ There is no setting for ambidextrous people, wise guy!

The Terror of Mouse Droppings

As with everything else in a PC, occasionally the mouse screws up. It does so by producing a trail on the screen, commonly called *mouse droppings*. This condition occurs when you move the mouse around and still see the cursor scattered all over the screen, typically more than one cursor that traces the pattern in which you're moving the mouse.

When you see mouse droppings, it usually means one thing: The computer is gaga. There is one solution to mouse droppings: Reset your PC. Refer to Chapter 5 for the details.

Chapter 15

Using and Abusing Your Keyboard

*N*othing beats the full responsiveness of a real keyboard when the keys punch down evenly and are light to the touch, maybe even clicking loudly when you press them. Clackity-clack-clack. A loud, clicky keyboard really makes it sound like you're getting a lot of work done. (If only the mouse made noise. . . .)

> ✔ This chapter deals with everything about your keyboard, save for one key: Print Screen. Because that key has Screen in its name, refer to Chapter 13 (on PC monitors) for information on what it does (see the section, "What's a screen dump?"). Then refer to Chapter 16 for information on actually using the Print Screen key.

Knowest Thine Keyboard

Your keyboard is the direct line of communication between you and the computer. The computer has no ears. You can try yelling. You can wave your arms. But the computer hears nothing unless you type something to it on the keyboard. The typical PC keyboard is shown in Figure 15-1. The nerds call it the *Enhanced 101-key keyboard*. Yes, there are 101 keys on it. You can count them yourself, if you have the time.

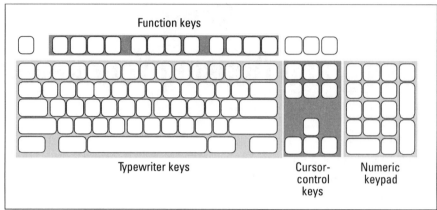

Figure 15-1:
The
enhanced
101-key
keyboard.

✔ Why name a keyboard? Because older PCs used different types of key-boards with different key layouts. Hopefully, all those models are in garages or landfills by now.

Basic keyboard layout

Four main areas are mapped out on your PC's keyboard. Refer to Figure 15-1 as you venture out to find them.

Typewriter keys: These keys are the normal-looking light-colored keys in the center of the keyboard. They include letters, numbers, and punctuation symbols.

Function keys: These keys are positioned on the top row of the keyboard. They are labeled F1, F2, F3, and on up to F11 and F12.

Cursor-control keys: Often called *arrow keys,* these four keys move the text cursor in the direction of their arrows. Above them are more cursor control keys — the six pack of Insert, Delete, Home, End, PgUp, and PgDn.

Numeric keypad: Popular among bank tellers with zippy fingers, the numeric keypad contains the calculator-like keys.

✔ The numeric keypad has a split personality. Sometimes it's used to generate numbers, other times it duplicates the cursor keys. See the section "The keys of state" later in this chapter for more information on this duplicity.

✔ The keys labeled F1, F2, and so on, are called *function keys.* Older key-boards may lack the F11 and F12 keys, but this isn't a major drawback because few programs use those keys anyway.

- ✔ The cursor-control keys are used to move the text cursor around, which typically looks like a blinking toothpick when you type or edit text in Windows. The mouse pointer is often called the cursor, though the cursor keys don't move it around.

- ✔ The PgUp and PgDn keys stand for Page Up and Page Down. The labels on the key caps may be fully spelled out or abbreviated.

- ✔ Insert and Delete are editing keys, often used along with the cursor keys.

- ✔ The Print Screen key may also be labeled PrtScr or Print Scrn.

So where is the Any key?

Nothing is more frustrating than hunting down that elusive *Any* key. After all, the screen says, `Press any key to continue`. So where is it?

Any key refers to, literally, any key on your keyboard. But why beat around the bush: When it says to press the Any key, press the spacebar.

- ✔ If you can't find the spacebar, or you think it's the place where you order drinks on the Starship Enterprise, press the Enter key.

- ✔ So why do they say "Press any key" instead of saying "Press the spacebar to continue"? I guess it's because they want to make things *easy* for you by giving you the whole keyboard to choose from. And if that's really the case, why not just break down and say, "Slap your keyboard a few times with your open palms to continue"?

"Must I learn to type to use a computer?"

No one needs to learn how to type to use a computer. Plenty of computer users hunt and peck. In fact, most programmers don't know how to type; they sit all hunched over the keyboard and punch in enigmatic computer languages using greasy, garlic-and-herb potato chip-smeared fingers. But that's not being very productive.

As a bonus to owning a computer, you can have it teach you how to type. The Mavis Beacon Teaches Typing software package will do just that. Other packages are available, but I personally love the name Mavis Beacon.

Trivia: A computer software developer once halted all development and had his programmers sit down and learn how to touch type. It took two weeks, but afterwards they all got their work done a lot faster and had more time available to break away and play DOOM.

For math whizzes only (like any would be reading this book)

Clustered around the numeric keypad, like campers roasting marshmallows around a fire, are various keys to help you work with numbers. Especially if you're dabbling with a spreadsheet or other number-crunching software, you'll find these keys come in handy. Take a look at your keyboard's numeric keypad right now just to reassure yourself.

What? You were expecting a x or ÷ key? Forget it! This is a *computer*. It uses special oddball symbols for mathematical operations:

+ is for addition

- is for subtraction

* is for multiplication

/ is for division.

The only strange symbol here is the asterisk for multiplication. Don't use the little X! It's not the same thing.

The / (slash) is OK for division, but don't waste your time hunting for the ÷ symbol. It's not there.

Where's the Help key?

There is no key labeled Help. There is one on a Macintosh keyboard, but this is *PCs For Dummies*, not *Macs For Dummies*. They're all fun. We're all-business, remember?

Whenever you need help in Windows, whack the F1 key. F1 equals help — no way to commit that to memory. However, I've included a little fake key cap cover on this book's Cheat Sheet. Clip it out and paste it over the F1 key on your keyboard. That way, you have a handy Help key, just like those Macintosh jokers.

The keys of state (or keys to change the keyboard's mood)

Several keys affect the way the keyboard behaves. I call them the keys of state. They are Shift, Caps Lock, Num Lock, and Scroll Lock.

Shift: No surprises here. The Shift key works just like it does on the typewriter. Hold it down to make capital letters. By pressing the Shift key, you also can create the %@#^@ characters that come in handy for cussing in comic strips. When you release the Shift key, everything returns to normal, just like a typewriter.

Know your ones and zeros

On a typewriter, the lowercase letter L and the number 1 are often the same. In fact, I remember my old Royal upright lacked a 1 key altogether. Unfortunately, on a computer there is a *big* difference between a one and a little L.

If you're typing 1,001, for example, don't type l,00l by mistake — especially when working with a spreadsheet. The computer will gag.

The same holds true for the uppercase letter O and the number 0. They're different. Use a zero for numbers and a big O for big O things.

Caps Lock: This key works like holding down the Shift key, but it only produces capital letters; it does not shift the other keys as a typewriter's Shift Lock key would do. (See the sidebar "The Caps Lock key doesn't work exactly like the typewriter's Shift Lock key " for more information.) Press Caps Lock again, and the letters return to their normal lowercase state.

Num Lock: Pressing this key makes the numeric keypad on the right side of the keyboard produce numbers. Press this key again, and you can use the numeric keypad for cursor control (for moving the text cursor around on the screen).

Scroll Lock: This key has no purpose in life. I've seen some old DOS spreadsheet programs use it. When Scroll Lock was pressed, the arrow keys moved the whole spreadsheet around, as opposed to moving a cell highlight. Scroll Lock does little else important or famous.

✔ The Caps Lock, Num Lock, and Scroll Lock keys have lights. When the light is on, the key's feature is turned on.

✔ When Num Lock is on, the numeric keypad produces numbers. Remember that fact when you use your spreadsheet. Otherwise, those numbers you thought you just typed in actually move the cell highlighter all over creation.

Various and sundry shift-like keys

You produce an uppercase S by pressing Shift+S, though no one needs to say "press Shift+S" because most typewriter-using people know that it works that way. But computer keyboards have two other shift keys to drive you nuts: Alt and Ctrl. Why? The answer is *pure greed.*

Like the Shift key, the Ctrl and Alt keys are never used by themselves. Instead, they give new meaning to a second key.

The Caps Lock key doesn't work exactly like the typewriter's Shift Lock key

Although the Caps Lock key allows you to type all-capital letters, it's not just like the typewriter's Shift Lock key. Here are the key [sic] differences:

1. The Caps Lock key only affects letters; it doesn't affect any other keys.

2. The Caps Lock key doesn't affect any punctuation marks.

3. If you type "This Text Looks Like A Ransom Note" and it ends up looking like "tHIS tEXT lOOKS lIKE a rANSOM nOTE," the Caps Lock key is inadvertently turned on. Press it once to return everything to normal.

4. If you press the Shift key while Caps Lock is on, the letter keys return to normal. (Shift kind of cancels out Caps Lock.)

Alt: The Alt key is used like the Shift key. For example, holding down the Alt key and pressing the F4 key (referred to as "pressing Alt+F4") closes a window on the desktop. You press and hold the Alt key, tap the F4 key, and then release both keys.

Ctrl: The Control key, abbreviated as Ctrl on the keyboard, is also used like the Shift key. In most Windows programs, if you hold down the Ctrl key and press S (press Ctrl+S, in other words), you save something. Likewise, in most programs, you press Ctrl+P to print (and so on for each clever letter of the alphabet).

✔ Even though you may see Ctrl+S or Alt+S with a capital S, this doesn't mean you must type Ctrl+Shift+S or Alt+Shift+S. The S is simply written in uppercase since "Ctrl+s" looks like a typesetting error.

✔ Don't be surprised if these shift keys are used in combination with each other. I've seen Shift+Ctrl+C and Ctrl+Alt. You use Ctrl+Esc to pop up the Start menu. Just remember to press and hold the shift keys first, and then tap the letter key. Release all the keys together.

✔ Some manuals use the term ^Y rather than Ctrl+Y. They both mean the same thing: Hold down the Ctrl key, press the letter Y, and release the Ctrl key.

✔ OK, I lied. With some programs, you do press the Alt key by itself. For example, you can press the Alt key to activate the menu bar in a Windows program. You can also press the Ctrl key by itself to switch off the Windows screen saver.

Enter and Return, the evil twin keys

Nearly all PC computer keyboards have two keys labeled Enter. Both keys work identically, with the second Enter key placed by the numeric keypad to facilitate rapid entry of numbers.

So what is the Return key? Many early computers sported a Return key. Essentially, it's the same thing as the Enter key. In fact, the Macintosh has both an Enter and a Return key.

I mention the differences here because I just saw a manual the other day that said to "press Return." There is no Return key! Press the Enter key when some dopey manual suggests you press Return. (Or just go out and buy a Macintosh and press the Return key on that keyboard when the PC manual says "press Return.")

✔ Pressing the Enter key is the same as clicking OK in a dialog box.

✔ In your word processor, you only press the Enter key at the end of a paragraph.

✔ Don't press Enter after filling in a text box inside a dialog box. Use the Tab key to move from text box to text box. This rule also applies when using some database programs; use the Tab key to skip merrily between the fields. La, la, la.

✔ The difference between Enter and Return is only semantic. Enter has its roots in the electronic calculator industry. You pressed Enter to enter numbers or a formula. Return, on the other hand, comes from the electronic typewriter. Pressing the Return key on a typewriter caused the carriage to return to the left margin. It also advanced the paper one line in the machine.

The Tab key

Like on a typewriter, pressing Tab moves the cursor over to the next tab stop, though on some computers pressing Tab causes the computer to produce a can of a refreshing diet beverage.

✔ To confuse matters, the Tab key sometimes isn't labeled Tab. Instead, it has two arrows on it — one pointing left and the other right. Weird stuff.

✔ The computer treats a tab as a single, separate character. When you backspace over a tab in a word processing program, the tab disappears completely in one chunk — not space by space.

✔ Use the Tab key to indent paragraphs; don't press the spacebar five times. You'll thank yourself later when your word processing program doesn't mangle paragraphs. (Or at least it gives your word processor one less way to mangle paragraphs.)

The mystery of the slash and backslash keys

Two slash keys are on your keyboard, and you can easily be confused.

The forward slash (/) leans forward (duh!), like it's falling to the right. This slash is primarily used to denote division, such as 52/13 (52 divided by 13). In English, it's used to divide various words or, most often, as an incorrect replacement for a hyphen.

The backslash (\ ) leans to the left. This character is used in *pathnames,* which are complex and discussed only near the end of Chapter 8, where no one can find them.

Don't confuse the two! If you do, the computer will become anxious, and it may leave a grease stain on your desktop.

The "Knock it off!" keys

Three "Hey! Stop that!" keys are on your PC's keyboard. Only one of them works in Windows; the other two are holdovers from DOS and don't work in Windows (though feel free to try).

Esc: The Escape key, labeled Esc on most keyboards, is supposed to enable you to escape from your current situation and seek higher ground. For example, if you don't like the Windows dialog box, press Esc and it's gone. Esc can be a good pinch hitter to try first when something goes awry.

Break: By itself, the Break key does nothing. But when you hold down the Ctrl key and press the Break key (Ctrl+Break), you can often break DOS's fascination with itself and get back to something constructive. This key combination is useless in Windows.

Ctrl+C: This key combination was DOS's hand brake. If you ever bother to fire up a DOS prompt window, you can use Ctrl+C to stop DOS from doing just about anything. (If not, try Ctrl+Break.)

✔ You may notice your keyboard has no true Break key. That key is often disguised as the Scroll Lock or Pause key. The word Break may be on the front, in a different color or written in Hebrew.

✔ Why is the key called Break? Why not call it the Brake key? Wouldn't that make sense? Who wants a computer to break anyway? Golly.

The secret behind the SysRq key

Simply pretend that the SysRq key isn't there. Don't mess with it. Windows doesn't use it. DOS never did.

IBM added the SysRq key to the keyboard many years ago to be used in a future version of DOS. Everyone is still waiting. So, although the SysRq key has kind of a cool name, it never really amounted to anything. Feel free to press it whenever you don't want to do anything. (It's Ctrl+Print Screen on your keyboard.)

Oh: SysRq stands for System Request, in case you were wondering.

Don't Bother with the Pause Key

Honestly, the Pause key doesn't work in Windows. In DOS, it would pause output. So if you were displaying a long file on the screen, you could press the Pause key and everything would stop. After you read a few lines, you could press the Pause key again, and everything would start up again. This process isn't necessary in Windows.

Pause does have a cousin of sorts. The Ctrl+S key combination is also used to freeze information, suspending it as it's displayed on the screen. Even so, about the only time you can use Ctrl+S is when you're online with your modem and some remote system is sending you text. Then it's OK to press Ctrl+S to pause the display. Press Ctrl+Q to get the text started again.

- ✔ I suppose Bill Gates is trying to tell us that there's no stopping Windows.
- ✔ The Pause key may also be labeled Hold.
- ✔ Ctrl+S pauses online text.
- ✔ Ctrl+Q resumes online text.

Common Windows Editing Keys

Almost any time text is selected in Windows it can be edited. For that task you need to know only one set of editing keys — the Windows editing keys. These are pretty easy to understand — at least compared with the ugly old WordStar cursor key diamond. I shudder at the thought. . . .

Enough shuddering! Table 15-1 lists the key commands used whenever text is selected in Windows.

Table 15-1	Windows Editing Key Commands
Key	**Function**
←	Moves the text cursor left (back) one character
→	Moves the text cursor right (forward) one character
Ctrl+ ←	Moves the text cursor left one word
Ctrl+ →	Moves the text cursor right one word
Home	Moves the text cursor to the start of the line
End	Moves the text cursor to the end of the line
Delete	Deletes current character
Backspace	Deletes preceding character
↑	Moves the text cursor up one line
↓	Moves the text cursor down one line
PgUp	Moves the text cursor up to the preceding page (screen)
PgDn	Moves the text cursor down to the next page (screen)
Ctrl+↑	Moves the text cursor to the preceding paragraph
Ctrl+↓	Moves the text cursor to the next paragraph
Ctrl+Backspace	Deletes current word (or Ctrl+Delete)

The Keyboard Follies

Keyboards aren't without their sticking points — and I don't mean what happens when you spill a cola in there. The following sections mull over some of the more trying times you may have with your PC keyboard.

"My keyboard beeps at me!"

Common problem. Many potential causes and cures.

Reason 1: You can't type anything! Whatever program you're using doesn't want you to type or expects you to be pressing some other key. Remember that in Windows you can only use one window at a time — even if you're looking at another window.

Reason 2: You're typing too fast. The PC's keyboard can only swallow so many keys at once. When its li'l stomach is full, it starts beeping at you until it can digest.

Reason 3: The computer is dead! Refer to Chapter 5 for information on resetting.

Keyboard templates

When trying to remember which key does what, many people put sticky notes on their keyboards. Entrepreneurs, recognizing a new market, created keyboard templates. A *template* is a piece of cardboard or plastic that fits around the keyboard. The keys stick up snugly from holes cut strategically through the middle.

The template contains a description of each key's function, conveniently placed next to each key.

- ✓ Because key commands change with each program, you need a different template for each program you use.

- ✓ No one on this planet ever learned how to use WordPerfect's 48-odd function key combinations without a keyboard template.

- ✓ Depending on templates can be dangerous, especially when the cleaning crew accidentally throws yours away, leaving you with no clues on how to operate your computer. Make a backup version by using the copy machine and a pair of scissors, and keep it in a safe place.

"Oops! I just spilled java into the keyboard!"

Sooner or later, you'll spill something gross into the keyboard. The grossest liquids are thick or sugary: soft drinks, fruit juice, cheap sherry, or St. Bernard drool (not sugary, but thick). These things can seriously damage the keyboard. Here's what to do:

1. **Pick up the glass or push the St. Bernard out of the way.**

2. **Save your work (if the keyboard is still functional), turn off the computer, and unplug the keyboard.**

3. **Turn the keyboard upside down and give it a few good shakes (away from your co-workers' keyboards, if possible).**

4. **Use a sponge to sop up as much stuff as possible, and then just let the keyboard dry out.**

   It usually takes about 24 hours.

✔ Surprisingly enough, the keyboard will probably still work, especially if there wasn't much sugar in the beverage.

✔ Unfortunately, spilling something in a keyboard probably cuts its life expectancy in half. The dried gunk beneath the keys will attract dust and grime, making the keyboard get dirty much more quickly than normal.

✔ If you find the keys stickkkkkking when you try to type, compare the cost of a new keyboard with the cost of having the old one professionally cleaned.

✔ Some companies sell plastic keyboard covers. These covers are custom fitted to the keyboard and work quite well. Smokers, especially, should consider purchasing one. (A simple sheet of plastic wrap works almost equally as well, but research shows that it lasts no longer than a few days.)

Ouch! My wrists hurt!"

Several years back, the *New England Journal of Medicine* published an article documenting "Space Invaders Wrist," a soreness caused by rapid hand movements at the controls of the Space Invaders arcade game.

Because typists move their fingers at a similarly rapid rate, they're subject to the same muscle soreness. In fact, Labor Department statistics show that a typist's fingers move farther in an hour than the fingers of every nose-picking commuter driving on the freeways right now.

Because of the strain, many typists suffer from Carpal Tunnel Syndrome, a soreness caused when muscles rub against each other in a small wrist passage called the Carpal Tunnel (the names Lincoln Tunnel and Holland Tunnel are already copyrighted by the State of New York). Some victims wear expensive, reinforced gloves that, if they don't actually help alleviate the pain, at least draw sympathetic stares from onlookers.

✔ A chair's seat and backrest should support a comfortable posture — a chair that can be adjusted to your own preference. When your hands are resting on the keyboard, the upper arm and forearm should form a right angle, with the hands extending in a reasonably straight line from the forearm. Many keyboards come with adjustable legs underneath for positioning the keys to a comfortable angle.

✔ If you can't adjust your desk or keyboard to the right height, buy a chair that can be adjusted up or down, or have your building supervisor install hydraulic lifts in the basement.

✔ Try using a palm or wrist pad. These foam or rubber devices rest in front of the keyboard and support the palms while you're typing.

✔ Hire Mrs. Grimwold, my old piano teacher, to walk around the office and whack people's sagging wrists with a ruler.

Oui! Oui! Je Veux Taper en Français!

Since you have a computer in your hands, it's capable of just about anything. One of its magic tricks is the Chameleon Keyboard. By using the Windows Control Panel, you can tweak Mr. Keyboard into behaving like a keyboard in a downtown Paris café — minus the Marxists.

To type in a different language, follow these steps:

1. Open the Control Panel.

From the handy Start menu, choose Settings⇨Control Panel. This summons the Control Panel's main window.

2. Open the Keyboard icon.

Keyboard

Double-click on the Keyboard icon to open it. The Keyboard Properties dialog box is displayed.

3. Click on the Language tab to bring that panel forward.

You'll see the Language panel, as shown in Figure 15-2.

4. Click the Add button.

The Add Language dialog box is displayed.

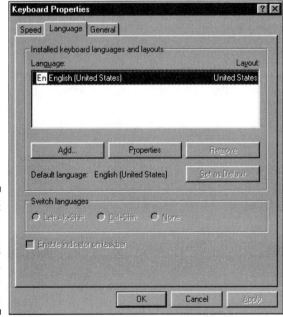

Figure 15-2:
The
Keyboard
Properties
dialog box,
Language
panel.

5. Choose your language from the drop-down list.

There are quite a few languages to choose from, including some I've never heard of before. There are *five* variations of French to choose from, *nine* variations of English. No Klingon, though.

Choose your language.

Click the OK button.

6. Meanwhile, back in the Keyboard Properties dialog box. . . .

The second language has been added to the list. Pay special attention to the Switch languages area of the dialog box. That area tells you which keys you use to switch between your various keyboard languages.

For example, press the Left Alt+Shift keys together to switch from one keyboard language layout to another. Or if you'd rather use the Ctrl+Shift key combination, click on that radio button instead.

7. Close the dialog box.

Click the OK button.

At this time, Windows may beg for its installation disks or CD-ROM disc. You have to put the proper disk into the drive to complete the operation.

You may even have to reset the computer.

✔ Alas, these steps merely switch your keyboard over to a different language *layout.* Your words won't magically appear in a foreign tongue.

✔ You can switch between the normal keyboard and the foreign language keyboard by pressing the left Alt and Shift keys together. A small, boring, two-letter indicator in the system tray (on the right side of the taskbar) tells you which keyboard layout is active.

✔ I have no idea where Microsoft is hiding the list of the keyboard layouts. They used to be in the Windows manual, but not anymore. Anyway, the keyboard layouts show you which new, funky keys are where. This is strange if you're just messing around, but if you seriously need to type in another language, it's incredibly handy.

What about Dvorak's Keyboard?

The first typewriters were piano-sized beasts with a few mechanical problems. If anybody tried to type faster than about ten words a minute, the keys jammed.

To slow people down, the designers made the typewriter's keyboard as awkward as possible. They placed the most common keys along the outside edges of the keyboard, forcing a typist's fingers to move as far as possible. All the extra finger work slowed people down; nobody could jam the keys, and the repair people were happy.

✔ This antique key arrangement you have on your keyboard right now in the last moments of the twentieth century, is called *QWERTY* because the Q, W, E, R, T, and Y keys all sit along the top row, from left to right.

✔ No one ever thinks about this, but the keys on your PC's keyboard don't need to be staggered as they are on a typewriter. This is just more fluff to fill your brain.

Then along came Dvorak

By the 1930s, the engineers had the typewriter mechanics down pat. They didn't have to slow anybody down anymore. So a guy named August Dvorak designed a new keyboard layout.

Dvorak's new keyboard layout placed the most-commonly-used keys directly underneath the right hand so that it could do most of the work (see Figure 15-3). The other common keys appeared directly under the left hand's fingers. No more finger stretches!

✔ With Dvorak's layout, people could type much faster and with less finger strain.

✔ No, the Dvorak keyboard doesn't spell DVORAK like the QWERTY keyboard spells QWERTY. And August Dvorak is a cousin of the famous musical composer Antonin Dvorak. Also, nobody knows this, but Alfred Nobel invented plywood as well as dynamite.

✔ Although the general public has given up its 8-tracks for cassettes and betamaxes for VHS, few people want to give up their old keyboard for a new, more efficient layout.

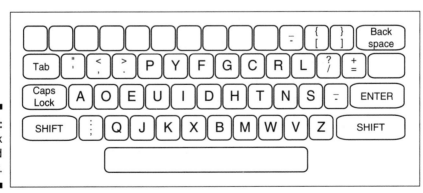

Figure 15-3:
The Dvorak
keyboard
layout.

"Hey! I want to try this Dvorak thing!"

If you're up for it, you can tell Windows to reconfigure your keyboard in the Dvorak layout. In the Keyboard Properties dialog box, Language panel (see Figure 15-2), in the Language list, click on English. Then click the Properties button. The Language Properties dialog box appears (see Figure 15-4).

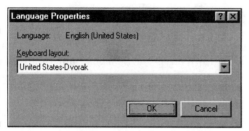

Figure 15-4:
The
Language
Properties
dialog box.

Locate United States-Dvorak in the drop-down list. Click OK to close the Language Properties dialog box. Then click OK to close the Keyboard Properties dialog box.

You may be asked to insert your Windows distribution diskettes or CD-ROM disc. Do so.

When the operation is complete, Windows has programmed a new keyboard for you. You have to relearn your typing skills, as well as move around all the key caps. Or you can buy a whole new Dvorak keyboard from a mail-order outfit.

Figure 15-3 shows you the new layout; if a key's meaning doesn't change (e.g., the number keys), it isn't marked in Figure 15-3.

- ✔ If you decide to learn the Dvorak keyboard, be sure to learn the QWERTY method, too, or you'll be lost when trying to use keyboards at libraries and offices (or any of the 99 percent of all keyboards you encounter).

- ✔ Unlike a foreign language keyboard layout, there is no handy key combination to switch between Dvorak and QWERTY. Heck, man, if you're gonna commit, commit.

- ✔ To restore your original keyboard, go through the steps described earlier in this section, but choose United States from the list.

- ✔ I don't know if there's a Mavis Beacon Teaches Typing Dvorak Style.

Chapter 16

The Printer, the Paper, the Document Maker

● ●

In This Chapter

▶ Different types of PC printers

▶ Compatible printers and PostScript

▶ Setting up your printer

▶ Installing your printer in Windows

▶ Using your printer

▶ Printing sideways (in landscape mode)

▶ Printing the screen

▶ Pulling a form feed

▶ Sending a fax

● ●

"Send this off to the printer," they say.
Then they wink their eye in a mischievous way.
Press Shift-F7 here, and F or 1.
Zip, zippity, zip, and your printing is done.
It's clean and it's quick, but not a memorable trick.
Yet why does it look like the printer is sick?
There are weird funny characters, an @ and a 4.
This just doesn't look like it did in the store!
You want hassle-free printing and envelopes to address.
But now you're not printing. Everything is a mess.

So many people worry about making a computer easier to use. But there's this rogue device: *the printer,* an equally ornery element of all computers, as tough to master as Windows and as fussy as any computer hardware. Your printer is like an unwanted relative: easily ignored most of the time but occasionally stopping by for an annoying visit.

Things are better than they used to be. Under DOS, you would have to tell each and every program you own about your printer. In Windows, you must toil with that task only once. It's nothing a few pages of text — or a large caliber weapon — can't solve.

Welcome to Printerland

Forget brand names and all the technical mumblings for a moment. There are two major types of printers: *impact* and *laser* (kind of like two characters you'd see on "American Gladiators"). The differences between the two types of printers are the quality of the image and the price.

Laser printers are more expensive and produce higher-quality text and graphics. Odds are fairly good that if you're in business, you want a laser printer.

Impact printers produce lower-quality images but are relatively inexpensive. They are ideal when quality and speed don't count, such as for the home or in the government or any other large bureaucracy.

- Impact printers are also called *dot matrix* printers. The name refers to the grid of dots used to create the image. On the really cheap printers this shows up annoyingly well.

- An older type of impact printer was the *daisy wheel*. This printer is essentially an electronic typewriter, and it produces similar output — but no graphics. The laser printer has replaced the daisy wheel as the printer of choice in business today.

- Specialty printers abound. One of the most popular is the ink-jet printer that actually spits ink onto the page. Contrary to that image in your head right now, the ink-jet printer produces clean, almost laser-printer-quality output. It's slower than a laser printer but much more economical. Also, some ink-jet printers can produce color images.

- Doinky little printers are available for laptop computers. They're called *thermal* printers because (like many fax machines) they print with heat on waxy paper. These printers are impractical for anything but portable computing.

- Another type of thermal printer is the *thermal transfer* printer. It's essentially a dot matrix printer but uses a special ribbon that prints on the paper using heat instead of pressure. Or at least that's how it was explained to me.

Only a die-hard computer geek would read this

Computer printers are like teenagers' cars: Speed and image are what count the most. Speed refers to how long it takes the printer to produce its image. Impact printers print one character at a time, so their speed is measured in cps (characters per second). A speed of 80 cps is about middlin', with smaller values indicating slower printers and higher values describing printers that would rip a hole in the wall if their little rubber feet weren't securely gripping the table top.

Laser printers print a sheet of paper at a time, so their speed is measured in ppm (pages per minute). A swift laser printer can crank out 8 ppm.

Image is referred to as letter-quality among impact printers. They try to approach the quality of a typewritten page but usually fall short. This earns them the moniker near letter-quality. Laser printers print much better than letter-quality. Their quality is measured by the number of dots they can laser beam into a linear inch. A laser printer with 300 dpi (dots per inch) is about average, and 600 dpi or more is possible with the proper hardware and sufficient funds. When you get up to 1,200 dpi, you're approaching the quality of a professional typesetting machine.

The object behind image is to create something that doesn't look as if it was made on a computer. Which makes you wonder why you've spent all that money when a typewriter's output ain't so bad. . . .

✔ Three important switches on the front of your printer (or on its control panel, wherever that may be) are the On-Line or Select switch, plus the Form Feed and Line Feed switches. The functions of these switches are covered later in this chapter.

The printer produces *hard copy.* That's anything you do on your computer screen that eventually winds up on paper.

"What's a Compatible Printer?"

Windows may claim it works with thousands of printers, but it secretly prefers certain brand-name printers. They are what you call "the biggies" — IBM, Epson, and Hewlett-Packard. Everything else will work, just as you can put any brand of tire on any car. It's just that the hassle rate rises when you stray from the major names.

A compatible printer is any make or model that works well with Windows. If you have an IBM, Epson, or Hewlett-Packard model, you're more than OK. With other printers, whether or not Windows will like them is an iffy situation. Most of the time, as long as you don't buy weird and non-Japanese-sounding printer equipment, you'll be OK. But, if you have one of the three biggies, you're doing just bitchen.

✔ You don't have to buy the same brand of printer as your computer. There are hundreds of different brands of printers. The one best suited to your computer is the one most compatible with your software (Windows) — not your hardware.

✔ All printers, whether or not they are the biggies, will plug into and operate with all PC software. The compatibility issue here describes how much you'll get out of the printer. Fancy printing, including graphics, is a touchy issue. If Windows really likes your brand of printer, that's great. And, if you have one of the three biggies, that's even better.

✔ Even if you don't have a big-name-brand printer, it may still be compatible with an IBM, an Epson, or a Hewlett-Packard printer. Check the manual, where the manufacturer usually boasts about such a feature right up front. It's referred to as *emulation,* which means one printer will behave like, or emulate, the features of another. (Emulation has nothing to do with a printer's setting itself on fire.)

✔ Your printer may have a row of tiny switches, called DIP switches (named after the French Dip sandwich). Some printers have a front panel with buttons and an LCD display instead of the switches. The object is to configure and control your printer. For example, if your Wannabishi printer can emulate the more popular Hewlett-Packard LaserJet, that's where you'd tell it to do so.

✔ Hewlett-Packard is often abbreviated HP. IBM is already an abbreviation. And Epson isn't an abbreviation at all, nor is it a type of salt. (Skip this following stuff if you're a busy executive.) The company that makes Epson printers used to make paper tape printers for calculators. The company called its printer the Electrical Printer-1 or EP-1. The second printer was the EP-2. And its first computer printer was the "son" of the EP printer line, hence EP-son or Epson. Amaze your friends at the next user group meeting with that piece of trivia. Maybe you'll win the Twinkie.

✔ Another type of printer compatibility is PostScript. If that concerns you, refer to the section, "What's PostScript?" Omigosh! Here it is:

"What's PostScript?"

A PostScript printer isn't a name-brand printer. It's more of a type of printer. PostScript printers — no matter who makes them — will work with all applications that support the PostScript printing language. This makes them a universal type of printer no matter who makes them.

- ✔ PostScript is actually a printing *language* — like a programming language — that tells the printer exactly what to do, what to print, and how it looks. The printing language can be very precise, which is why many printers support it and most applications will customize their output for a PostScript printer.

- ✔ All Apple (Macintosh) laser printers use PostScript. (At least the expensive, good ones do.) If that excites you, rush out right now and buy some Apple stock. (Ha, ha.)

- ✔ PostScript printers are expensive.

Gutenburg Never Had It This Rough (Setting Up Your Printer)

This is the easy part: To set up your printer, you plug it into your PC. Specifically, you find a connection called the *printer port* on the rear of the PC's console. It may be labeled as such or dubbed "LPT1." Plug one end of the printer cable into the printer port on the console and then plug the other end into the printer. If you get good at this, you can charge your friends fifty bucks to perform the same feat for them.

- ✔ The PC's printer port is also called a *parallel port*.

- ✔ There may be more than one printer port on your PC, in which case they're referred to as LPT1, LPT2, or even LPT3.

- ✔ If you have more than one printer port, plug your printer into LPT1, the first printer port.

- ✔ LPT is an IBM term. It stands for Line PrinTer.

- ✔ A single computer is capable of handling two printers, but you must have a terribly big ego to be that possessive.

- ✔ If you're using a printer on the network, then it doesn't need to be plugged into your PC at all. You access that printer through your PC's network hose. More on network printing later in this chapter.

Loading it with paper

Your printer needs to be loaded with paper. The days of printing on thin air are still in the future.

For impact printers, you feed in a continuous sheet of fanfold paper or line up one sheet at a time as you would with a typewriter.

Laser printers load up a cartridge of paper at a time, similar to a photocopier. Ink-jet printers also use a cartridge or often have you lay a sheaf of paper in a handy, easily-jamable paper tray.

- ✔ Always make sure that you have enough printer paper.
- ✔ You can buy standard photocopier paper for your laser printer.
- ✔ Some color printers require a special paper to get the best image. This paper is horribly expensive, so buy it in bulk. Avoid thin (under 20 lb.) weight paper since the ink bleeds through it like a wet sock.
- ✔ Special "laser paper" is available for a nicer output on a laser printer, but steer clear of the finer, fancier papers and especially of erasable bond. Those papers have talcum powder coatings that come off in your laser printer and gum up the works.
- ✔ *Fanfold paper* is a continuous piece of paper that snakes into an impact printer. This paper must be manually separated after you print on it: You tear off each sheet, as well as the "holes" on the sides of the paper. You can't put fanfold paper into a laser printer, but you can sit around all day and argue about what the little holes are called.

Loading it with ink (or the ink substance)

Your printer is like a banker. The banker takes your money and sticks it in a vault (or dumps it into shoddy real estate deals with powerful politicos). Your printer takes ink from some sort of storage device and transfers it onto the paper's real estate.

Impact printers require a ribbon. Loading it will get your hands all smudgy no matter how careful you are.

Laser printers require drop-in toner cartridges. These are easy to install and come with their own handy instructions. Just don't breathe in the toner or you'll die of cancer.

Ink-jet printers use little canisters of ink, which surprisingly make them the easiest to change of all. Just be careful with the old, used canisters, which may be inky on their tip. I put mine in a ziplock baggie and dispose of them according to proper EPA hazardous PC waste procedures.

This is the last time this information on serial printers will appear in this book (maybe)

Not all printers plug into the PC's printer port. The exception is the serial printer, which, surprisingly enough, plugs into your computer's serial port. These printers work just like parallel printers, but they're getting old and few people have them any more. Here are my final comments on serial printers for the two of you left in the United States who use a serial printer with your Windows 95 computer:

✔ Some serial printers are a dual-mode type. They can be run as a serial printer or as a parallel printer. Unless there's some grave

need to run the printer as a serial printer, hook it up in the parallel mode.

✔ Setting up a serial printer in Windows is easy; just set it up like any other printer and Windows figures out the rest. Hopefully.

✔ Serial printers require special serial cables. These are radically different from the standard serial cable you may use to connect to an external modem. When buying a serial printer cable, make sure that it's labeled as such.

✔ I suggest buying rubber gloves or those cheap plastic gloves that make you look like Batman when changing a ribbon or toner cartridge.

✔ Even if you're environmentally unconscious, you should consider recycling your old toner cartridges. Some new cartridges even come with return mail slips so you can send them back to the factory for proper reintegration into the earth's ecosystem.

✔ Another option for an old toner cartridge is recharging. You can take it to a special place that will clean the old cartridge and refill it with toner. This actually works and is often cheaper than buying a whole new cartridge. Even so, it should only be done once. Make sure the recharging place follows this policy, or take your used toner cartridges elsewhere.

Telling Windows about Your Printer

Windows may be smart when it comes to adding Plug-n-Play expansion cards, but the Plug-n-Play printer is still a few light-years away. You must set up a printer deliberately.

Connect your printer to the PC (if you haven't already). Make sure your printer is on, loaded with paper, and ready to print.

Now you're ready to tell Windows all about your printer. Heed these steps:

1. **Open up My Computer.**

   Double-click on the My Computer icon. This displays a window chock-full of your PC's disk drives, plus two (or more) weird folders.

   One of those weird folders is named Printers.

2. **Open the Printers folder.**

   Printers

   Double-click on the Printers folder icon. A window appears listing all the printers you may already have connected to your PC, network printers, plus a special Add Printer icon.

3. **Open the Add Printer icon.**

   Double click on the Add Printer icon to open it.

   Look, Ma! It's the Add Printer Wizard!

   Add Printer

4. **Click the** Next **button.**

5. **If you're not setting up a network printer, click the** Next **button.**

   If you are setting up a network printer, click on Network printer, and then click the Next button.

6. **Describe your printer's make and model to Windows.**

   Using the dialog box (shown in Figure 16-1), click on your printer's manufacturer and then pluck out the model number.

   If your printer isn't listed, you'll need a special installation disk that (hopefully) came with the printer. If so, click the Have Disk button and browse for the disk using the Open dialog box techniques described in Chapter 9.

Figure 16-1:
Choose your printer's make and model from this dialog box.

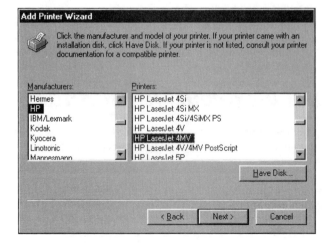

7. **Click the** Next **button.**

8. **Pick the printer port from the list.**

    It will probably be LPT1, your first printer port.

9. **Click the** Next **button.**

10. **Click the** Next **button again.**

11. **Click** Finish.

    You're done.

You can print a test page on your printer if you like. Personally, I'm shocked the test page isn't a catalog and order form for Microsoft Products. But it ensures that your printer is connected properly and everything is up to snuff.

✔ Unlike DOS, where you had to install your printer for every stinkin' application, you only need go through these steps once in Windows.

✔ Network printer? Let someone else set the thing up.

Basic Printer Operation

Here are the steps required to turn your printer on:

1. **Flip the switch.**

✔ Always make sure that your printer is on before you start printing. Like, duh.

✔ Your printer doesn't need to be on all the time. Only turn it on whilst you print. When you're done printing, you can turn the printer off. (This is economical for laser printers, which use up to 1,000 watts of electricity when they're on.)

✔ An exception to the on-while-printing rule is for those Energy Star printers. Energy Star means the printer will run in a low-power mode while it's not working. You can leave those suckers on all the time if you like. I do.

Going on-line

Your printer has two on-like buttons. The first is the power switch. That turns the printer on. The second switch is the On-Line or Select button. That must be turned on before your printer can print.

So why bother? Some things your printer can do by itself, such as eject a page, print a list of its fonts, or do a graphics test. It must be off-line or deselected to do that. Then, when your PC needs to print again, you must switch your printer back on-line.

Printing something, anything

Under Windows, printing is a snap. All applications support the same print command: Choose File⇨Print from the menu, click OK in the Print dialog box, and — zit-zit-zit — you soon have hard copy. This is why Chairman Bill (as in Gates) bestowed Windows upon the masses.

✔ The common keyboard shortcut for the print command is Ctrl+P. This is true for all Windows 95-specific programs; some older Windows programs may use a different key combination.

✔ Always save your stuff before you print. Not that anything bad may happen; it's just a good reminder to save.

✔ Many applications sport a Print toolbar icon. If so, you can click on that button to quickly print your document.

✔ It's usually a good idea to preview your printing before you condemn even more of our North American forests to death. Many Windows programs have a File⇨Print Preview command that lets you pour over the page before it's splattered all over a tree slice. Save an owl. (Or something like that.)

"I want to print sideways"

Printing on a sheet of paper long-ways is called printing in the *landscape* mode. Almost all Windows programs are capable of this.

From the Print dialog box, click on the Properties button. The very first panel in your printer's Properties dialog box is Paper (see Figure 16-2). Click on the Landscape option. Click OK to close the dialog box, and then click OK in the Print dialog box to print in the landscape mode.

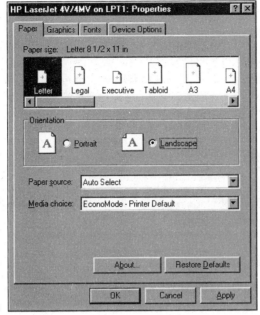

Figure 16-2:
The Paper
panel in the
Properties
dialogue
box.

Printing the screen

Even though there's a button on the keyboard named Print Screen, it won't send a copy of the screen to the printer. At least not directly. If you really need a printed copy of Windows desktop or some window on the screen, follow these steps:

1. **Arrange the screen so that it looks the way you want it printed.**

2a. **If you want a snapshot of the whole screen, press the Print Screen key.**

2b. **If you want a snapshot of only the top window on the screen, press Alt+Print Screen.**

3. **Open the Paint program.**

   From the Start menu choose Programs⇨Accessories⇨Paint.

   The Paint program appears on the screen.

4. **Choose Edit⇨Paste.**

   This pastes the image into the Paint program.

   If a warning dialog box tells you the image is too big, click the Yes button.

5. Print the image.

Choose File⇨Print.

The Print dialog box appears. Click OK to start printing.

If the image is very large, you might want to take advantage of the File⇨Print Preview command. It will show you how the final image will look, as well as how many pages it will print on (if it's incredibly huge).

Form feeding

A form feed is the process of spitting a page — or the rest of a page — out of the printer. This is done for an obvious reason: to see what you've printed.

To make the printer eject a page (a form feed), take the following two steps:

1. Press the printer's On-Line or Select button.

The little light will go out, which puts the printer into its "command mode."

2. Press the Form Feed button on the printer.

This may also be labeled "Eject." You might also have to select Form Feed from a menu on the printer's tiny LCD screen.

With an impact printer, one whole sheet of paper will pop out. On a laser printer, the printer will warp up to speed, drag in a piece of paper, print on it, and then slide it back out.

➤ Remember to press the On-Line button after you're done. The computer won't talk to the printer until it's on-line again.

➤ Never use the advance knob on an impact printer when the printer is on. If you need to use the advance knob to adjust the paper, turn the printer off, adjust the paper, and then turn the printer on again. (The reason here, in case you're itching to know, is that the advance knob is engaged when the printer's motor is on. Turn the motor off, and the advance knob just elopes.)

➤ Doing the form-feed is the only way to see what you've printed in a laser printer. Laser printers do not print until you either print an entire page or give the printer the form feed command.

➤ Form-feeding paper also gives you a blank sheet of paper if you need one.

Important Printer Things to Remember

Printers don't come with cables! You must buy the cable separate from the printer.

The printer cable can be no more than 20 feet long. That's ridiculous, of course, since the best place for your printer is within arm's reach.

Printers don't come with paper. Always buy the proper paper for your printer. And stock up on it too; go to one of those discount paper warehouse places and buy a few boxes.

Never let your printer ribbon get too old and frayed. You may think this saves you money, but the printer wears out faster if it has a threadbare ribbon.

For laser printers, there is a "toner low" light or warning message. When you first see it, you can take the toner out of the printer and rock it from side-to-side. This redistributes the toner and gets more mileage from it. But it can only be done once! Replace the old toner as soon as you see the "toner low" light again.

Most printers have little pictures on them that tell you how the paper goes into the printer. Here is how those symbols translate into English:

✔ The paper goes in face down, top side up.

✔ The paper goes in face down, top side down.

✔ The paper goes in face up, top side up.

✔ The paper goes in face up, top side down.

If there is an arrow on one side of the paper, it usually indicates whether the top side is up or down. Then again, this could all be wrong, and what they're telling us is that we need to start using stone tablets all over again.

Faxing a Something Works Sorta Like Printing

No, this section isn't in the wrong chapter. The truth is that sending a fax with your computer is similar to printing, but then again it's not.

Faxing in Windows is similar in that you're essentially sending a document to a fax/modem connected to your computer, dialing up a fax machine somewhere else on the planet Earth, and printing it. It's a convoluted long-distance way to print, but it works.

Faxing in Windows is different from printing in that you must use a special fax program to make it all happen. Needless to say, this is a major pain in the keister.

I'm not going into detail on faxing in Windows primarily because there are other programs out there that do it better. (More on that in a moment.) Basically, in Windows, you follow these three hazy steps:

1. **Choose Programs⇨Accessories⇨Fax⇨Compose New Fax.**

   This fires up an annoying series of dialog boxes for which you enter or choose the name of someone to send the fax to and compose the cover page.

   Don't be lulled into thinking that the Windows Address Book is a handy thing. It's as frustrating as a tax form.

2. **Attach a document.**

   Somehow, you must pick the document you want to send from disk. This means you don't write a fax "on the fly." Instead, you use WordPad or some word processor to write the thing for you. Then you must save it to disk, close it, and *then* send the fax. Hey! Multiple steps! In the old days, took only one!

3. **Send the fax.**

   Give up now and buy a third-party fax program.

   Third-party fax programs work like printing. The fax/modem is merely another "printer" on your computer. In Windows, you choose the File⇨Print command in any application. From there you choose the fax/modem from the drop-down list of printers in the Print dialog box. Click OK to print as you normally would.

   Instead of sending the document to your printer, however, the fax/modem software takes over. It asks you for a phone number and some other details. Basically you just fill in the blanks. Eventually you'll see a Send or some such command. Choosing that command sends your fax.

   This "old" method is much easier than wrestling with Microsoft's "new and improved" fax nonsense. I can tell you, nothing makes me want to punch a computer in the face more quickly than Windows 95's stupid, inane, disgusting, poorly designed, and rude Microsoft Fax software.

✔ Okay, so I hate it.

✔ Obviously, to send a fax, you'll need a fax/modem. See Chapter 17 for more on modems.

Chapter 17

The Modem Chapter

In This Chapter

▶ Understanding what a modem does

▶ Looking at internal and external modems

▶ Judging a modem's speed

▶ Connecting an internal modem

▶ Connecting an external modem

Communicating with a modem is one area of computing that has taken off faster than a lawn chair with 50 weather balloons attached. Personally, I'm shocked. In days of yore, having a modem and dialing up another computer was complex and laden with jargon. Then, after you were connected to another computer, you had nothing but diehard, rude nerds to talk to. It wasn't very encouraging.

Things change, however. Presently, having a modem and becoming part of the online universe — cyberspace, the Internet, what have you — is a reason for owning a computer. The jargon is still there. And it's technical. And all the nerds I remember from 1982 are still out there, on the Net, playing God, and insulting everyone. Still, it's worth a quick dip, even if you're only mildly interested. This chapter will show you the ropes (or cables).

✔ Fair warning: Telecommunications is not simple, and nothing I can do in writing will make it simpler.

✔ Using communications software is covered in Chapter 21.

✔ Modems can be messy, and computer communications causes a lot of headaches. Rather than spoil this uplifting chapter with that information, I've shoved it all off until Chapter 24, which discusses computer agony in depth.

✔ There's also a mountain of modem terminology to climb. These terms are all sanely described in this book's handy Glossary, somewhere in the back.

What Does a Modem Do?

A modem is a device that takes the digital information from your computer and translates it into audio signals that can be sent over common phone lines (see Figure 17-1).

In a way, the computer sends painful bits and bytes to the modem, which then converts them into sounds and sings them over the phone line (and I'm not talking opera here). Using a modem, you can send information to another computer by calling its modem on the phone.

You control a modem, and therefore talk with another computer, by using communications software. It controls the modem, dials up other computers, sends information, and does just about everything in a complex and confusing manner.

- ✔ The most common device to plug in to a serial port is a modem. In fact, the serial port is often referred to as a modem port. Refer to Chapter 11 for the lowdown on ports.

- ✔ Modem is a contraction of the words modulator-demodulator. But instead of calling it a lator-lator, they chose mo-dem. Also, there are more modem jokes in the computer world than anything else, typically "How many *modem* do you want?"

- ✔ Modems are judged by their speed — how fast they can talk to each other. Your computer can chat with the modem at blistering speeds, but the modem is limited (by design and price) as to how fast it can talk. More on this speed thing later in this chapter.

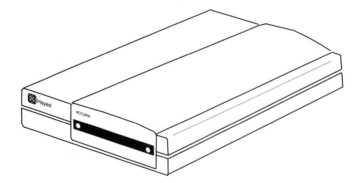

Figure 17-1:
A typical PC
external
modem.

Types of Modems

There are a bazillion different types of modems. There are internal and external models, models with different speeds and features, different brand names, and prices from super cheap to down-payment-on-a-house expensive. It's modem madness!

The most important type of modem is the Hayes-compatible. Just as being IBM-compatible was important for a computer, being Hayes-compatible was important for a modem. It's not really a big deal anymore since, like all PCs, all modems are now Hayes-compatible. That term means they use and understand the same type of commands the Hayes brand modems do.

✔ Do you need to know the Hayes modem commands? Nope. But your communications software does. It uses those commands to control the modem. Non-Hayes-compatible modems tend to ignore popular communications software.

✔ Only real pricey modems tend not to support the Hayes commands. These modems are used by computer nerds who know what they're doing and can afford not to be compatible.

Do it live inside or outside the computer?

Modems come in two breeds:

Internal: This type of modem fits inside your computer console.

External: This type of modem lives in its own box that sits outside your computer console.

Both types work in exactly the same way; the external modem just has a little plastic box housing the mechanism, plus an extra power cord and cable connecting it to a serial port.

✔ Internal modems are cheaper. They plug into an expansion slot inside your computer. The back of the card is visible at the back of your computer; that's where its phone line connectors hang out.

✔ External modems cost more because you have to pay for its little plastic box. You'll also have to buy a serial cable to connect it to your serial port, just as with a serial mouse.

Although external modems cost a little more and take up shelf space near your computer, they have the following advantages:

✔ External modems have a little row of lights along the front that correspond to the online action. A light goes on when the modem is connected to another computer, for example. Other lights convey similar informational tidbits.

✔ Most external modems have a better speaker. You can listen when the modem dials, and you can hear if you have a busy signal. (This feature comes in handy when using the modem on rapid re-dial to win radio station giveaways.)

✔ Because the external modem sits on a shelf, it's easier to reach its volume control knob.

✔ External modems are transportable. They're easier to take to the repair shop, for instance. You can also use them with other computers or take them to a friend's house. (This is a serious step toward computer nerddom, however.)

✔ Finally, anyone can install an external modem: Take it out of the box and peel back the Styrofoam and wrapping. Set it on your desktop. Plug the power cord into the wall. Plug the phone cord into the wall (and optionally plug the phone that was plugged into the wall into the modem). Plug one end of a modem cable into the modem. Plug the other end into your PC. *Plug, plug, plug your modem, gently into the wall; merrily, merrily, merrily, merrily, comm is such a ball!*

Internal modems have the following advantages:

✔ They don't junk up your desktop. Unlike the outboard modem, internal models have only one cable; the one that goes to the wall (and maybe another one to your phone). They don't have a power cord or serial cable.

✔ Internal modems are always ready. You have to remember to turn on an external modem; internal modems are on all the time.

✔ Internal modems usually come with cool software, such as a communications program, faxing software, and maybe even some Internet stuff.

I feel the need for speed

Just as some computers are faster than others, some modems are faster than others. But all modems are relatively compatible: The fastest modems can still talk to the slower ones.

Modem speed is measured in bits per second (bps), or how many bits they can toss across the phone line in one second. I've thrown all that nonsense into Table 17-1, where it's easier to skip over.

✔ Which modem speed is best? Why, the fastest, of course. Today, a 14.4K modem is considered average. A 28.8 modem is fast. I assume some faster modems exist, but they probably cost more than the first moon shot.

✔ Don't bother with anything less than a 9600 bps modem.

✔ Some people use the word *baud* to describe modem speed. That's inaccurate. The correct term is bps. Correct them enthusiastically if you want to sound like a true computer geek.

Table 17-1	Modem Speeds
Speed	**Possibly Helpful Information**
300 bps	Almost all modems can communicate at this snail's pace; almost none of them do.
1200 bps	Although this speed is four times as fast as 300 bps modem speed, it's still regarded as too slow by today's standards.
2400 bps	Most major online services still connect at this slow speed, but they're no joy to use that way.
9600 bps	The former champ and second most popular speed. Nearly all the online services, including Prodigy, America Online, and CompuServe, let you call at this speed — unless you live in North Idaho.
14.4 kbps	The reigning champion, though the national online systems are still catching up to this speed. This would be the minimum speed you need to connect to the Internet, however.
19.6 kbps	An older fast standard, used by some Internet servers, but one that never truly caught on in the mainstream.
28.8 kbps	Just riding into town is the 28.8 kbps standard. A must for the Internet, though nothing else supports it yet.

Fax modem malarkey

The latest rage, these modems can send and receive information from fax machines, as well as from other computers. You tell the software what file you want to send, along with the fax machine's phone number. The software converts your file into a graphic image and passes it to the fax/modem, which calls up the fax machine and sends the picture over to the fax machine.

You can receive faxes, too. Your fax/modem will answer the phone when a fax machine calls. It will receive the transmission and store the picture on your hard drive for later viewing or printing.

I want to push my modem even faster!

It's possible to have Windows tweak your 14.4K or 28.8K modem to a faster speed. I don't know why it works, but for calling the Internet, these illegal adjustments are a real boon. And this is techy stuff, so I'm not being comfy with my explanations here.

Open the Control Panel, and then open the Modems icon to display the Modems Properties dialog box. Choose your modem and then click the `Properties` button.

If you have a 28.8 kbps modem, choose `57600` from the `Maximum speed` drop-down list.

If you have a 14.4 kbps modem, you can choose `38400`.

Those speeds will be used when your communications software dials out. Be sure to tell your communications software, or Internet dialer program, to use the faster speeds. The Internet will be as fast as it can go, without you having to add an expensive ISDN or T1 or fiber-optic or subspace phone line.

✔ Refer to Chapter 16 for information on sending faxes with your fax modem. (It's in the printer chapter, since sending a fax works a lot like printing with a computer.)

✔ Faxes are graphic images: They're pictures of pieces of paper. When you receive a fax of a letter, you won't be able to put that letter into your word processing program unless you have special software. That's pretty expensive and complicated stuff.

✔ If you're serious about faxes, hook your fax/modem up to its own phone line so it can receive faxes all the time. It's a drag to pick up your phone at 3 a.m. only to hear the whine of a fax machine on the other end.

The Joys of Using a Modem

Using a modem itself is cinchy. It's the communications software that will drive you up the wall.

Setting up a modem is so easy a 45-year-old could do it. The following sections tell you how.

✔ Using communications software and dialing out with your modem is covered in Chapter 21.

✔ If you're bold enough to try the Internet, see Chapter 22.

✔ The best way to use a modem is with its own phone line. Just about every house or apartment has the ability to have a second line added without paying for extra wiring. If so, have the phone company hook that line up and use it for your modem. Why? Because. . . .

✔ You can't use your phone while your modem is talking. In fact, if somebody picks up another extension on that line, it will garble the signal, possibly losing your connection — not to mention they hear a horrid screeching in their ear.

Hooking up an internal modem

Let someone else plug the internal modem into one of your PCs expansion slots; or maybe it just came that way from the factory. Your job is to connect only one thing: a phone cable from the modem into the phone wall socket or *phone jack*.

Figure 17-2 shows what the back of the internal modem looks like. Two phone jacks are there. Plug one end of the phone cable into the `Line` hole. Plug the other end of the phone cable into the wall jack.

What do you do with your modem?

Most of the subject of using a modem is covered in Chapter 21. Most people use their modems for two things: calling online services and calling the Internet. In the olden days, calling local bulletin boards was popular. Though those systems still carry a local flavor you can't find anywhere else, they're becoming antiquated by the gargantuan Internet.

Online services: An online service is a huge computer that's hooked up to a whole bunch of modems. From your end, an online service looks like any other software program. But, although most programs make you feed them information, the online service sends you information.

Like magazines, online services are subscribed to. Expect to pay anywhere from $5 per month to $20 per hour for the joy of using one.

Internet: See Chapter 22.

BBS: Short for bulletin board system, a BBS can be considered a tiny online service. It's usually a PC some hobbyist has connected to a modem in his or her living room. Most BBSs offer forums, just like the commercial online services, but they typically don't charge anything for access.

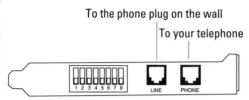

Figure 17-2:
Important
stuff on the
back of an
internal
modem.

Phone connectors have a little release lever on them. When properly connected, they click into place. Ain't no way that sucker's falling out of there.

It doesn't matter which end goes into which; plugging in a modem is just like plugging in a phone. If a phone is already plugged into the wall, unplug it. Then plug it into the Phone hole in the back of your modem.

Table 17-2 offers a quick summary of what plugs into what. Symbols may also be used instead of names for the various connectors on your modem's rump.

Table 17-2	Plugging What into What for Your Modem
Hole Name	**How It Goes**
Line	Plug a phone cable from this hole on your modem into the phone jack on the wall.
Line in	Same as the Line jack.
Phone	Plug your telephone into this jack on the modem.
Line out	Same as the Phone jack.
DTE	Plug a serial cable into this connector on the back of your modem; plug the other end into a serial port on the back of your PC.
Power	Plug the power cord into this hole on the external modem; the other end plugs into a power strip or wall socket.

Hooking up an external modem

Unlike an internal modem, anyone can connect an external modem. It doesn't even require a screwdriver. You do have more cables to connect, but that's not a true bother. Besides, once it's all hooked up, you'll never have to mess with it again.

There are four things to connect to the back of an external modem. Figure 17-3 shows them all, though they may appear differently on the back of your modem.

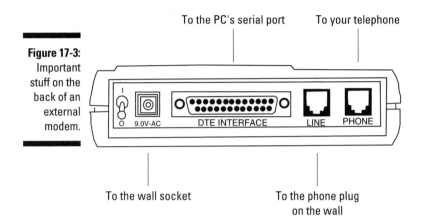

Figure 17-3:
Important
stuff on the
back of an
external
modem.

To the PC's serial port   To your telephone

To the wall socket   To the phone plug
on the wall

Start by plugging one end of a serial cable into the rear of your PC. Plug it into either COM1 or COM2. Plug the other end of the cable into the back of your modem. The cables only go one way. You can't screw it up.

Next, plug the modem into the phone jack on the wall. Stick one end of the phone cord into the wall jack; stick the other end into the Line hole on the back of the modem. You notice the connector snaps into place so it won't accidentally fall out.

If you had a phone connected to the wall jack, plug it into the modem's Phone hole. If not, if you're just using the modem on that line, nothing needs to be plugged into the Phone hole.

Make sure the modem is turned off. (The switch is either on the side or back.) Plug the power cord into the modem, and then plug the power cord into a wall socket or power strip.

- ✔ Refer to Table 17-2 for a quick summary of what plugs into what.

- ✔ You notice that the serial port on the rear of your PC uses 9 wires, but the plug on the rear of the modem uses 25. (Don't bother counting them; I did that for you.) The modem only needs 9 wires. It has a 25-wire connector for tradition.

- ✔ Some modems use symbols instead of names for the connector holes.

- ✔ Sometimes you may find the names or symbols on the bottom of the modem instead of the back.

- ✔ Familiarize yourself with the modem's on-off switch. Also look for the volume control, which may be behind the modem or under one of the sides.

- ✔ It's OK to leave your external modem on all the time. You can turn them off to save power, but remember to turn them back on before you use them. If you don't, your communications software will become bewildered.

Installing your modem with Windows

After setting up your modem, you must tell Windows about it. This task isn't as painful as it used to be, thanks to Windows hardware installation wizard.

The subject of the hardware installation wizard is covered in Chapter 18. Skip up there for more information on what to do next.

Chapter 18
Just Hanging Around (Peripherals)

● ●

In This Chapter

▶ What is a peripheral?

▶ Using the Windows 95 plug and play feature

▶ All about scanners

▶ All about sound cards

▶ Assigning sounds to various Windows tasks

▶ All about joysticks

▶ All about magneto-optical disk drives

▶ All about tape backup units

▶ How, when, and what to upgrade on your PC

▶ Thoughts on buying and selling used PC stuff

● ●

*T*he major parts of an IBM-compatible computer are fairly boring: the monitor, the console box, the keyboard. The interesting parts are the *peripherals:* gizmos you can add to your computer to make it more useful or more fun — and certainly more expensive.

If you play your cards right, your PC can become a fax machine, jukebox, video arcade system, or all three (even at the same time). This chapter takes a look at some of the more popular peripherals that attach to a PC.

✔ Even though anything outside of the console box would be considered a peripheral, this chapter covers only those peripherals not mentioned in the previous chapters.

It's Just Extra Stuff for Your Computer

Peripheral refers to anything outside of the main. For example, the *peripheral nervous system* is all the nerves in your body outside of your brain (which is called the *central nervous system*). *Peripheral vision* includes things you can see without looking directly at them. And *peripheral nervous vision* is what first-time computer buyers get when they enter the store. With a computer, however, a *peripheral* is any accessory or auxiliary equipment you may buy and connect to the computer.

Peripherals enable you to expand your computer system without having to buy a totally new computer. You can add these extra hardware devices yourself or have a guru, computer consultant, or some other highly paid individual do it for you.

The variety of peripherals you can buy for your computer is endless. Common peripheral items include the computer's printer, although this peripheral is more or less considered part of any standard computer; a *modem,* for calling up other computers or the Pentagon by using a standard telephone; a *scanner,* for reading text or graphics images; a device for making the computer play music; and numerous other fancy — and pricey — items.

- ✔ If you were a computer, your arms and legs would be considered peripherals. However, you're restricted by design to only two arms and legs each, so your upgrade options are limited.

- ✔ All peripherals are hardware.

- ✔ Although the word peripheral refers to things outside of a computer, you can also add peripherals internally — inside the PC's console. (In a way, peripheral refers to anything beyond what comes standard in the computer.)

Telling Windows about All This Stuff (The Miracle of Plug and Play)

Wiggling in an expansion card sounds easy. Plugging in a desktop scanner is a snap. And — don't tell — it really is. You just turn off the PC, unscrew this and that, plug it in like a Tinker-toy, and wham — there it is.

Unfortunately, only the physical part is a no-brainer. The software part is far more difficult. That's where you have to get your expansion card to get along with other expansion cards in your computer, as well as your software. That process is a truly brain-numbing exercise.

In order to remove some of the pain from adding expansion cards to a PC, the industry has devised yet another standard. This one is called *plug and play.* The idea is that you should be able to plug in an expansion card and it, or your software, should be able to figure everything out and set itself up automatically.

When you think about it, shouldn't a computer do this automatically anyway?

Well, whatever, the day of plug and play is supposedly upon us. More and more expansion cards and options are being advertised that way, and Windows 95 offers plug and play as a feature.

Anytime you add any new piece of hardware to Windows, Windows instantly recognizes it the moment you turn your PC on. That hardware is then configured using a program called the hardware wizard.

Add New Hardware

In some rare cases, you may have to run the hardware wizard yourself. For example, when you add an external modem, you must have Windows hunt for it. In that case, you open the Control Panel by choosing Settings⇨Control Panel from the Start menu. Then double-click on the Add New Hardware icon to run the hardware wizard. In mere moments, your new hardware should be up and running, and everything will be groovy.

And to think computers were around only 40 years before the programmers thought of this!

✔ Keep your eye out for plug-and-play happy peripherals. Most new computers are plug-and-play friendly, and in a few years just about every hardware doohickey you buy will be the same way.

✔ Actually, the Macintosh computer has had plug and play for years. It's only the PC with its stuck-in-the-past original IBM PC architecture that makes plug and play such a boon.

✔ According to Microsoft, Windows 95 can identify and properly configure 90 percent of the expansion cards and peripherals out there. It can guess at another 9 percent. And only 1 percent leaves it baffled.

✔ Yes, you'll probably end up being in that 1 percent.

✔ Plug and play isn't fool-proof. For that reason, many in the industry have dubbed it "plug and pray."

"Scan, Scan, Scan," Said the Scanner (The Unprinter)

If you're into graphics, a nifty peripheral you can add to your PC is a scanner. It works like a photocopier. But instead of producing a duplicate of a sheet of paper, the scanner converts the image to bits and bytes and stores it in your computer.

Scanners have two very useful purposes. The first is to scan graphic images for inclusion in documents and for desktop publishing. The second is that software can *read* the documents you scan, converting the image into text for input in the computer. This is truly amazing stuff.

Scanners come in two basic styles: hand-held and desktop.

A *hand-held scanner* looks like a miniature vacuum cleaner. You slide the scanner across a picture, and the picture appears on your screen. After it's on the screen, the image can be dropped into party flyers, faxes, newsletters, books, or any other printed material.

Larger scanners, known as *flat-bed* or *desktop scanners,* work more like copiers. You place the paper on top of the scanner, close the lid, and push a button. The image appears on your screen, ready to be saved to disk.

- Hand-held scanners work best for importing small images: logos, signatures, or small pictures.

- If you don't move your hand smoothly while sliding the scanner over the image, the resulting picture will look like one of those curvy mirrors they have at the circus.

- Desktop scanners can import images more clearly and much more expensively.

- All scanners come with special expansion cards; you won't find any serial port scanners. Bribe a guru to do the dirty installation work.

Reading in text with a scanner isn't as easy as it sounds. Scanners understand only the image they scan. To convert that image into text, you need special software called Optical Character Recognition (OCR) software. Even then, the software can read only certain types of characters. Although OCR software is getting better — it's even tossed in with most fax software to read text from incoming faxes — be sure to run your spell checker afterward.

Making Your PC Sing

Do, re, mi, fa, so, la, ti, DOS!

IBM and compatible computers have always treated sound as something to be avoided. The computer beeps rudely when you've pressed the wrong button or when your spreadsheet figures don't add up. The PC's tiny speaker can barely be heard; there's not even a way to adjust the volume. Luckily, a few companies began creating *sound cards,* mostly so game players could hear music and antediluvian space grunts.

Today, sound cards have become one of the most trendy add-ons in the IBM computer world. People say they're buying them for *business presentations* and *educational uses,* but that really means they want to hear the sound of a club swinging in the Microsoft famous Golf game.

✔ For you to hear the sound of a golf club swinging, your sound card must be capable of playing *digital audio.* Digital audio is a sound that's been examined by a computer, translated into a string of numbers, and stored to disk. For example, your compact discs contain digital audio.

✔ Most sound cards can synthesize music, as well. When a sound card plays music, it's usually using its own built-in synthesizer, just as if it were an electric organ. Instead of playing back actual digital sounds, the sound card just generates musical tones on the fly.

✔ Sound cards don't come as a complete package. To hear them, you need speakers or some cables to connect the sound card's output into your home stereo. If you want to record sounds, you need to buy a microphone. Plus you'll need cables to hook up a small radio to the auxiliary port if you want to hear music in the background.

✔ Two standards dominate the sound card market: AdLib leads the synthesized sound/music market, and Sound Blaster leads the digital sound market. Make sure that your sound card is compatible with AdLib and Sound Blaster, or most software won't recognize it.

✔ Even if your CD-ROM drive can play digital sound, you probably need a sound card, too. When your CD-ROM drive is playing back digital sound, it's very busy — much too busy to access any other data on the disk. So companies usually store the sounds on the CD-ROM drive but route them through a sound card so that the CD-ROM won't be tied up.

✔ If you put speakers on your desk, remember that they contain magnets. If any stray floppy disks come too close, they may lose their data.

✔ Digital sound takes up huge amounts of room on a disk. That's why most digitized sounds are limited to short bursts like golf swings and grunts.

Having Fun with Sound in Windows

If you have time to waste, you can turn your smart business computer into a goofy business computer by adding sounds to Windows. I'm not going into any detail here, because this is an area wide-open for play. But I will show you the playground:

1. Open the Control Panel.

From the Start menu choose Settings⇨Control Panel.

2. Open the Sounds icon.

Double-click on the Sounds icon to open it. The Sounds Properties dialog box is revealed (Figure 18-1).

Sounds

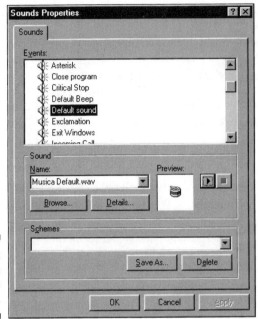

Figure 18-1:
The Sounds
Properties
dialog box.

3. Mess around.

In the E̲vents list are various things Windows and some of your applications do. To each one of these things you can apply a specific sound. So, for example, when Windows opens a window, you can have the sound of something unzipping (or a balloon popping or rubber band snapping) play on your PC's speaker.

Ah, yes. Fun.

You choose sounds by using the Sound area in the dialog box. This area is rich for fiddling.

You can pluck out a sound scheme in the S̲chemes area. Schemes are collections of sounds that came with Windows or the Plus! package. I enjoy the Robotz Sound Scheme, but I mix in a little Musica and Utopia for my own pleasure.

4. Click OK to get back to work.

You can create your own sounds using a microphone and your sound card. If you want to record stuff from a sound effects CD or your stereo, use the sound card's Line In jack, not the Microphone jack.

Oh, there's tons of sound software to mess with. It would take another book to cover it all. *PC Sound For Dummies*? Maybe.

- ✔ Don't feel like a goof when you call tech support for some reason and they tell you to open this or that window and Mary Poppins says "Spit-spot" each time you do.

- ✔ Never, under any circumstances, play the Microsoft Sound sound. It will make you gag.

The Joys of Joysticks

Joysticks get no respect in the computer world. IBM released some joystick specifications in volume two of its reference manual for the PC XT, and that antique joystick had only one button. Manufacturers have had to group together to find some sort of standard.

- ✔ IBM was very sneaky when it designed its first joystick expansion card. It referred to the card as an *analog to digital card* and mumbled something about scientific experimentation. Yeah. Meanwhile, all those guys in white lab coats were busy killing aliens.

- ✔ Not all joysticks are created equally. Most joysticks from other computers (or even game machines) won't work on an IBM computer. Those joysticks use a different format for transmitting data. (They use different plugs, too.)

- ✔ In order to use a joystick, you need a joystick port, usually called a game port. These ports come on expansion cards and plug into expansion slots.

- ✔ Luckily, most sound cards come with a built-in game port, so you don't have to buy a separate game card.

- ✔ Joystick ports have their own unique size. You will never plug a joystick into anything other than a joystick port.

- ✔ Some expansion cards geared toward the game player have two ports on the end — one for each joystick. Others have only one port. You can plug two joysticks into a single game port by using a Y adapter, available at most computer stores. Don't try installing a second game card to get a second port; that attempt will only befuddle the computer.

- ✔ If your game allows it, be sure to calibrate your joystick before playing. All joysticks are slightly different, and the game must be customized to each joystick's individual quirks.

The Very Cool Magneto-Optical Drives

The traditional type of optical drive in a computer is the CD-ROM. However, there are other types of optical media as well. The most popular is the MO, or magneto-optical drive. This is kind of a CD-ROM drive, though the disks are smaller and slower and you can actually write information to the disk, just like a floppy or hard disk.

MO drives come in several flavors, depending on what you want and how much you're willing to spend. Some drives are known as WORMs, which means Write Once, Read Many. These drives can be written to, but the information can never be erased or overwritten later. It's kind of a one-shot deal, perfect for someone who wants to make copies of something that never changes.

On the highest end of the scale are special writable CD-ROM drives. These drives can both play and write CD-ROM discs. Of course, that doesn't make the CD-ROM like a hard drive. No, you must create a CD-ROM all at once, not in little bits and pieces like you put information on a hard drive. And not only do writable CD-ROM drives require all that advanced preparation, they are also expensive as all heck.

> ✔ Ideally, if you want a writable optical drive, one that you can use just like a floppy or hard drive, you want an MO drive; a simple magneto-optical drive that can read, write, and erase.

> ✔ I don't know about you, but I think there's something very cool about the word *magneto*.

Tape Backups

Remember the old computers from the '60s? I bet you envision this room full of refrigerator-sized devices, each with two huge tape reels on it, spinning back and forth in tight jerks. Blinking lights everywhere. Men and women in lab coats. Ah, those were the days. . . .

Sorry to burst your bubble, but those refrigerator-sized devices with the tape reels were not the computer. Those were really the disk drives. Back then, computers stored all their information on magnetic recording tape — a slow and cumbersome process.

Floppy disks eventually replaced tape, but you still find tape used for one purpose: backup copies of data. A tape backup unit plugs into the back of your computer (like everything else) and copies the information from your hard drive to tape.

Peripheralitis: something you'll probably never get

A disease many computer owners get is *peripheralitis*. That's the overwhelming desire to spend more and more money on your computer, typically by buying peripherals.

PC beginners are relatively immune to this disease; most prefer to just use the darn thing and then quickly shut it off. Still, it's amazing what computers can do, provided that users have the cash or VISA credit line to pay for it all.

Why? For security. If anything ever happens to the hard drive — such as someone shoots it or Fred's nephew erases all the files — you can rescue your stuff from the tape backup copy. A sound idea, rarely practiced in real life.

✔ Tape backup drives are an optional extra on all PCs. Most don't require their own expansion card; these drives use your PC's floppy disk expansion card instead.

✔ Some tape drives are external, and some are internal. The external ones are more expensive but have the advantage of being mobile enough to put on a cart and wheel around to different computers.

✔ Tape backups generally aren't faster than floppy disk backups, but they are less time-consuming. As long as the tape is large enough, you won't have to switch them as often as you do floppy disks. Also, tape backups can be automated to take place after-hours.

✔ Most of the time, you find a tape backup on a network file server. This way, all the company's files can be backed up on one system, as opposed to a tape backup unit for each PC.

"I Have Some Money, and I Want to Upgrade My Hardware"

Most people don't trade in their cars each year. TVs, VCRs, blenders, and clock radios usually stay put until they break, and then you buy a new one. Even the office typewriters are probably several years old; there's just no point in buying a new one all the time.

The computer world, being bizarre and different as we know it, offers updates and upgrades on a monthly basis, if not weekly. It's technology! There's something new and better! And you still have $1,500 in credit on your VISA!

What to buy first

Instead of buying a new computer, it may be easier to upgrade the old one. Or, rather, have somebody else upgrade your old computer for you. But where do you spend your money first? Too many enticing things can get in the way of a sane decision. Let me help:

Memory: Your first upgrading priority should be memory. It's expensive, but it's still the cheapest component to buy and the one with the least amount of headaches. Just about all your software will enjoy having more memory available.

> ✔ Increased memory can make these programs work faster and handle larger chunks of information. It also lets the computer handle more graphics and sound.
>
> ✔ More memory is the best thing you can buy for your PC.
>
> ✔ For more information about memory stuff, read Chapter 12.

Hard drive: Buy a second hard drive. Make it a big one. Most PCs can handle two hard drives. And by the time you need another one, you'll know exactly how many more megabytes of storage you need.

> ✔ If you don't have room in your PC for a hard drive, you can always replace one of your current drives. This is a complex process, because you must copy all the files off the old hard drive and onto the new one. Personally, I'd rather do the following:
>
> ✔ If you have a SCSI hard drive system, buy an external hard drive. You can have up to six hard drives with a SCSI system. Chances are your PC's CD-ROM and maybe even your disk drives right now are SCSI, so adding an external hard drive is cinchy.
>
> ✔ By the way, larger hard drives don't take up any extra room in the computer's case, so don't worry about buying a bigger case.

Monitor: Buy a big monitor, like a 21-inch jobbie. These things are *great.* You can really see a lot of windows on the screen at once without feeling crowded. Oftentimes, it's easy to just replace the old monitor. In fact, you can do the whole operation yourself, but have someone with an expendable back hoist the thing up for you.

> ✔ For more information on monitors, see Chapter 13.

When to buy a new computer

Plan on this: Every four or five years, replace your PC. By then, the cost of a new system will be cheaper than any upgrading you do.

Your PC is essentially out of date the moment you purchase it. Somewhere right now in Silicon Valley, they're devising new microprocessors and better motherboards that will cost less money. Maybe not the *minute* you purchased your PC, but sooner or later your leading-edge technology will be yesterday's kitty litter.

But do you really need to buy a new computer? Maybe not. Look at the reasons you bought it in the first place. Can the computer still handle those needs? If yes, you're doing fine. Upgrade only when you desperately need to. No sense in spending more money on the monster.

✔ Computer technology grows faster than fly specks on a clean windshield. But, unless your computing needs have changed drastically, your computer can still handle the tasks you bought it for.

✔ Most people buy newer computers for the increase in speed. Yet speed doesn't always mean increased productivity. For instance, most word processing time is spent pondering the right choice of words. A faster computer can't help there. Faster computers do help those applications that need the extra horsepower: graphics, animation, desktop publishing, and programs of that ilk.

✔ Compare the price of a new computer with the amount of time you'll save at a faster processing speed. If you spend a lot of time waiting for your computer to catch up with you, an upgrade may be in order.

✔ Avoid the lure and seduction of those techy computer magazines that urge you to Buy! Buy! Buy! the latest PC. Remember who most of their advertisers are.

Buying and Selling Used Gear

When people upgrade their computers piece by piece, the old stuff turns up in the classified ads. This is where you can find some bargains, but only if you really, really know what you're doing. After all, the old stuff isn't as good as the new stuff. And, quite often, the new stuff is cheaper than what they're asking for the old stuff.

Should you buy used gear? Only if they're selling *exactly* what you need. For example, you've used the Zot 101 printer for years and yours broke. If there's a Zot 101 for sale somewhere — and it still works to your satisfaction — then buy it used.

✔ Test drive before you buy. This approach is like kicking the tires, but it ensures that whatever you're taking home works. (Well, it worked at least once.)

✔ A big problem with used equipment you're not familiar with is that you may not get any manuals, and there is no technical support or warranty from the selling party. Although it's important to test drive old equipment, don't expect any of the service or support you find with new stuff.

✔ Never buy a used computer as your first computer purchase. It's just much better to pay a store for the service and support you need. (And don't shop for the cheapest price, either! Service and support are important and worth paying a bit extra for.)

✔ PCs have no resale value, so wipe away those visions of selling your used system for anything more than 10 percent of its purchase price. The new stuff is just better and cheaper.

✔ A better option is to donate used equipment to a charity or a local school. The tax write-off is far greater than the resale value ever will be.

✔ If you're selling used computer parts, try to keep all the manuals together, along with support software — the same stuff you got new with the product. Also, accept only cash. For major items, ask for a cashier's check.

✔ Some stuff you never get rid of. Start a collection! Make jewelry from it! I must have enough junk in my back office to make six or more computers. I actually did cobble together a PC for my son. It's the only system in the house that doesn't have a case, and rubber bands hold the hard drive in. There should be a prize for such creativity.

Part V
The Non-Nerd's Guide to Software

The 5th Wave
By Rich Tennant

"THIS SECURITY PROGRAM WILL RESPOND TO THREE THINGS:
AN INCORRECT ACCESS CODE, AN INAPPROPRIATE FILE REQUEST,
OR SOMETIMES A CRAZY HUNCH THAT MAYBE YOU'RE JUST
ANOTHER SLIME-BALL WITH MISAPPROPRIATION OF SECURED
DATA ON HIS MIND."

In this part...

OK, so if software is so important, why is this part of the book *after* the part on hardware? Easy: Because you need one before you need the other. Software needs hardware like a symphony needs an orchestra. After all, what's the point of bassoons and oboes without a foot-high stack of music for them to play?

This part of the book is about PC software. You can't avoid it. You need it. Your computer needs it. Heck, the environment needs it too, what with all the air they put into those software boxes. Another thing covered here: online communications. Difficult stuff. Requires *two* chapters.

Chapter 19

Software: the Real Brains

. . . .

In This Chapter

▶ Word processors

▶ Spreadsheets

▶ Databases

▶ Graphics software

▶ Multimedia

▶ Utilities

▶ Office software

▶ Shareware and public domain software

. . . .

Computers need software like the Frankenstein monster needs an electrical storm. It gives the big, hulking, beast of a computer life! *Life!* And without it, the computer would just be a collection of, er, *parts*.

This chapter describes the variety and flavors of software available. After all, there's more than one way to bring the creature alive.

✔ Software needs the computer as much as the computer needs it. It's kind of a yin-yang thing, though I promise not to delve too deeply into Eastern philosophy at this point in the book.

✔ The plural of software is *software*. If you say "softwares," you'll sound like a foreigner.

✔ Mary Shelly wrote *Frankenstein* when she was 19 years old. It was her first book.

The Wordy Stuff

Just about everybody wants to use his or her computer to write something. Whether it's a thank-you note to Aunt Sally, a letter to the wacko liberal editor of your local paper, or a 500,000-word sweeping romance novel about two entomologists in Paraguay, computers make the writing process much easier.

- ✔ Word processing is writing.

- ✔ There are three types of word processing software: text editors, word processors, and desktop publishing software.

- ✔ If this were *USA Today,* there would be a little box nearby that would say that 70 percent of all computers are used for word processing.

- ✔ The best part about writing on a computer is that you can change what you've written without messing up the printed page. Editing "on the screen" means that each printed page will be perfect. Or as near perfect as you and the computer can make it.

Text editors

A text editor is a bare-bones word processor. It probably won't let you set the margins, and forget about formatting the text or using different fonts. So why bother with a text editor?

Text editors are so simple that they're fast and easy to use. Instead of writing a gargantuan novel on the history of the paper clip, you would use a text editor to create or edit a plain text (or ASCII) file on disk. Sound dumb? Well, it turns out there are *lots* of plain text files on your disk, quite a few of which you'll end up editing from time to time.

- ✔ A text editor is basically a no-frills word processor.

- ✔ Text editors save their documents as plain text or ASCII files. No fancy schmancy stuff.

- ✔ In Windows, the plain text editor is called the Notepad. You will have this program only if you upgraded to Windows 95 from an older version of Windows. Otherwise, you can use the WordPad program as a text editor.

- ✔ Actually, any word processor can be a text editor. The secret is to save the file as a *plain text* or *text only* type of file. Refer to Chapter 8 for more information on saving files of a certain type.

- ✔ Why should Freon cost anything?

Word processors

The word processor is the natural evolution of the typewriter. No more are words written directly on paper. Instead, they're *words electric,* which you can toss around and fiddle with on the screen to your heart's content. Editing, fixing stuff up, spell-checking, formatting — computers were made for this stuff. It's no wonder IBM sold off their typewriter division.

✔ The files that word processors save are commonly called *documents*.

✔ In the early part of this century, Vladimir Nabokov wrote by hand while standing up. In the latter part of this century, he probably would have used a word processor — but standing up anyway.

✔ Some word processors let you create *form letters*. You type a letter, save it, and then type a list of all the people who should receive the letter. The word processor will automatically mangle everything together, producing a fresh letter to each person on the list. This is known as *mail merge*.

Desktop publishing packages

The second phase of the word processor revolution was the addition of pictures and graphics. New word processors could arrange text in columns and add headers and footnotes and all sorts of typographical nonsense. Soon, these high-end word processors became their own, new software category: *desktop publishing*.

Today, desktop publishing programs create the fancy pages you see in newspapers, magazines, and helpful newsletters that come with the electric company bills. The fruits of these applications are ubiquitous. Figure 19-1 shows the author's Christmas newsletter, which was done in PageMaker. Yeah, that's a little much for a Christmas letter, but it does show what you can do with this stuff. Didn't take much time to toss together, either.

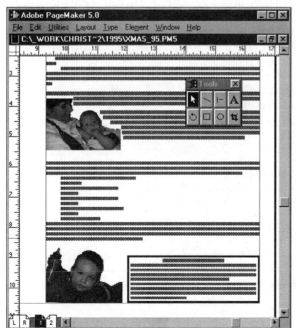

Figure 19-1:
Merry
Christmas
using
desktop
publishing.

✔ If you're cool, you'll say DTP instead of desktop publishing.

✔ Typically you create your text in a word processor, and then *place* it into the desktop publishing program. Desktop publishing is primarily used to arrange words and graphics. Composing the words (as well as the graphics) is done beforehand using other software.

✔ Today's more expensive word processing software includes many of the features of desktop publishing programs. Unless you're in the publishing business, your word processor can probably handle your desktop publishing needs.

✔ This book was created using PC software. The original text was composed in Microsoft Word. Graphics were created by HiJaak, Adobe Illustrator, and PC Paint. And the desktop publishing work is done in PageMaker.

✔ Ubiquitous = everywhere.

The Numbery Stuff

Because word processors mangle words, other special software is required to mangle numbers. That software is generically referred to as spreadsheet software.

A spreadsheet uses a large grid of box-like *cells* on the screen (see Figure 19-2). Into those cells you can put text, numbers, or formulas. The formula part is what makes the spreadsheet so powerful: You can add various cells, compare values, and perform any number of odd or quirky mathematical operations. The whole thing is instantly updated, too; change one value and see how it reflects everything. Millions of dollars have been embezzled this way.

Figure 19-2:
A typical
spreadsheet.

	A	B	C	D
1	**Paper route income**			
2	Household	Rate	Vig	Total
3	Thompson	61%	$ 10.00	$ 18.15
4	Davis	77%	$ 10.00	$ 19.67
5	Jones	18%	$ 10.00	$ 13.77
6	Brown	6%	$ 10.00	$ 12.55
7	Matthews	45%	$ 10.00	$ 16.50
8	Burns	15%	$ 10.00	$ 13.48
9	Simpson	72%	$ 10.00	$ 19.25
10	Johnson	19%	$ 10.00	$ 13.91
11	Roberts	71%	$ 10.00	$ 19.12

TIP

"You can use a computer to balance your checkbook"

The old reasons for getting a computer were quaint and impractical: You could balance your checkbook, keep track of your recipes, and create a Christmas mailing list. Sheesh. They should have said: You can meet the mate of your dreams, dial up the Pentagon and launch a weapon, or kill a million space monkeys without getting blood on your tunic.

Even so, one of the most popular software packages of all time is called Quicken. It's essentially a home (and business) accounting package that makes keeping track of your money easy and fun — yes, fun, in that most people actually sit down and balance their checkbooks since it's so dern easy.

There are many home and business accounting applications available. I'm not trying to push Quicken over the others (whose names I forget at the moment). And no, I don't own any Quicken stock or anything, but I do use the software and find that everyone else I show it to seems to say the same thing: "Jeez, Dan, your car payments are outrageous!"

✔ The files saved by spreadsheets are called *worksheets*. A worksheet is created by a spreadsheet. Even so, many people refer to worksheets as spreadsheets. Ain't no crime in that.

✔ Most spreadsheets can convert the numbers into graphs and charts, making it easier to visualize how much money the CEO is *really* making.

✔ All worksheets you create are blank, ready for you to fill them in. Some worksheets are not blank. They're called *templates* and have been pre-created and customized to do specific tasks.

✔ Don't think spreadsheets are all numbers and no excitement. A popular 1-2-3 template at one time was called the Template of Doom. It was a game.

The Databasey Stuff

Because the word and number processing chores are snapped up by word processors and spreadsheets, database programs are required to mangle every other type of data out there.

Databases do two things: sort and report. They handle any type information, whether it is words, numbers, or little-known bits of trivia (the *Lawrence Welk Show* was originally called the *Dodge Dancing Party* or the scientific name for a gorilla is *Gorilla, gorilla, gorilla*).

- Databases contain three main parts: *fields, records,* and *files.* A *field* is a single piece of data: a person's last name on a form, for instance. A *record* consists of several fields: names, addresses, and phone numbers, all together. A *file* consists of a bunch of records stored on disk.

- Just remember to press Tab when you want to move from field to field in a database. (Hold down Shift and press Tab if you want to move backward.)

- Like spreadsheets, databases can be customized to match specific needs. Rather than toil on your own, you can hire a programmer to create a database perfectly suited to your line of work.

- Oh, heck, just put the programmer on the payroll; those guys never finish their work.

- Databases and spreadsheets can sometimes replace each other's jobs. If the fields in a database contain mostly numbers, a spreadsheet may work better. If a spreadsheet contains more labels and text, a database may be in order.

The Drawing and Painting Stuff

As any parent of a preschooler knows, nothing makes a mess faster than artwork. With a PC, however, all the mess stays on the computer screen — they're not Crayola marks or paint drippings. Hundreds of graphics warriors, in fact, have already swapped their oils and acrylics for a computer. Graphics programs come in varying degrees of sophistication, each with a different target audience in mind:

Database programs come in three unimportant types

Free-form database. Perhaps the simplest database, it works best when you're organizing a big file that is full of random information. When you type the word *eggs,* the database will retrieve every paragraph mentioning eggs, whether it is a grocery reminder, a favorite recipe, or the stock quote for a software store.

Flat-file database. A flat-file database helps retrieve information that's been organized into fields, records, and files. So you can type in a request or query, and the database then retrieves information about people named Thomas who drive Yugos and vote Democratic. It's more powerful than a free-form database, but it requires the information to be relatively organized to begin with.

Relational database. The most powerful database, which I don't know much about, but they tell me it's expensive.

Simple paint programs: These are on the level of the Paint program that comes with Windows. You can draw interesting and often useful pictures, but there is limited control and variety of the things the program can do or paint.

Drawing programs: These programs create images as objects. So you can create a box object, a circle object, and text object. The objects can be edited and changed, unlike in a paint program where you're essentially spraying pixels on the screen.

Advanced painting programs: These painting programs have a wide variety of painting tools to create all sorts of interesting effects. I have one I could show you, but my CD-ROM drive broke and I can't make an illustration of such a painting program. Figure 19-3 would have shown you what it looks like.

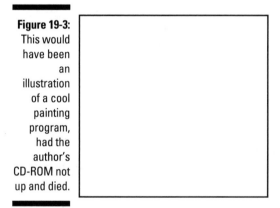

Figure 19-3:
This would have been an illustration of a cool painting program, had the author's CD-ROM not up and died.

Illustration programs: These programs combine the tools of drawing and advanced painting programs. They're primarily used by graphics artists to create illustrations — like the ones you see in *USA Today* or on wine bottles or posters advertising art shows. You know the type.

CAD: This software handles extremely detailed or technical drawings. They let engineers do such scientific things as design new, three-tray microwavable containers for frozen New Orleans-style chicken and broccoli.

✔ Most of the best drawing and painting programs come on the Macintosh, which is why the beret-heads prefer that computer. The software is also available on Windows and works just as well.

✔ I had to spend 90 minutes on the phone with the tech support guy to convince him my CD-ROM drive was dead. They're sending me a new one. Don't know when it will get here. Last time I buy a PC from those bozos.

Multimedia Stuff

Multimedia describes any sort of flashy graphics mixed with sound. Some of the latest Windows multimedia applications come very close to a television set in terms of sound and pictures. The computer industry is excited about it; the television industry is totally freakin' out.

- ✔ *Multimedia* incorporates two "mediums" — in the computer world, a computer plays sound while it displays something flashy on-screen.

- ✔ Multimedia applications require a powerful computer, a top-quality monitor, a large hard disk, a sound card, and typically a CD-ROM drive (see Chapter 7).

- ✔ With my CD-ROM drive kind of dead now, I suppose I have a Monomedia PC.

- ✔ What good is multimedia? Mostly, it's used for games, though educational programs like Microsoft's Encarta encyclopedia could be considered educational. Some corporations use multimedia for business presentations.

The Utility Stuff

Most software is designed to help you get to work. Utility programs help your *computer* get to work. Basically, a utility helps a computer accomplish a chore, whether it's organizing its hard drive or figuring out why it's not working right. In fact, most utilities are disk utilities.

Windows comes with many of the utilities you'll need. To see its portfolio of disk utilities, right-click on a disk drive and choose Properties from the pop-up menu. Click on the Tools tab, and you see three disk utilities you can (and should) run from time to time. Figure 19-4 shows the Tools tab in the disk drive Properties menu.

- ✔ Windows comes with a few handy utilities, but that doesn't mean you shouldn't buy any more. A lot of the third-party utilities are tons better than the stuff Windows has.

- ✔ One utility Windows doesn't come with is a virus-checker. These utilities scan your hard drive for any evil programs and wipe them out before the viruses try some nasty trick. See Chapter 24.

- ✔ Even though Windows can, supposedly, uninstall software, you might consider buying an un-install program. These programs do a much better job than Windows by itself, often saving you lots of disk space in the process.

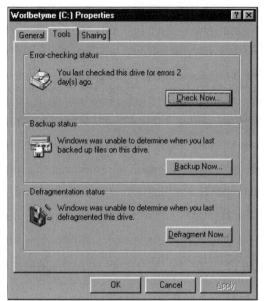

Figure 19-4:
Windows
disk utilities.

Those Office-Type Programs

To make even more money, the software developers have come up with so-called Office Suite types of programs. These are actually several packages all sold as a single unit. You can buy them cheaper that way, plus the software company makes oodles of money selling you upgrades from time to time. (More on upgrading in Chapter 20.)

Office packages are great when you're starting out. But you might not consider one if you're buying it for just one piece of pie. For example, if you're just buying Microsoft Office to run Excel or Word, consider buying them separately. There's no point in junking up your hard drive with stuff you'll never use.

"What About Shareware and Public Domain Software?"

Frustrated by the system, some programmers give away their programs free. Seriously! But there's a catch: They ask you to send them money on the honor system if you like their program. Because they're bypassing the traditional, expensive way to sell software, they don't ask for much; most charge from $5 to $45 for their *shareware*. When you mail in the check, the programmer mails back the latest version of the software and a manual.

Other programmers give away their programs but don't ask for money in return. They figure that they're making a humble contribution toward making the world a better place to compute. This free software is called *public domain software*.

Ask your computer guru for more details on shareware and public domain programs. Or check with any local computer user groups. Or, if you're feeling particularly adventurous, buy a modem and join an online service. (See Chapter 21.)

Chapter 20
Getting Used to Software

• •

In This Chapter

▶ How to buy software

▶ Stuff in the software box

▶ Installing software

▶ Uninstalling software

▶ Updating software

▶ Whether or not to upgrade Windows

▶ Learning software tips

• •

*U*sing software means using your computer. You may punch the Enter key on the keyboard, but it's some piece of software that gives that action significance, either running a word processor, launching an intercontinental ballistic missile, or erasing every last file on your hard drive. Yeah, verily, software hath the power.

Tons of tomes have been written on how to make software work for you. It would be silly of me to document all that here. Instead, this chapter focuses on the getting-started aspect of software. How to buy it, set it up, get used to it, and uninstall it if you hate it.

A journey of ten thousand steps starts off with a good supply of bunion pads.
— Lao Tsu

A Few Words on Buying Software

Buying software is part of the computer buying process. You pick out your software *first,* and then pick the hardware to match. But there's so many software packages out there, it's easy to feel like you're making a dopey decision.

To prevent that foreboding and dread, you can always comparison shop software. Better still, I recommend seeing what other people are using. What do they use at the office? What do your computer-literate friends enjoy using or recommend? Make sure you get what's right for you, not just what's cheap and popular.

- ✔ Try before you buy software.
- ✔ Have someone at the store demonstrate the software for you.
- ✔ Always check out a store's return policy on software.
- ✔ Check the software's requirements. They should match your computer's hardware inventory.
- ✔ For buying software, use the same techniques mentioned in the companion booklet on buying hardware.

What's This Stuff in the Box?

Surprisingly, many large software boxes contain air or cardboard padding to make the boxes look bigger and more impressive in the store. I suppose the idea is to push the competition off the shelf. It also gives you a sense of worth, since paying $279 for a compact disc and flimsy booklet seems more important if it's in a hefty box.

The most vital things inside the software box are the disks. There will either be one compact disc in there or — if your PC doesn't have a CD-ROM drive — you'll have the version with anywhere from 2 to 36,000 floppy disks. You'll probably find a manual and a few other goodies, too. Here's the rundown:

Disks: Never toss these out! I always keep them in the box they came in, especially after installation.

The Horrid Manual: Most programs toss in a printed manual, typically the size of a cheap trade paperback. There may be more than one manual. Look for the "Getting Started," "Installation," or "Setup" section of the manual first.

Registration card: Resembling a boring postcard, this usually sits right on top. You fill out your name and address and answer a few questions about the software, and then you mail the card back to the company. The company then (supposedly) notifies you of any defects, including nonfunctional commands or air-bag problems. Some companies require you to fill out the registration card before they'll offer technical support over the phone.

Quick reference card: The manual works fine for explaining everything in great detail, but you'll find yourself continually repeating some commands. A quick reference card contains those useful commands; it can be propped up next to the keyboard for quick sideways glances. Not all software comes with these cards, however.

Quick installation card: Computer users thrive on instant gratification: Push a button and watch your work be performed instantly. Nobody wants to bother with slow, thick manuals, especially when installing the software. A quick installation card contains an abbreviated version of the manual's installation instructions. By typing in the commands on the card, you can install the software without cracking open the manual. Victory!

License agreement: This extensive batch of fine print takes an average of 3,346 words of legalese to say four things: 1) Don't give away any copies of this program to friends — make them buy their own program. 2) If you accidentally lose any data, it's not our fault. 3) If this software doesn't work, that's not our fault, either. 4) In fact, you don't even own this software. You merely own a license to use the software. We own the software. We are evil. We will one day own the world.

Sometimes the licensing agreement is printed on a little sticker on an envelope; you have to tear apart the agreement before you can get to the disks inside. Whether this means you agree with it or not is up to a battalion of attorneys to uncover.

Read me first: When the company discovers a mistake in its newly printed manual, it won't fix it and print out a new one. It will print the corrections on a piece of paper and slap the headline "Read Me First!" across the top. Staple that piece of paper to the inside cover of your manual for safekeeping.

✔ Thank goodness software boxes aren't junky like those magazine publisher sweepstakes things. You can never find the things you need to fill in, stickers to place over the TV set or on Ed's head, options to clip. What nonsense! Software boxes are much neater by comparison.

Software Installation Chores

The first step in installing software is simple:

1. **Get someone else to do it for you.**

   Maybe you have a computer guru (see Chapter 23). Maybe there's an office MIS guy. If not, the following guidelines may help. All software packages handle the details a bit differently, so don't be surprised if you find yourself surprised.

Why are computer manuals so horrid?

Computer manuals have a bad rap. Things are better today than they were 15 years ago. Back then, everyone was a nerd. Most manuals just began "Flip these switches to enter base hexadecimal address pairs for IPL." And *that* was considered user-friendly.

Why are the manuals so bad? Many reasons. Primarily the manual is written as an afterthought. The software developer spends more time and attention on building the product. The manual is given to someone reluctant to create it, often the product manager or programmer. They're far too familiar with the product to compose a useful manual, nor do they care about getting it done properly.

Manuals must also be completed well before the product is done. It takes longer to print 10,000 manuals than it takes to copy off 10,000 disks. Therefore, the manual is often inaccurate or vague.

Size is an issue. Most manuals are slim because their weight adds to the product's shipping cost. Some places don't even bother with a manual, instead putting everything on disk in "read me" or "help" files.

People who write computer manuals are paid by the hour or on salary. No one in that position is going to put their heart into creating the best possible work. This is why books on the subject are far better than manuals; the author is trying to make money by writing a successful book. The writers at the software company pick their noses and watch the clock.

Or

1. **Read the "Read Me" blurb.**

   When you first open the box, scrounge around for a piece of paper that says "Read Me First!" and follow the first instruction: Read it. Or at least try to make some sense of it.

   Sometimes the Read Me First sheet contains a sentence or two left out of the manual's third paragraph on page 127, "Dwobbling your shordlock by three frips." If you don't understand it, don't throw it away. It may come in handy after you've started using the program.

2. **Set the manual(s) aside.**

   Say "There" when you do this.

3. **Put the Installation disk into your disk drive.**

   Find the disk marked with the words "Installation" or "Setup" or "Disk One," and place that disk in the disk drive where it fits.

A few paranoid words about sending in the registration card

You won't find this in any software manual: Be wary of sending in a registration card! I'm not recommending against it entirely, I just don't think it's absolutely necessary. Call me paranoid, but I find it odd that after I send a registration card to some outfit, I get a lot of junk mail related to the product I just registered. Also, even though I get promises to be notified of a new version, I never do. I registered six copies of one program at my office and got nothing in the mail about the latest version. My suspicions grow.

I do recommend registering any product that comes with a unique serial number. All of Adobe's software (PageMaker, Illustrator, and so on) requires this. They won't give you support or special deals on software upgrades unless you register. For them, plus a few other companies that really do notify you of new software releases, registration is a must. For most everyone else, it's iffy.

Here are some thoughts and suggestions:

- ✔ If you don't register your software, keep the registration card and any serial numbers handy. You may need them in the future.

- ✔ Never tell one software company about the programs you own from another company. For example, if you just bought a utility program, don't list all the other utility programs you use on the registration card. This is a marketing ploy; if you follow through, you will be bombarded with competitive upgrade offers.

- ✔ Never register using your modem. Any program that registers you by modem might go through your computer, gather information on all the software you own, and send that information away. That information is your *personal* business. No other organization should know about it.

- ✔ It's OK to register by fax, but print the fax on your printer so you can edit it before sending. Use a marker to blot out any information that's none of their business.

- ✔ Consider filling out the registration card using a unique middle initial or first name. For example, I registered a utility program using the name *Dan U. Gookin*. Now I know where junk mail for *Dan U. Gookin* comes from.

Hopefully it will be a compact disc. If not, it will be a 3 ½-inch (or maybe even 5 ¼-inch — ugh!) disk. Like cockroaches, it's the first of many.

If it's a 5 ¼-inch drive, remember to close the drive door latch after inserting the disk.

If you're installing from floppy disks, put them in a neat stack in order, first disk on top. That way you can easily feed them, one after the other, into the disk drive without having to rummage for the next disk later.

4. Start the Installation program.

Open the Control Panel; choose Settings⇨Control Panel from the Start menu.

Add/Remove Programs

Double click on the Add/Remove Programs icon. The Add/Remove Program Properties dialog box is displayed (Figure 20-1).

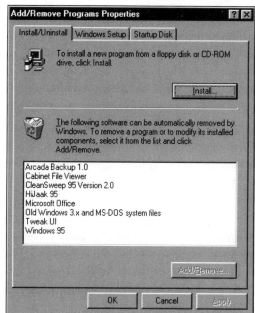

Figure 20-1:
The Add/
Remove
Program
Properties
dialog box.

Click on the Install button.

Windows goes out to your disk drives and searches for the proper installation disk. It then runs the Install or Setup program.

This is all the Add/Remove Programs icon does. It merely looks for the Install or Setup program that truly installs your software. After that, it's your new program's installation program that takes over.

5. Read the screen carefully; click the Next button as necessary.

The installation program will start placing instructions on the screen.

Watch them carefully; sometimes they'll slip something important in there. My friend Jerry (his real name) just kept clicking the Next button instead of reading the screen. He missed an important notice that said an older version of the program would be erased. Uh-oh! Poor Jerry never got his program back.

6. Choose various options.

The software will ask your name and company name, maybe ask for a serial number. Type all that stuff in.

Don't freak if the program already knows who you are. Windows is kinda clairvoyant in that respect.

When asked to make a decision, the option already selected (the *default*) is typically the best option. Only if you know what's going on and *truly care* about it should you change anything.

7. Files are copied.

Eventually, the installation program will copy the files from the diskettes or CD-ROM drive onto your hard drive for full-time residence.

If you're unlucky enough to be installing from floppy disks, keep feeding them, one after the other, into the floppy drive. Make sure you get them in the proper order (they're numbered). Make sure you remove one disk and replace it with the next disk.

8. It's done.

The installation program ends. The computer may reset at this point. That's required sometimes to install special programs Windows needs to know about. (Windows is pretty dumb after it starts.)

Start using the program!

✔ These steps are vague and general. Hopefully your new software comes with instructions more specific.

✔ Keep the quick reference card next to your computer immediately after installing the program; it will be more helpful than the manual.

✔ Should you keep the "old" version of your software? Maybe. I always do. But then I put a sticky note on my monitor, reminding me to delete the old version in a month or so.

Uninstalling Software

To remove any newly installed program, you use an Uninstall program. This is not a feature of Windows, though Windows makes it easier. Apparently your program must have its own uninstall feature for it to work. Otherwise, you're stuck with it.

Do not attempt to uninstall *any* software by deleting it from your hard drive. You should never delete any file you did not create yourself. (You can, however, delete any shortcuts you create.)

Uninstalling software is done the same way you installed it: Open the Control Panel's Add/Remove Programs icon. This displays the Add/Remove Programs Properties dialog box, as shown in Figure 20-1.

The list of programs Windows knows about and can uninstall is listed at the bottom of the dialog box. Click on one of those programs, the one you want to uninstall. This selects the program for action. Then click the Add/Remove button.

A warning dialog box is displayed before Windows yanks the cord on your program. Click Yes to zap it to Kingdom Come.

- ✔ Need I say anything about being careful with this?

- ✔ Third-party uninstall programs do a better job than Windows does. For one, you may notice that not all of your programs are listed in the Add/Remove Programs Properties dialog box. Those third-party uninstallers can hunt down rogue files and safely eliminate all their bits and pieces.

- ✔ See Windows 95 on the list? Yup, you can get rid of it, too. I wouldn't, if I were you.

- ✔ The item titled Old Windows 3.x and MS-DOS system files (or something similar) appears if you upgraded to Windows 95 from an earlier version of DOS or Windows. Choose this item for removal to free up an extra few megabytes of hard disk space.

- ✔ The Add/Remove button can also be used to add individual components to your programs. For example, you could click on Microsoft Office to add a new component or piece of that software, something you didn't choose to install way back when.

- ✔ For adding components missing from Windows, choose the Windows Setup panel in the Add/Remove Programs Properties dialog box.

Upgrading or Updating Your Software

When a novel's written, it's finished. Subsequent reprints correct a few misspellings, but that's about it. But software's never finished. It's too easy to change. Most software packages are updated about once a year.

Why update? Sometimes the company fixes a few problems, or bugs. But most often, the software contains new features so that it can compete with the other guy's software. This is why new versions appear. The upgrade gives you access to the newer, bug-free software and its features. It also lets software companies grow rich by charging you all over again for something you already own.

My advice: Only order the update if it has features or makes modifications you desperately need. Otherwise, if the current version is doing the job, don't bother.

- ✔ Consider each upgrade offer on its individual merits: Will you ever use the new features? Do you need a word processor that can print upside-down headlines and bar charts that show your word count? Can you really get any mileage out of the "network version" when you're a sole user sitting at home?

- ✔ Something else to keep in mind: If you're still using DoodleWriter 4.2 and everybody else is using DoodleWriter 6.1, you'll have difficulty exchanging documents. After a while, newer versions of programs become incompatible with the older models.

- ✔ In an office setting, everybody should be using the same software version. (Everybody doesn't have to be using the *latest* version, just the *same* version.)

- ✔ If the book industry worked like the software industry, Tom Clancy would have gotten a phone call several years back: "Hey, Tom, babe, you know the old Soviet Union has collapsed? Time to rewrite *The Hunt for Red October!* Maybe change the bad guys to Iraqis or something. Get with the times!"

What about upgrading Windows?

Yeah, Windows is software, just like other programs on your computer. And Windows gets updated every so often. Only, when it does, it's a *big deal.* Why? Because everything else in your computer relies on Windows. Therefore it's a major change, something to think long and deep about.

Often the newer version of Windows has many more features than the older version. Do you need those features? If not, don't bother with the update.

One problem you may have if you decide to upgrade is that your software may not work properly. None of my Adobe applications worked with Windows 95 when it first came out. I had to wait months and pay lots of money for upgrades before things got back to normal.

After a time, you may notice newer software packages coming to roost on the newest version of Windows. The new stuff will be better than your current stuff, meaning you'll need to upgrade if you want to take advantage of it.

So where does this leave you? Don't bother updating Windows until at least six months after the newest version is out. By then, it should have all the bugs worked out and major applications updated and fine-tuned. Heck, wait a year if you have to. The old version will always work as long as you own it. Bill Gates himself is (or was) fond of saying, "Software never gets obsolete." I might add: as long as you're using it.

Some Tips for Learning a Program

Using software involves learning its quirks. That takes time. So my first suggestion for learning any new software is to give yourself plenty of time.

Sadly, in today's rush-rush way of doing everything, time isn't that easy to come by. It's a big pain when the boss sends you down to the software store expecting you to come back and create something wonderful before the end of the day. In the real world, that's just not possible (not even if you're an "expert").

Most software comes with a workbook or a tutorial for you to follow. This is a series of self-guided lessons on how to use the product. It also tells you about the program's basic features and how they work.

I highly recommend going through the tutorials. Follow the directions on the screen. If you notice anything interesting, write it down in the tutorial booklet and flag that page.

Some tutorials are really dumb, granted. Don't hesitate to bail out of one if you're bored or confused. You can also take classes on using software, though they may bore you as well. Most people do, however, understand the program much better after the tutorial.

After doing the tutorial, play with the software. Make something. Try saving something to disk. Try printing. Then quit. Those are the basic few steps you should take when using any software program. Get to know it and then expand your knowledge from there as required.

✔ Some businesses may have their own training classes that show you the basics of using the in-house software. Take copious notes. Keep a little book for yourself with instructions for how to do what. Take notes whenever someone shows you something. Don't try to learn anything, just note what's done so you won't have to make a call should the situation arise again.

✔ Never toss out your manual. In fact, I recommend going back and trying to read the manual again several weeks after you start to learn a program. You may actually understand things. (Consider that the fellow who wrote the manual knew the product about as well when he first sat down to write about it.)

✔ Computer books are also a good source to learn about programs. They come in two types: references and tutorials. The tutorial is great for learning; references are best when you know what you want to do but forgot how.

✔ This book is a reference. All *...For Dummies* books are references.

Chapter 21

Going Online

*W*hen the reporter asked the old hermit why he didn't have a phone, the hermit replied "Why do I want a bell in my house that anyone in the world can ring?" Well, when you have a modem, you can use your computer to ring any number of bells in people's homes all over the world. Of course, it really helps if the bell is connected to another computer, one that can pick up the phone and start chatting amiably with your PC. That's the essence of online communications.

This chapter provides an outline of the modem process. You dial. You do something. You hang up. It works like that, but with many more details and confusing jargon thrown in along the way.

✔ This chapter covers using your modem to dial up a BBS or online service. It does not cover using the Internet. Refer to Chapter 22 for information on that.

The Horror of Communications Software

A communications program is software that controls the connection between your computer and some other remote computer system, such as an online service (like America Online, CompuServe, or Prodigy) or a local BBS (like the other services but cheaper — and free — and run by some kid in your neighborhood).

Communications software does a great deal, which is probably why it's so darn cryptic. Basically, it has to coordinate several elements:

✔ Your computer's serial port

✔ The modem itself

✔ Setting things up to call another computer

✔ Talking with the other modem that answers the phone

✔ Doing interesting things while you're talking to the other computer

✔ Odd terminology

The nice part is that once you've set the various options, using the communications software and your modem is a cinch. The ugly part is that most of this stuff hasn't changed much in 20 years. When you use an online system, odds are it's probably text-only. No graphics! No mouse!

And don't think the odd terminology is only a minor part. Online things have strange descriptions. Those in the know are generally patronizing when it comes to helping out a beginner. It's intimidating. But don't let that stop you. Everyone else out there faced the same hurdles.

✔ Some online services, such as Prodigy or America Online, require special software rather than a general-purpose program like the HyperTerminal program that comes with Windows or a third-party communications program.

✔ What you're doing with communications software is calling another computer. That computer's modem answers the phone, talks to your modem, and then the two computers start sending information back and forth to each other. But while you're connected, you're essentially running a program on that other computer. This is the weird part of communications that makes some people sit in their chairs for hours without moving.

Dialing Up a Something with Your Modem

To use your modem, you need two things:

1. **Communications software**

2. **The number of another computer to call**

Communications software is a special program that controls your modem. You have such a program included with Windows, one called HyperTerminal. Or you may have another favorite program, one that came with your modem (included "for free!"), with your computer when you bought it, or it may just be hanging around. You can also buy such software at the store.

The other thing you need is a phone number. After all, your modem doesn't just yell out the window. It needs to use the phone just like you do.

The best place to get computer phone numbers is the store from which you bought your computer or modem. Local computer magazines list numbers, and user groups also maintain lists.

✔ Windows comes with a decent communications program called HyperTerminal.

✔ Some technical information about the other computer's modem is often included with the phone number. This information isn't required by HyperTerminal but may be necessary to other communications software. This information includes the other modem's speed and its *data word format,* which means even more technical information! Windows' HyperTerminal program is smart enough to do without this extra mumbo jumbo.

Running HyperTerminal

Windows comes with an OK communications program called HyperTerminal. In keeping with the fine, confusing tradition of communications programs past, HyperTerminal works like no other application that comes with Windows. The following demo will drive that point home.

Start HyperTerminal by doing the following:

1. **From the Start menu choose Programs⇨Accessories⇨HyperTerminal.**

   You'll notice that HyperTerminal is a *folder,* not a program. When you choose that item from the Start menu, a folder appears, similar to the one shown in Figure 21-1.

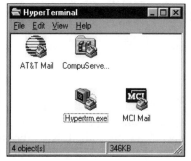

Figure 21-1:
Windows'
HyperTerminal
folder.

The HyperTerminal program is the icon named Hypertrm or Hypertrm.exe.

The other icons in the HyperTerminal folder are called *session files.*

2. **To dial a session file, open its icon.**

Those icons you see in the HyperTerminal folder represent other modems and computers to call. They've already been set up so that all you have to do to call the computer is open the proper icon. That runs HyperTerminal, which then obeys the instructions in the session file, dialing the other computer.

For example, in Figure 21-1, you could double-click on the AT&T Mail icon to dial up the AT&T Mail service. (Don't, since this is just a demo.)

If you don't see an icon for the system you want to call, you must create it from scratch. This is gone over in the next section.

If you do see an icon you want to open, open it. The modem will dial, and eventually you'll be online and chatting with another computer. (Skip up to the section titled "Logging in" after reading this section.)

3. **You're online!**

Now you do online things, which are covered in the section "Logging in," as well as other sections throughout the remainder of this chapter.

4. **You're done.**

You say good-bye to the other computer, which is covered in the section "Saying Bye-Bye" at the end of this chapter.

Creating a new session file in HyperTerminal

Before you call another computer, your communications software must tell your modem about the computer system you're calling. This must be done for each other computer you call, since each computer that answers the phone is different (and that's probably due to some arcane law passed during the Bush administration). Fortunately, it needs to be done only once.

In HyperTerminal you shove all the required information into a special session file. You need to know the following basic (yeah, right) information about the other system — the one you're about to phone:

▸ The system's name

▸ The system's phone number

Other, technical information may be required by other communications programs. Not so with HyperTerminal.

Hypertrm.exe

In the HyperTerminal folder window, open the HyperTerminal icon by double-clicking it. This displays the HyperTerminal program's New Connection dialog box. Time to fill in the blanks!

The first thing to do for the session you're creating is choose a name and an icon for it (see Figure 21-2). Silly stuff. Must be done.

Figure 21-2:
The
Connection
Description
dialog box.

In the Name input box, type a name that will help you recognize the system you're calling. Type something like pnet or pro-sol or Harry's Softwarez or whatever is the name of the system you're calling.

Press the Tab key.

Choose an icon for the system. I don't mess around here; I choose the Big Red phone icon every time.

Click OK. The Phone Number dialog box appears (see Figure 21-3).

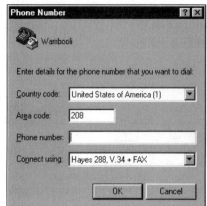

Figure 21-3:
Type the
phone
number in
this dialog
box.

Three items in the Phone Number dialog box have already been entered for
you; you told Windows your country, area code, and modem type when your
modem was first installed (or it was done at the factory or by your PC guru).
You need to type in the phone number.

Type in the phone number. Enter the area code in the Ar̲ea code box if it's
required.

Click OK. The Connect dialog box appears.

If you have an external modem, make sure it's on; the little lights on the front of
the modem should be on, and the modem should look happy and content.

Click the Dial button to dial the modem.

Hurry up to the next section to see what happens next.

✔ Modems work just like phones: They dial a number. Another modem
should answer, in which case both modems start singing to each other,
they get all operatic, and then a connection is made.

✔ Dialing up long-distance with your modem incurs long-distance charges
just as if you were calling a person. Otherwise, the phone company does
not charge you more for a modem call.

✔ When you're using your modem, no one else can call you. I know, this
sounds dumb, but few people realize they're using the phone because it's
not immediately in their ear. Incidentally, if you pick up the phone while
the modem is working, you'll hear a horrid high-pitched squeal — the
modem in action. If you talk, you'll see random characters on your screen,
or you may break the connection. (Other people in the house will do this
more often than you.) Because of this, I recommend getting a second
phone line for your modem.

Dialing woes (what happens next)

Your software is dialing. And then . . . and then you can experience one of five things:

First, and least terrible, is a busy signal. Modems get busy a lot more often than human phones. Try dialing again later.

Second, there's no answer. Call back right away. The modem is probably bored, or the computer may be doing something else. (Some systems are part-time and only answer the phone during certain hours.)

Third, and not as bad as it seems, is getting a long stream of *garbage characters* across the screen. If so, wait. Your communications program may hang up or you may eventually see some readable text. You can try calling again, which sometimes works. (Hey, modems are moody.)

Fourth, and most terrible, is that a human answers. If this happens, do them a favor and don't call back using your modem. The places that publish modem numbers frequently make mistakes. Don't bug poor Mrs. Henderson by redialing her phone every 30 seconds from midnight to 2 a.m.; she probably hates computers more than you do.

Fifth, and best, is that the other computer answers — which is great and what you want. Skip up to the next section.

- ✔ Sometimes the other system may not respond right away. If so, press the Enter key to "wake it up."

- ✔ Garbage characters:

  ```
  } }4}"}&}  }  }  } }%}&cJ}-}'}(}"%}>~~
  ```

- ✔ Repeated garbage characters or bursts of random characters in the midst of normal text are signs of a bad connection, and it's worth calling back.

- ✔ Consistent garbage characters may induce your phone company (or an overenthusiastic electrician) to rewire your house with fancy-schmansy phone wire. Don't! It's terribly expensive and probably won't help. (I know this firsthand.)

Logging in

When the modem you're calling answers, it says "Hey, wake up!" to its computer. That computer then runs special software, which you use remotely. Oh, it's all so magical. But everything typically starts with logging in:

```
LOGIN:
```

You need to tell the other computer who you are. Type your full name or nickname at a login prompt. Sometimes the prompt says LOGIN; other times it just may ask for your full name or first and then last names:

```
First Name:
```

```
Last Name:
```

If you've never called the system before, read the instructions on the screen to see how you can become a member and get your own account.

After you enter your login or ID, you'll be prompted for a password:

```
Password:
```

Type in the secret word. This is used to ensure that you are who you logged in as. Once that's entered and verified, you continue to use the online system.

- ✔ What happens next? Why, you're online. You're in cyberspace! Refer to the section "Doin' the Online Thing" for what else you can do.

- ✔ When you're done, you'll need to properly say good-bye to the other computer. This is covered in the section "Saying Bye-Bye" at the end of this chapter.

- ✔ Many systems have interesting ways to log in. Some just come up right away; others require you to press Enter first.

- ✔ In the olden days, CompuServe had you press Ctrl+C to get a prompt asking for your ID and password. If any such system requires something unique to type, there will probably be a note of it.

- ✔ Read the screen! It usually tells you what to do next.

Quitting HyperTerminal

This should be a no-brainer, but it's not. To quit the HyperTerminal program (after you say bye-bye and the modem hangs up), you choose File⇨Exit from the menu. No problem.

But, ah-ha! There is still a HyperTerminal folder open on the desktop. To truly clean things up, close that folder by clicking on its X close button in the window's upper-right corner. There. You can go to bed now.

Doin' the Online Thing

Online means something is connected. Your printer is online when it's actively paying attention to your computer and printing whatever the computer tells it to print. With a modem, you're online when you're actively conversing with another computer.

Most of what you do online is dictated by the other computer. You can read messages, peruse your mail, chat, and so on. The remote computer thinks, so you just sit there and type. But there are times when you need to tell your computer to do something. There are two big issues I can think of:

Downloading: This is the art of having the other computer send you a file, say an animated cursor file with which to entertain yourself.

Uploading: This is where you send a file to the other computer. For example, every chapter in this book was uploaded to IDG's massive computer system from the author's puny PC.

- ✔ You don't spend all your time online passing files back and forth. Most of the time you'll be reading.

- ✔ The first thing most people do once online is check their electronic mail — e-mail.

- ✔ A bulletin board is an open area where many people post messages. It works like e-mail, but it's public. For example, you may want to read messages in a forum about your favorite TV show, hobby, political interests, or just idle chatter.

- ✔ Chatting online is where two or more people get together and type at each other at once. It's silent chaos!

- ✔ Most of the so-called "cybersex" takes place in the online chat rooms of Prodigy and America Online. Not that I would know anything about that, of course.

- ✔ Another way to pass the time online is to capture a file. This is where you direct your communications program to start recording what you're receiving from the other computer. You can send the information to a file on disk or to your printer. Imagine, a transcript of your online infidelity. Is that admissible as evidence in divorce court yet?

Downloading something

One of the most popular things to do online (aside from sending nasty letters to your philosophical enemies) is to download or "grab" software. This is where you order, nay, *demand* that the other computer send you something from one of its hard drives. The software is then beamed into your computer, where you can then mess with it.

Downloading is a bit confusing, which is why I've outlined the basic steps as follows:

1. Search for a file to steal, uh, download.

Most places you call will have a collection of files or library. Use whatever commands to go there and hunt for a particular file you want to download.

Make a note of the file's name or ID so that you can tell the other computer to send it.

2. Tell the other computer which file to send.

Use whatever commands to have the other computer send you the file. For example, the command may be as dumb as D for Download. The computer will then ask for the filename or ID. Let it know.

3. Tell it how to send it (the *protocol*).

Next the other computer will ask you how to send the file, which *protocol* to use. It's a confusing subject that need not be so.

A protocol is a method for sending a file between two computers. It ensures that the file gets there exactly as it was sent.

If you're using HyperTerminal, always choose the Z-Modem or ZMODEM protocol. Simple enough.

If you're using some other communications program, you may want to check to see which protocols it supports. If it supports Z-Modem, use that. Otherwise, find a protocol common between your software and the other computer's.

The most common denominator is the X-Modem or *binary* protocol. It's not as sophisticated or speedy as Z-Modem, but pretty much all computers and communications software support it.

4. Tell it to start sending.

This is one of the trickier points to remember: Always tell the other computer to start sending the file *first*.

It will wait patiently until your communications software is ready to receive something before it gets all mad and walks off in a huff.

5. Tell your communications software to receive a file.

On your end, tell your communications program to receive, or download, a file.

In HyperTerminal, choose Transfer⇨Receive File. The Receive File dialog box appears. Click the `Receive` button.

In other communications programs, you may have to press the PgDn key (page down for download) to download. You then need to give your program a name for the file as it will be saved on your computer.

If you're using the Z-Modem protocol, you don't need to tell your software the filename. This is because Z-Modem automatically saves the filename properly, which is another reason why it's so popular.

6. **Downloading.**

It takes a while to download the program. A progress indicator on the screen will tell you how you're doing. Just sit back and wait. Or if it's going to take a long time, you can get up and do those stretching exercises you're supposed to.

✔ When you're done downloading, you can continue your online frolic, or tell the other computer good-bye, quit your communications package, and go out to play with your new files.

✔ Downloading takes time. The larger the file, the more time it takes. At 2400 bps, a 100K file may take about seven minutes to download. At 9600 bps, it takes about a minute and a half. And at 28.8 kbps (the current fastest speed), it will only take a matter of seconds.

✔ Technically, the "other computer" is called the *host.* You download from the host. It helps to think of the heavenly host, since they're "up there" and you're "down here" — and if they sent you anything, it would travel down. That's how I remember that downloading is the other computer sending you a file.

✔ Downloading is not stealing. Most online systems exist to give you files. However, they usually want something in return. If you have any files to upload, or send the other computer, it's not required but is appreciated. And, by the way:

✔ Don't download software you know is stolen. This includes anything that you would otherwise have to pay money for at the store. For example, downloading a copy of 1-2-3 is illegal. It's theft. Also, such programs are usually infested with viruses, which can wreak more havoc on your computer than a toddler with a bat.

✔ Special software is available that scans anything you download for a virus. Most of the time, however, you can rest assured that programs you get aren't infected. All of the major online services and most reputable BBSs pre-scan their files to prevent against viruses.

✔ You really need to get some kind of reward for successfully downloading a file the first time. Then you discover the file is an *archive,* or ZIP, file. Back to the drawing board! And refer to the sidebar, "ZIP-a-dee-do-da, UNZIP-a-dee-ay."

TECHNICAL STUFF

ZIP-a-dee-do-da, UNZIP-a-dee-ay

Most files you download will be *archives*. These are single files that hold even more files — like a single beehive holds hundreds of bees. Before you can get at the files and really do something, you must crack the archive nut.

Fortunately most archive files are "self-extracting." For example, you may have downloaded the game NINJA.EXE. When you run it, the self-extractor takes over automatically, unpacking and "exploding" the various files in the archive like you'd unpack after moving. So where you had one file before, you have several (dozens sometimes) other files, each of which makes up the Ninja-whatever you downloaded. Only then can you start playing the game.

Why archives? Well, considering that this is a techy sidebar and I am allowed to spout off here, the history is rich and tradition-filled. Actually, in the old days, it used to take several hours just to download one file. The solution was to compact a file into a smaller size for easy downloading. Then, as computer programs grew more advanced, the compacting programs allowed more than one file to be packed and shrunk at the same time. The end result was the archive.

The term ZIP comes from one of the programs that makes archives. ZIP archive files end in ZIP and you need the UNZIP program to unpack them. However, if the archive ends in EXE, it unpacks itself.

Uploading something

The opposite of downloading is uploading, just like the opposite of eating is, well, never mind.

To upload is to send a file to another computer. It works a lot like downloading, though the roles are reversed: You tell the other computer to prepare itself to receive a file, and then you tell your communications software which file to send. As it goes with downloading, you instruct the other computer first, and then tell your communications program to kick everything into gear.

Briefly, here are the steps:

1. **Tell the other computer to prepare to receive a file.**

   This command can be found somewhere in its menus. You may also need to give a name to the file and describe it briefly.

2. **Tell it how to receive (the *protocol* stuff).**

   Settle on a way of sending the file; both computers must agree on this.

   As with downloading, the best and most popular protocol is Z-Modem. Be sure to pick a protocol that both your computer and the host understand.

3. **It's ready to go.**

The other computer now sits and waits for you to send the file. Even though you aren't ready, it will sit and wait for you to move into action.

4. **Search for a file to upload.**

In HyperTerminal, choose Transfer⇨Send File. This displays the Send File dialog box.

Use the Browse button to hunt down a file to send. Make it something fun, say that collection of radical, leftist feminist poetry you want to send to the Rush Limbaugh forum on CompuServe. Click the Open button when you've found your file. (See Chapter 8 for more information on the Browse/Open dialog box.)

In other communications programs, you need to pick a file to send using whatever uploading commands they have. The PgUp key is the uploading key for most communications programs.

5. **Choose a protocol.**

Select the protocol you've already told the other computer you were going to use. Use Z-modem, if possible.

Sometimes this step and the previous step are combined. You may have to choose the Z-modem menu item from the Upload menu, for example.

6. **Tell your communications software to send a file.**

Click the Send button in HyperTerminal.

Do whatever else is required in other programs.

Since the other computer is ready and waiting for the file, everything moves forward smoothly.

✔ Only upload software that's public domain or shareware. Don't upload anything you paid money for.

✔ You can upload anything you created yourself.

✔ It's a good idea to ZIP or archive large files before uploading. That way you don't spend too much time uploading and the file won't take up that much space on the host computer.

Online Attitude

Online telecommunications is a new and exciting way to communicate. Just as with learning a foreign language, however, there are some rules about online communications you should be aware of before you take the plunge. Don't get me wrong; this can be fun. I do it all the time and have made quite a few enemies of my friends.

✔ Happy people go modeming.

✔ You can't "see" anyone you "meet" online, so don't assume anything about them. Modem people are old, young, and come from diverse backgrounds, though studies show they're typically male, upper income, and Republican. Still, don't hold that against them.

✔ Please don't type in ALL CAPS. Type your letters and comments in mixed case — like you do when writing a letter. To most online people, all caps reads LIKE YOU'RE SHOUTING AT THEM!

✔ Don't "beg" for people to send you e-mail. Participate in discussions or just be obnoxious, and you'll always have a full mailbox.

✔ The art of written communication is lost on the TV generation. People use the phone to communicate where you hear inflection and gather extra meaning. Unfortunately, an online message lacks such nuances. And since we don't all have the written vocabularies we should, a joke, side remark, or kidding can easily be taken seriously (way too seriously). Remember to keep it light. Adding "ha, ha" occasionally lets people know you're having fun instead of being an online jerk. Speaking of which. . . .

✔ There are many online jerks (ha, ha). The best policy to take with them is to ignore them. No matter how much they steam you, no matter how ludicrous their ideas or remarks — golly, even if they're a Libertarian — don't get into a "flame thrower" war with them.

✔ In an online debate, ignore anyone who quotes "the dictionary" as a source. I hate to break it to you, but there is no National Institute of English that defines what words mean. Dictionaries are written by people as ignorant as you and I. Heck, I could write and publish a dictionary if I wanted to and make up entirely new definitions for words. Nope, the dictionary is not a source to be quoted.

✔ Buy *The Illustrated Computer Dictionary For Dummies,* available from IDG Books Worldwide and written by yours truly and the honorable Wallace Wang.

✔ An online debate isn't over until someone compares someone else to Adolf Hitler. Calling the person a Nazi or the generic "fascist" also counts.

✔ Never criticize someone over spelling. English is a beautiful and rich language, utterly lacking in logic or spelling rules. Phonics, ha! *It* starts with a P for Pete's sake! There's no sense in drilling people on their spelling (unless it's truly awful, in which case you're probably dealing with a 12-year-old).

Saying Bye-Bye

When you're done using the remote computer, you should tell it good-bye — which is only polite. Use whichever command it has to hang up the phone.

Remember: You're telling the other computer good-bye. You're not telling your software to hang up. For example, the other computer may have a menu system that's as ugly as this:

```
(ABDFGIJKLMPQRSTVWZ?)
```

```
Command:
```

Type a ? (question mark) to see a longer description of the command options. You may find that, lo, **G** means Good-bye. Type **G** at the prompt:

```
Command: G
```

Press the Enter key. The other computer may say:

```
Why are you going? Do you hate me? Do you really want to hang up? (Y/N)?
```

Type **Y** for Yes. You *really* want to hang up now.

There. You've told the other computer good-bye.

- ✔ Always let the other computer hang up first. This enables it to properly clear your call, stop charging you online access fees, and so on.

- ✔ Sometimes the good-bye command is on a menu. It may be H for hang-up, G for Good-bye, O for Off, or E for Exit.

- ✔ If you have a command prompt, you may have to type in the command. For example, you may have to type in **BYE** and press Enter. Other variations include **EXIT**, **LOGOFF**, **LOGOUT**, and **QUIT**. When in doubt, type **HELP**.

- ✔ Only if the other computer appears dead or just totally confused should you hang up on your end: Tell your communications software to hang up the phone. In HyperTerminal, that's <u>C</u>all⇨<u>D</u>isconnect.

Chapter 22
The Internet Chapter

In This Chapter

▶ How to connect to the Internet

▶ Deciphering your Net address

▶ Using electronic mail (e-mail)

▶ Browsing the World Wide Web

▶ Reading news (USENET)

▶ Sending files with FTP

▶ Searching for stuff with Archie and Gopher

▶ Various Internet tidbits

*W*ant to impress someone? Then go out and buy your own private island. Want to join the latest trendy computeroid thing? Then sign up for the Internet.

The Internet is the Next Big Thing in computing. But don't believe the hype. Buried in the hoopla is a loose connection of government, educational, and high-tech industry computers that all chat with each other. There are millions of things to do and see on the Internet, plus you may actually get to meet some of the rudest people in all of humanity. No wonder everyone is nuts about it!

✔ The Internet isn't a product, it's more of a thing.

✔ If you really need stock quotes, news, and information, then you should connect with CompuServe, America Online, or Prodigy.

✔ Researching on the Internet is iffy. It's like a voluntary library without a librarian. There is some great stuff there, but most of it is trivial.

✔ This chapter is not an end-all Internet discussion. You really need an entire book on the subject to understand it completely.

✔ "Searching for stuff with Archie and Gopher" sounds like a lost episode of the *Andy Griffith Show.*

Connecting to the Internet

Computer pundits are always looking for the latest trend, the next "big" thing to take over. It was 1-2-3, then desktop publishing, then Windows, then the Internet. It's cool. It's hot. Everyone wants on! Get a modem! Sign up now! Don't be left behind!

A-hem.

If you're dying to become a member of cyberspace, you're going to need two things:

- ✔ An Internet provider, or someone who offers Internet or World Wide Web (WWW) access. This might be a local outfit that does nothing else, a national online service, or maybe even some type of connection right at your office.

- ✔ Special communications software. Unlike the HyperTerminal program in Windows, you need about half a dozen programs to do the Internet. One program dials, one reads your mail, one *browses* the Web, another reads news, and so on. It's massively confusing, so don't expect things to get any easier.

Finding a provider that doesn't charge a lot of quatloos

To hoist yourself up into the Internet saddle, you need a provider. This is because the Internet is not like a BBS. It's a collection of computers, and what you need is access to one of those computers or, more likely, access to one of those computers that talks to one of those computers — a provider.

Don't read this brief history of the Internet

The Internet is not the Information Superhighway that was praised in the early '90s. It started out as a way for UNIX computers to communicate with each other, locally at first and then over the phone lines.

The roots of the Internet are in the old ARPAnet, a network of military and civilian computers in the '70s, where today's Internet software was hashed out. From there it grew to a network of government and university computers, and eventually PCs as they became more powerful and able to run UNIX software.

So keep in mind when you use the Internet that it's the result of evolution, not creation. And as such, it has all the earmarks of things evolved and little of the elegance of that which was created.

Some of the providers are local systems or computers. Heck, your computers at work may be able to tie into the Net somehow. Some of the newer providers exist only to give rabble like you and me Internet access — at a cost. And finally, some of the traditional, national online services — Prodigy, CompuServe, America Online, and others — provide access to the Internet.

Every provider is going to charge you something for the privilege of accessing the Internet. Sometimes, as when your work or school computers have access, it should be free. But most of the time, especially for using some of the more interesting Net features, there will be Big Coin to pay.

✔ The information superhighway has many on-ramps.

✔ It's also rife for punnage: Roadkill on the information superhighway; Potholes on the information superhighway; Stuck in a traffic jam on the information superhighway; and so on.

✔ There is no off-ramp on the information superhighway.

✔ The best Internet providers also supply you with a "getting started" disk and maybe a helpful setup booklet. Setting things up involves lots of busy work, copying down numbers and cryptic words. The more help they give you, the better. If not, shop around.

✔ No one provider is *the* provider. In fact, no one or no thing is in charge of the Internet. There are some committees and folks who oversee much of it, but there is no large glass building downtown that houses the Internet Corporate Headquarters. (This also means there's no one to complain to, which is one of the Internet's major foibles.)

✔ The Internet is free. This means, of course, that everyone pays for it. Your tax dollars go to the government, military, and educational systems that serve as the backbone of the Internet.

✔ Yet, while the Internet is free, you pay money to access it. This is the service your provider offers. You pay them to access a free service. (Don't weep, even students at universities pay for access. And government workers? Well, it's hard to type and hold a donut and coffee cup at the same time.)

✔ There were three Providers on the planet Triskellion.

Special communications software

In the olden days, all you needed to talk to the Net was a dumb terminal program. In fact, I used a program I wrote myself to access the Internet in the early '80s. Today, the Net is more sophisticated. To use many parts of it, you need special software: viewers to see things, browsers to surf things, mail and news reading programs to make life easier, and so on.

If you access the Internet from a service like CompuServe or Prodigy, the special software you use to access those systems will act as your Internet software (and expect to pay a premium for the service). Some Internet providers, such as the Pipeline in New York City (NEW YORK CITY!?), come with their own special software.

The best place to find this software is at a software store or computer bookstore. Often several of the packages you need are bundled into one large box, complete with manuals and books that offer lots of suggestions and tips.

Pretty much the all-around best software to get is Netscape. It lets you browse the Web, read your mail, read newsgroups, and do file transfers (FTP). About the only thing Netscape doesn't do is something called *telnet,* which is too geeky to try anyway.

Your Net Address

After you get set up on the Internet, you'll be blessed with your own Net address. This is a location where anyone in the universe can send you mail. For example, your address may be:

```
president@whitehouse.gov
```

It just looks so cool! In fact, I personally think a Net address should have many more doohickeys in it. How about:

```
pres(ident)@**white{ho}use!—::—=!gov(&)^^
```

After a while it looks like a swear word in *Mad* magazine. But I digress. Most Net addresses work like this:

```
you, at, provider, dot, domain
```

First comes your name, your supercool Net name. Then comes the @ sign and then the provider or the system you dial into. Then comes a dot and finally the domain, which is a code word that tells the rest of the Internet what type of organization you use. So president@whitehouse.gov is the address of the President of the United States, which is an account on the computer whitehouse and is a government Internet site.

Here is Bill Gates' Net address:

```
billg@microsoft.com
```

That's Bill Gates, who is known as `billg` on the Net, and he's at microsoft-dot-com, the Microsoft company.

- ✔ Your Net address is just about the coolest thing you can put on your business card.

- ✔ The domain says what type of computer system you're using: `com` for company; `org` for non-profit organizations; `gov` for the government; `mil` for the military; `edu` for educational whatevers; and so many more that it would be too nerdy of me to list all of them here.

- ✔ Yes, `president@whitehouse.gov` is really his address. By the way, you can get a book called *E-mail Addresses of the Rich & Famous* by Seth Godin (Addison-Wesley). It lists the names of all sorts of folks "on the Net," from politicians to comedians to movie stars to famous nerds and geeks the world over.

- ✔ Since I'm neither rich nor famous, my Net address isn't in the book. If you want to write me, to ask a question or just say "hi," I can be reached at: `dgookin@wambooli.com` (that's *dgookin*, me, Dan Gookin, at Wambooli, my online company).

Internet Pieces Parts

Internet isn't a thing as much as it's a collection of things. The following sections cover some of the more popular things. Yes, there are even more, but these are the most common.

Letters, O, we get letters! (E-mail)

When you have your hallowed Net address, you can get mail. One of the first things any Internet users do once they're "on" is to check their mail.

- ✔ You use a unique program to both read and send mail. The Eudora program is popular, though I can't understand why. Netscape can also read and send mail.

- ✔ Most of the major online services offer Internet mail, which is how they communicate with each other.

- ✔ At the end of your Internet mail most people put a *signature*. This is a small (hopefully small) bit of text to end your message. For example

```
********************************************************
*   Billy Smith ! Cool net dood ! UCSD Rules !    *
* ---------------------------------------------    *
*   "I'm a doctor, not a moon shuttle conductor!" *
*      Buckaroo Banzai is cool!                    *
*   I think I've wasted enough net bandwidth       *
*      But Maybe Not!                              *
* ---------------------------------------------    *
*      Barney Sucks! Power Rangers Suck!           *
********************************************************
```

This is definitely not the earmark of a civilized Net denizen.

The World Wide Web

The World Wide Web, which I can type more easily as WWW, is yet another way to organize and make sense of information on the Internet. In a few years, I predict, the entire Internet will be the Web. The other Internet pieces parts are rapidly becoming Web-ized.

On the Web, information is organized via *hypertext;* various words and whatnot on a WWW page are linked to various parts of the Internet. That way you could view a page of the Web with the word *Klingon* on it, select that word, and soon you'll see a document describing trekkie bathing habits. Something like that.

To make the best use of the WWW, you need a Web browser (see Figure 22-1). This is a program that presents information on the Web in a graphical, mouse-driven, or easy-to-use fashion. That way you can see the hypertext words highlighted or underlined and then click on them with a mouse. Various and sundry Web browsers exist, but Netscape is the best.

- ✔ If you want to "surf the Net," you'll want to use the WWW.

- ✔ Web page addresses usually start with the cryptoglyph `http://` and then something that looks very Netish followed by a dot and `html`. Essentially it's just another Net address, one that contains a Web page document. Look up in a real Internet book if you want to know what all the jargon means.

- ✔ The best way to access WWW is with a very, very fast modem. Since it tends to be graphical, the Web can be unbearably slow when you're using anything less than a 28 kbps modem. Sorry.

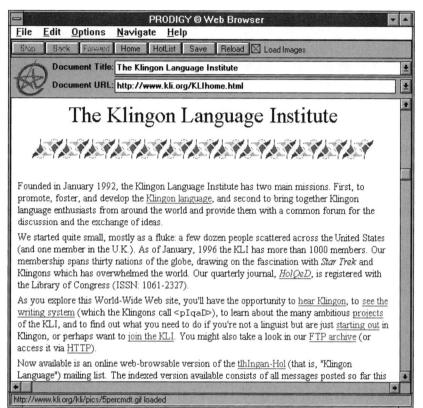

The Klingon Language Institute

http://www.kli.org/KLIhome.html

The Klingon Language Institute

Founded in January 1992, the Klingon Language Institute has two main missions. First, to promote, foster, and develop the Klingon language, and second to bring together Klingon language enthusiasts from around the world and provide them with a common forum for the discussion and the exchange of ideas.

We started quite small, mostly as a fluke: a few dozen people scattered across the United States (and one member in the U.K.). As of January, 1996 the KLI has more than 1000 members. Our membership spans thirty nations of the globe, drawing on the fascination with *Star Trek* and Klingons which has overwhelmed the world. Our quarterly journal, *HolQeD*, is registered with the Library of Congress (ISSN: 1061-2327).

As you explore this World-Wide Web site, you'll have the opportunity to hear Klingon, to see the writing system (which the Klingons call <pIqaD>), to learn about the many ambitious projects of the KLI, and to find out what you need to do if you're not a linguist but are just starting out in Klingon, or perhaps want to join the KLI. You might also take a look in our FTP archive (or access it via HTTP).

Now available is an online web-browsable version of the tlhIngan-Hol (that is, "Klingon Language") mailing list. The indexed version available consists of all messages posted so far this

http://www.kli.org/kli/pics/5percmdt.gif loaded

Figure 22-1:
Browsing
the Web.

There's no place like a home page

One aspect of the WWW that everyone's nuts about is the *home page*. Normally that's the first page you see when you use the Web. And you can create your own custom home page if you like. For example, you can have a home page that tells about yourself, maybe has some hypertext links to your favorite parts of the Net, maybe even a button you can click — and then those so equipped can hear your dog barking. Then you can encourage others to visit your home page so they, too, can hear your dog barking at all hours.

News (or USENET)

News on the Internet should be put into quotes: "News." What constitutes news is really up to the people who publish it. On the Internet, that's anyone and everyone. So if you're expecting Paul Harvey, forget it. What you get when you want "news" on the Internet is really a collection of public forums on varying topics. For example, there are groups out there who discuss politics, science fiction, off-color jokes, genealogy, history, and a wide variety of interests.

In one way, the "news" is more of a subculture of cyberspace. You'll see "news" tidbits (called *postings*) from anyone. It could be an expert in the field, or it could be the most dreadful of all Net beasts: the college freshman with his brand new Net account. *Run for the hills!* So while you can use "news" to post a message and get responses from knowledgeable people all over the world, you can also use it to argue the subtleties of the Klingon language with people who have way too much time on their hands.

✔ Internet "news" is really more like the chitty-chat you get on a local BBS or the forum messages on CompuServe. They consist of *postings* — like public mail messages — from whoever happens to be perusing the news group at the time.

✔ "News" is divided up into various news groups. For example, `rec.arts.startrek` is where you can actually see people who devote large parts of their brain to figuring out how fast Warp 9 really is. Other groups devoted to specific subjects are given equally terse, period-peppered names.

✔ To read the "news," you need news reading software. This tool is hopefully part of your Internet software suite. Some providers offer their own news readers, and some news readers are better than others.

✔ Netscape and a few other Web browsers can actually read news.

✔ News grows. Internet news groups sometimes have hundreds of new postings a day. It's next to impossible to keep up (unless you have a cushy job where you can read news all the doo-da-day). On the pleasant side, you don't really have to read everything because the "news" is rather capricious (and experience will prove this to you).

FTP (Sending files on the Internet)

FTP as a noun: I just got this file from FTP.

FTP as a verb: You can FTP that file from the university's archives.

FTP as an acronym: It's File Transfer Protocol, a way to move files between two UNIX computers on the Internet, which also means you can move files between some remote location and your own PC. In fact, a recent trend to is to say such-and-such a file is available by FTP (noun) from some Internet address. You can then use your Internet provider to help you FTP (verb) the file to your own computer.

↙ You can use FTP (noun) to log into a remote UNIX computer, one that has a whole archive of files. Once there, you can select files for downloading.

↙ You can also use FTP (again, noun) to automatically snatch files for downloading. This is what you do when someone says to FTP (verb) a file from some remote machine.

↙ Other FTP-ish terms: *Archie* and *Gopher.* They're covered next.

↙ Pray to God that your Internet software has some form of easy FTP "shell" or a user-friendly guide to help you. It's not a cinch. Hey. This is UNIX. If it was supposed to be easy, *everyone* would be using it.

Everything's Archie

Thanks to FTP and, of course, to millions of megabytes of hard disk storage at major universities (supported by U.S. taxpayers), there are lots and lots of files out there on the Internet. Bazillions, in fact. To make that job easier, you need Archie.

Archie is a program used to help you locate files on the Internet. It's an index that holds millions of entries, each one of them a file buried somewhere in cyberspace. Essentially Archie is like the librarian who knows where every book is so you never have to bother with the card catalog.

To use Archie, you can either contact an Archie Server or mail Archie directly. The Archie servers let you run the Archie program, which helps you locate your file. To mail Archie, you just send him (and I'm not being overtly sexist here since Archie is a male name) your file finding request and he'll respond shortly.

How does it all work? I haven't the foggiest. But if you're willing to try, I advise picking up a good book on the subject or referring to your Internet provider's documentation before messing around.

↙ Archie isn't an acronym. It comes from the root word *archive,* which means to store something. And the old Archie comics had something to do with it as well.

✔ Since it's called Archie, other Internet look-up programs have similar names: Veronica and Jughead. I'm sure there's a Betty and Ronnie coming to a computer near you soon.

✔ Archie drove a jalopy. Does anyone under 70 ever use that term?

✔ Veronica is a program you use to search gopherspace, a part of the Gopher program covered in the next section.

✔ By the way, Archie finds only files stored on various Internet computers. To find people, you use a program called — and I'm not making this up — *finger.* My publisher forbids me to make any finger comments here.

Gopher it

The Internet Gopher is a fun tool that lets you browse through all of the Internet to look for stuff. It's like a combination of other Internet tools — FTP, Archie, whatever — that lets you look for information by topic and doesn't care which aspect of the Internet the information is located on or how to get there.

To use Gopher, you need a Gopher client, which should be part of your Internet software or something your provider offers. You then contact a Gopher server, which is the program that does all the gophering.

There's much more to the Internet Gopher than all this (as there is with all of the eclectic Internet). I can tell you from personal experience that I've actually used Gopher to help me find an archive of lyrics to old TV show theme songs. Believe it or not, your tax dollars are being spent right now to maintain such information on a university computer somewhere in gopherspace.

✔ *Gopherspace* is Netspeak for a place the Gopher searches.

✔ A gopher is a subordinate whom you would send on errands, telling this person to "go fer" this or that. Ha, ha.

✔ Veronica is a mouse-based program that helps you use the Internet Gopher. It stands for Very Easy Rodent-Oriented Net-wide Index to Computerized Archives. I'll bet they thought of the acronym first, huh?

✔ Jughead is a software tool used to search various Gopher servers from only one area of gopherspace — for example, looking for stuff only at the local university. Other than that definition (which I stole from IDG Books' *Illustrated Computer Dictionary For Dummies,* by the way), I have no clue how it works.

A Quick Roundup of Internet Stuff

 The following terms are closely associated with the Internet. As with everything else, this stuff is in a state of constant flux; new Internet goodies will doubtless appear, and some of these old chestnuts will fade into the ether. Until then, you can use these definitions as a guide for getting started — or at least to familiarize yourself with the terms, lest you venture out there and feel like an utter dolt.

Internet Phone: A way to bypass long-distance phone companies by using Internet connections instead. You speak into your computer's microphone, and someone else in the world hears you moments later. Sure, everyone sounds like a recording of Apollo astronauts in the early '70s, but it adds no cost to your Internet bill.

IRC: An acronym for Internet Relay Chat, a chat-at-once thing for typing at people on the Internet. Crazy. Insane. Makes the America Online chat rooms look like afternoon tea in Victorian England.

PPP: An acronym for Point-to-Point Protocol, a method of using a high-speed modem and a phone line to talk to the Internet just like you were another Internet computer. This method is rapidly replacing SLIP as a direct way to get on the Internet for PC users. (Oh, you still need a provider to get on the Net, but after that, the rest of the Net thinks you're another Internet site, not just someone using a provider.)

SLIP: An acronym for Serial Line IP (Internet Protocol), a method of hooking your computer directly up to the Internet using a high-speed modem and standard phone line.

TCP/IP: An acronym for Transfer Control Protocol/Internet Protocol. One of the file transfer protocols (a la Z-Modem) by which the Internet sends and receives information between its various computers. A completely geeky term to know.

Telnet: Essentially a UNIX modem program, one that lets you call up other UNIX computers and use them just as if you were sitting there. Telnet is how you can achieve *remote login,* which sounds a lot cooler than it really is.

UUCP: The UNIX-to-UNIX Copy Program, essentially a hyped up version of the copy command (called *cp* on UNIX) that allows your computer to copy files to and from other computers, either on a network or through a modem. If your computer can do UUCP, then it can dial up any Internet site and get mail and news. However, this is basically a UNIX-only thing.

WAIS: An acronym for Wide Area Information Servers, this tool allows you to search through information on the Internet. For example, suppose you knew the line of a poem but forgot who wrote it. You could enter the line, and WAIS would find any text containing that line, eventually leading to your poem. Hopefully.

The Internet has even more terms and jargon associated with it, a lot of which you'll find out is popular among the Internet natives (especially on "news"). To help you cope, you should pick up a copy of IDG Books' *The Illustrated Computer Dictionary For Dummies,* the second edition of which is rife with Internet terminology.

Part VI
Something's Wrong!

"ALRIGHT, STEADY EVERYONE. MARGO, GO OVER TO TOM'S PC AND PRESS 'ESCAPE',...VERY CAREFULLY."

In this part...

"There I was, just sitting there, minding my own business, when all of the sudden — for no reason whatsoever — the computer up and died. What did I do wrong?"

Computer owners are too quick to blame themselves for the folly of their PCs. We always assume its our fault, that we somehow offended the delicate sensibilities of the PC. Wrong! Computers foul up on the slightest whim. Don't mistake their flakiness for anything you've done. Instead, refer to the chapters in this part for remedies. Make this part of the book your place to turn to when the computer up and dies — or just crosses its eyes and says "Blean!"

Chapter 23
When to Scream for Help

. . . .

In This Chapter

▶ Finding yourself a PC guru

▶ Getting computer help from others

▶ How to tell if something is really wrong

▶ Properly explaining the problem

▶ Food with which to bribe your guru

. . . .

*Y*ou may be a major executive, a teacher, a mad scientist, or any smart, talented, gifted individual. But this computer thing makes you feel like a dummy. No problem. That's why this book was written. I'm not going to argue against computer literacy; everyone should know how to use an automated teller machine, and not being afraid of a computer is important. But should you memorize everything about a computer? Naaaaa. There's no need to. Plenty of other people have already done that. Your task is to use those people's skills, thank them profusely, and then get on with your work.

This chapter discusses how to get help from PC-knowledgeable friends and office comrades. Regardless of whom you decide to ask for help, call that person your *PC guru*. This chapter also discusses the differences between major problems that require assistance and things you can quickly remedy yourself.

Who Is Your PC Guru?

Your personal computer guru is someone — anyone — who loves computers and knows enough about them to offer help when you need it. Your guru is an important person to know and respect. Everyone has one — even the gurus themselves! If you don't have one, you need one.

At the office, the guru is probably the computer manager, but you should ask around to see whether anyone else can do the job. Quite a few computer zanies may be lurking around the office. If you find one, he or she may be able to offer help, suggestions, and advice more quickly than the computer manager (who goes by a schedule). Especially for help on particular types of software, turn to people who use the programs regularly; they may know tricks that they can pass along.

For the home, finding a guru can be more difficult. Usually a neighbor, friend, or relative will know enough about computers to help you install hardware or software, or at least give you advice about some program.

Whatever your situation, identify your guru and keep that person in mind for troubled times or for extracting advice and tips. It's like having a good mechanic handy or knowing a friendly doctor. You may not use your guru all the time, but knowing that he or she is available makes computing easier.

✔ Remember that a certain amount of finesse is involved when using your computer guru's talents; a line must be drawn between getting occasional help and taxing your guru's patience.

✔ Computer gurus can handle remarkable computer geekistical operations but only if they know what you're talking about. If you ask them to "check the Kyoowooi for you," they shrug and move off to floss their RS-232 ports. Learn the bare basics of pronunciation; a *queue* is pronounced *Q,* for example. When in doubt, write it on a card and wave it slowly over your head.

Other Places You Can Look for Help

Computer gurus aren't everywhere. Suppose you live on Pitcairn Island, and your PC just came mail order from PC's Limited (along with your absentee ballot for the 1988 Presidential Elections). Who's going to be your guru? Definitely not the lady who makes festive pot holders out of palm fronds.

When you don't have a real guru handy, there are alternatives. Here's a bunch I can think of right off the top of my head:

✔ Some computer stores may offer classes or have coffee groups where you can ask questions. But keep in mind that this is a limited source of information.

✔ Local computer clubs dot the nation. Don't be afraid to show up at one and ask a few questions. You may even adopt a guru there or learn about special sessions for beginners. Many computer clubs or special interest groups (SIGs) are designed specifically for questions and answers. Check the local paper or computer flier at the store for more information.

✔ Community colleges offer introductory courses on computers and some software programs. Come armed with your questions.

✔ Check your bookstore or newsstand. Although this book and other *...For Dummies* books may be all you need, other self-help texts exist. I'm a personal fan of *PC Novice* magazine, which always has plenty of tips and questions and answers for new computer owners. Other magazines have similar features, but keep in mind that most are very technical in nature.

✔ Don't forget the gurus you already paid for: the technical-support people at your computer store or the telephone support you get with every piece of software you buy. Everything comes with support; it's part of the purchase price (or so they claim). Especially for software, call the support department if you're having trouble. (But don't abuse phone support; it's not an excuse for not reading the manual.)

✔ If these traditional avenues fail, consider the unconventional. If you're a member of the Prodigy online service, try there for help. Or try one of the other numerous online services, such as CompuServe and America Online. (Of course, this advice assumes that you know how to wrestle with a modem in the first place.)

Is Something Really Wrong?

You need to call someone else for help in two circumstances. The first circumstance is when you want to do something and need to know how it's done. For example, you want to use columns in WordPerfect but don't have a clue how to do it. That's when you need a true guru — someone who has mastered the PC or its software and, if he or she doesn't know the answer, can sift through the manuals and discover it quickly.

The second circumstance is when something runs amok in a computer. This situation happens all the time, even to the gurus. Computers are like garden hoses in a way; they can tie themselves up into twisty tangled knots with little or no effort on your behalf. I call it the "It worked yesterday" syndrome. Because learning about a PC or knowing the innards of Windows or some piece of software is beyond a normal person's abilities, it's time to call for help when you need this kind of expertise.

What about them thar computer consultants?

A computer consultant is someone who likes computers and charges you a fee because of it. They help you get out of any circumstance, offer suggestions, buy things for you, set up your system, train you about software, and create custom programs — all for a fee. Having a consultant might be worth the cost. I should warn you, however, that most of these gurus for hire do no more than the free, bribable gurus, and you typically pay them by the hour, one hour minimum. That's a lot of money to have someone come to your office to plug in a phone cord.

Some really great questions to ask your guru

Darn, I'm in a good mood today. Here are some questions you can ask a computer guru that will turn the tables. At once, you'll have the feeling of superiority as the so-called guru stands there baffled, not knowing what you're talking about. Use these sparingly:

- I keep losing my document through an intermittent data fistula. Can you patch it up?

- My PC has a coolant leak. Do you know anything that can remove liquid nitrogen stains?

- The frangellico dirigible osmosis is tweaked.

- The biotransfer filter on my keyboard is popping out. Can I stuff it back in using a flat-edge screwdriver?

- Something in the error induction coils is transducing my document while it's being printed.

- Where is the "Frane" key?

- The Canis Familiaris virus gormandized my homework.

- I hear that new encephalophage virus is carried in common cerumen.

- My pixels are converging due to negative ion density. Is that a software or a hardware problem?

- The manual says to "depress the Enter key." Which put-downs work best?

- Before calling your guru for assistance, try working through the problem again. For example, if you're trying to print and it just doesn't work, try again after a few moments. Working out a problem ahead of time lets your gurus know that you're not abusing their help.

- Use your application's online help. There you may find suggestions, advice, and hints about using the program. The big-selling programs offer more help than no-name (or *el cheapo*) programs. Try this method of getting help first before calling someone else. If this method doesn't work, you could try the manual. (Yeah, right.)

- Press the key labeled F1 to get help.

- Don't be too quick to blame yourself if you can't do something. If you've done it the way the manual says and it still doesn't work, either the manual or the computer program is wrong. What you have is a genuine bug, and your guru — or the software manufacturer — should be made aware of it.

- Some computer gurus operate for free. Never take advantage of their generosity. Refer to the section "Common Bribes for Computer People" later in this chapter if you want to thank them in an appropriate way (well, appropriate for them).

How to Scream for Help

Approaching your guru with a problem requires skill. You don't just say "It doesn't work" and toss up your hands. Unless you're a soap opera star or royalty, don't expect much help from that approach. Instead, try the following:

1. **Relax.**

   Everyone has things to do and deadlines to meet. Don't dump your stress on the computer guru. If that's a problem for you, arrange to have your guru look at the PC when you're not there. No guru will help a rude user. (Who would want to?)

2. **Document what's going on.**

   When something doesn't work, write it down or be very detailed when you recite the problem.

   For example, don't just say, "I tried to start my computer, and it won't boot." Instead, write down any messages you see, such as `Not a system disk`. Or, if the computer beeps, write that down. If the printer doesn't print, yet the light is flashing, make a note of it. This kind of information helps the guru determine the problem — and it also shows that you care.

3. **Demonstrate the problem.**

   If you happen to be with your guru, show what the computer does. Your guru may want to sit in your chair. That's OK. Just tell your guru what you wanted to do and demonstrate how it didn't work. For example, print your spreadsheet and show your guru the odd characters that appear.

   When the guru can't be there, try to be near your computer when you're on the phone. Type in commands as the guru instructs you. Try to be accurate about describing your situation or what appears on-screen.

4. **Offer a suggestion.**

   This step is optional. Obviously, you don't know how to fix the problem. But, by offering a suggestion, you're showing the guru that you care. If you can't think of anything to say, make something up: "The disk drive needs a new steering wheel" or "The printer is in Italian mode" or "I think it needs to be plugged into a 220-volt socket." The best suggestion to make is "Something needs replacing."

   ✔ Nobody will help you if you ask the same questions over and over again. After telling you three times how to print sideways in your spreadsheet, your guru may become understandably rude and uncooperative. Instead of letting that happen, write down the answer and keep a log book handy if you need to.

> ✔ You don't really want to learn anything about a computer. Even so, some
> gurus may try to teach you something. If so, grab the old yellow pad and
> write down everything your guru says. True, you may never use those
> instructions. But writing them down makes the guru happy.

Common Bribes for Computer People

Those who love diddling with computers are an odd lot. In addition to thanking
them when they help you, consider offering a treat every so often. That way,
you dupe them into believing that they're not being abused.

Forget about giving your computer gurus money or software programs for their
favors. Instead, consider the following foodstuffs:

> ✔ Any Mexican or Thai prepackaged prepared foodstuffs with a nearly all-red
> thermometer on the side of the box.

> ✔ Anything made by Hostess — Twinkies, Ding Dongs, Fruit Pies (especially
> the ones with pudding in them), and so on. The Dolly Madison line of
> snack cakes is also OK but only when Hostess is unavailable.

> ✔ Doritos — preferably nacho-cheese flavored.

> ✔ M&Ms — the 2-pound package. You get bonus points if you pick out all the
> brown ones.

> ✔ Oreos with Double Stuff. More stuff. More cholesterol. Computer people
> like that.

> ✔ Cheetos. This prize is the primary reason that computer nerds have yellow
> stuff between their teeth.

> ✔ That 4-pound bag of fortune cookies you see at Sam's Club.

> ✔ Doughnuts. Don't be afraid to offer a computer person a stale doughnut. In
> fact, banging a doughnut on a table is one of the ways most computer
> people wake each other up in the afternoon.

> ✔ Ritz crackers and peanut butter, a.k.a. Ritz Bits. Sometimes, just giving
> computer people a 4-pound tub of generic peanut butter is best. Hand it to
> them along with a butter knife — but turn away quickly.

> ✔ Jolt Cola — all the caffeine and twice the sugar. (Another favorite beverage
> is Diet Coke; for the most part, computer zanies don't drink much beer.)

> ✔ Pizza — perhaps the ultimate choice. Slide a pizza under your guru's door
> if you fear to venture inside.

Avoid giving healthy food, although all-natural potato chips are OK. Steer clear of vegetables or anything green (except for M&Ms). Meat is OK, if you want to fix dinner for your gurus. But don't ask them how they want it (the answer is usually raw).

The jury is still out on Olestra.

The author and publisher of this book will not be held responsible for any health conditions that may result from this diet. Further, if you decide to throw a party and serve this junk, please display this book proudly or at least mention it in a favorable way.

Chapter 24

(Trouble) Shooting Your PC

In This Chapter

▶ Understanding why and how a PC up and dies

▶ Fixing various problems by resetting

▶ Removing a dead program from Windows

▶ Checking for a virus

▶ Fixing monitor problems

▶ Fixing printer problems

▶ Unjamming a printer

▶ Fixing modem problems

*W*hy is it that computers run amok? If cars had the same troubles, no one would drive. Heck, no one would walk, sit, or play anywhere near a road. As humans we count on things to be reliable and consistent. Life is supposed to be that way. Heaven must be that way. Hell? It's probably wall-to-wall computers down there.

There can be millions of reasons why computers go insane and turn on their owners. (Calling Stephen King! Are you dry on ideas?) I can't list them all here. But I can list a lot of common ones, plus a few steps to take for regaining control of the beast. That's all listed here, as much as I could squeeze into this book (which they tell me is already getting too fat).

▸ The problems listed in this chapter are all easily fixable by either you or your PC guru.

▸ Before you consider taking your computer into the repair shop, refer to Chapter 25, "Servicing Your PC."

The "It Was Working Yesterday" Syndrome

Computers should make funny noises before they go south. The car? It makes noises. The squeak turns into a whine, then a thumping noise, then something metal and dripping with hot oil pops up through the hood. That's the car's subtle way of letting you know something is awry.

With a computer, they just stop working. You do the same things you did yesterday, the day before, all week, month, and year long and then — maybe it's the phase of the moon? — the computer becomes uncooperative. It's maddening.

Just resetting

Anytime something *weird* happens, just reset. Follow the instructions in Chapter 4 for resetting your PC. Do it. When the computer comes alive again, the problem might just be automagically fixed.

- ✔ Why does this work? I have no idea. I think, maybe, the computer just gets tired. It needs to be reset every so often to keep itself awake.

- ✔ *Tired* is not the proper term, of course. Typically, what happens is that the PC's memory gets mangled. This never happens on purpose; over a period of time, programs with subtle faults induce memory errors. These errors grow until you need to reset to fix them.

- ✔ Some programs are memory hogs and prevent other programs from working properly — even though you may have megabytes of RAM. The ugly finger of blame gets pointed squarely at Microsoft Word here. It's a big memory hog. If you notice that other programs don't seem to function when using a memory hog like Word, quit the memory hog program and start it up again later.

Think about the past

Sometimes the "It was working yesterday" syndrome has a cause, only you just forgot it. Ask yourself the following questions:

- ✔ Did I add any new PC hardware recently?
- ✔ Did I add any new software?
- ✔ Have I changed any software?
- ✔ Have I reset any of the Windows options?
- ✔ Did I uninstall anything?

Oftentimes you find yourself remembering what happened, that is, "Oh, yeah, I set the printer to print sideways yesterday. No wonder all my correspondence came out looking so funky."

Killing off a program run amok

Programs can up and die. They don't even wave good-bye or make that "Eugh!" sound kids make when they play army. They just go. Sometimes one program can bring down the entire PC. I experienced this a lot when I was learning to program in the C language. Even some well-meaning programs may collapse the system if they're pushed too hard. To see if you still have control, try moving the mouse around. That's a good sign if it still works.

Next, try popping up the Start menu in Windows: Press Ctrl+Esc to do so, which ensures that your keyboard is still functioning. (Press the Esc key to make the Start menu go away.) You may have to wait for Windows to respond; sometimes a misbehaving program numbs your PC's operating system for a time.

After that, press the Alt+Tab key combination to switch to another program or window. If that works, chances are you can safely kill off a program that ran amok. Here's how:

1. **Press Ctrl+Alt+Delete.**

   This brings up the Close Program window (see Figure 24-1).

2. **Sniff out any recently deceased programs.**

   You see the words *not responding* in parenthesis after the dead program's name in the list. For example:

   ```
   Sheriff (not responding)
   ```

Figure 24-1: The Close Program window.

Click on that program's name in the list.

If more than one program is not responding, repeat all of these steps to rid yourself of each of them.

3. Click the __E__nd Task button.

The program is killed off.

- ✔ If you ever do kill off a program with the Close Window, it might be a good idea to go ahead and restart Windows 95 just to be safe. Usually a dead program isn't fully killed, and pieces of it will get lodged in Windows' teeth and start to rot. (That's kind of a metaphor.)

- ✔ If you can't use the mouse or your keyboard, you have to manually reset your computer. Refer to Chapter 4.

"Does my PC have a virus?"

A common question that zips through the mind of a bewildered user facing a silly PC is, "Could this be a virus?" I hate to say it, but yes it could — especially if you can answer yes to any of the following:

- ✔ I download files from the Internet or a local BBS.

- ✔ I started a game on my PC from a boot disk in drive A.

- ✔ I use stolen software my friends and co-workers give me.

- ✔ Other people use my PC.

The answer may be yes in all of those situations, and you might not have a virus. But the odds are pretty good you do if you follow those nasty habits. Sadly, Windows doesn't come with any antivirus software. You need to run down to the Software-o-Rama to buy some. The antivirus software will remove the virus from your PC, as well as assist you in spotting such nasty programs before they invade again.

- ✔ Most PC viruses display nasty messages on the screen. The one I got said `Arf! Arf!` and that was it — right after it erased the hard drive.

- ✔ Some users are too quick to blame the virus. Don't be. The media loves to hype PC virus stories since folks in the media are paranoid about computers anyway (and feel you are more so).

- ✔ Believe your antivirus software when it tells you no viruses are in your PC.

- ✔ No, you can't give your PC a virus by sneezing on the monitor. But you should have a box of Kleenex handy for when that does happen.

"I Can't See Anything on the Screen!"

Sometimes, the monitor appears totally blank. Other hints may tell you the computer is on — it's making noise, its lights are on, and so on — but the monitor appears to be broken. If so, follow these steps:

1. **Make sure that the monitor is plugged in.**

2. **Make sure that the monitor is turned on.**

   Some monitors have on-off switches separate from the computer's main on-off switch.

3. **Touch a key.**

   Sometimes special programs called screen blankers turn off the display. Touching a key — either a Shift key or the spacebar — restores the image.

4. **Check the brightness knob.**

   Someone may have turned it down, in which case adjusting the brightness (or contrast) knob brings back the image.

   Another problem may be the software you're running. Some software is dumb. It won't let you know, if you don't have the proper graphics adapter. Instead, you see a blank screen. If you try the steps we just mentioned and they don't seem to work, reset your computer by following the instructions in Chapter 4.

Printer Trouble

Nothing induces woe like the printer. First, there are so many types of them. Second, printers are very mechanical, which leads to programs mangling and jamming paper. Third, you may use a printer only once in a blue moon, and you can forget how it works. All this and more can lead to printer trouble.

Weird characters at the start of the document

Occasionally, you may see some odd characters at the top of every page or just the first page you print. For example, you may see a ^ or &0 or E@, or any number of ugly-looking characters that you didn't want there and that don't show up on your screen. It requires a major "Hmmm."

Hmmm.

Those characters are actually secret printer-control codes. Normally, the characters are swallowed by the printer as it prepares itself to print. The problem is that the software on the computer is sending your printer the wrong codes. Since your printer doesn't understand the codes, it just prints them as is. Hence, you see ugly characters. The solution is to select the proper printer driver for Windows. You want a printer driver that knows your printer and how to send it the proper codes. This stuff is best done by the person who (supposedly) installed your software on the computer. It can be changed in most cases. But better make someone else do that for you.

A common problem may be choosing a wrong printer in the Print dialog box (see Chapter 16). If your PC uses more than one printer, make sure you pick the proper one from the list *before* you print.

"The page didn't come out of my laser printer!"

Laser printers are unlike their more primitive impact printer cousins. With an impact printer, aside from getting mediocre text quality, you get to see what you print as it's printed (even hear it, too!). Laser printers are quiet. But they don't print until one of two situations occurs:

1. **The laser printer will print if you printed a whole page full of text, not before.**

   Unlike the dot-matrix printer, nothing is really put down on paper until you fill up a sheet.

2. **You can always force a laser printer to print what's been sent to it so far by giving it a form feed: Push the printer's online or select button to take it offline (the Ready light will turn off).**

   Then click on the Form Feed or Page Advance button. Remember to put the printer back online when you're done.

In a jam?

Paper flows through your printer like film through a projector; each sheet is magically ejected from a laser printer like the wind blowing leaves on an autumn day. Poppycock! Paper likes to weave its way through the inner guts of your printer like a three-year-old poking his fingers into your VCR. When this happens, your printer can become jammed.

For impact printers, you can unjam most paper by rewinding the knob. But turn off the printer first! This action disengages the advancing mechanism's death grip on the paper platen, which means it makes it easier to back out the jammed paper. If the paper is really in there tight, you may need to remove the platen. When that happens, you need to take the printer apart to get at the problem; call someone else for help unless you want to take it apart yourself.

For laser printers, a light flashes on the printer when the paper gets jammed. If the printer has a message read-out, you may see the message Paper jam displayed in any of a variety of languages and subtongues. Make your first attempt at unjamming by removing the paper tray. If you see the end of the paper sticking out, grab it and firmly pull toward you. The paper should slip right out. If you can't see the paper, pop open the printer's lid and look for the jammed sheet. Carefully pull it out either forward or backward. You don't have to turn the printer off first, but watch out for hot parts in the printing mechanism.

Sometimes printers jam because the paper you're using is too thick. If that's the case, removing the paper and trying it again probably won't help; use thinner paper. Otherwise, paper jams for a number of reasons, so just try again and it will work.

Printing on one line or massive double spacing

Two common impact printer flubs are the "Everything is printing on one line!" expression of panic and the "Why the heck is everything double-spaced all the time?" annoying interrogation. Both problems are related, though solving them doesn't involve lying on a couch and talking about your mother.

Somewhere on your printer is a series of tiny switches. The computer weenies call them DIP switches. Flipping one of those tiny switches will solve your problem, whether everything is printing on one line or you're seeing all your text double-spaced. (Both situations are actually the same problem, which is covered in the information that follows, which you can ignore.)

The switch will be identified in your manual. It has the name "Add linefeed" or "Automatic linefeed" or "LF after CR" or something along those lines. To fix your problem, flip the switch. It's a tiny switch, so you may have to mutilate a paper clip to reach in and flip it (turn off the printer first).

- ✔ If flipping this switch is something you don't feel like doing, have someone else do it.

- ✔ If you cannot locate the switch on the back of your printer, it may be inside, under the printing mechanism. If so, turn the printer off when you're in there fumbling around.

- ✔ If this doesn't fix the problem right away, turn the printer off, wait, and then turn it back on again.

TECHNICAL STUFF

Printing problems explained, which you can ignore

Each line sent to the printer ends in two special codes: the carriage return and line feed. The carriage return tells the printer to start printing on column one again — on the left side of the page. The line feed, following the carriage return, tells the printer to print down on the next line of the page. Simple enough.

The problem is that not every computer sends the printer a carriage return/line feed combination. Some computers only send a carriage return. When that happens, no line feed takes place and all your text is printed on one ugly, ink-stained line.

To solve the problem of printing on one line, the printer can be told (via a switch) to supply its own line feed automatically after each carriage return received. That way, if your computer is dumb enough to send only the carriage return to end a line, the printer supplies the line feed and everything prints as you intended.

The problem of double-spacing happens when that same add-a-line-feed switch is on and the computer is already sending a carriage return/line feed combo. In that case, at the end of the line, the printer adds its own line feed, giving a double-spaced effect. Turning the tiny switch off fixes that problem.

Modem Mayhem

Once you get going with your modem, telecommunications can be easy. Yeah, and I've heard some weirdos can rip out their toenails without any sensation of pain. You may encounter some problems from time to time. Chances are they'll probably be one of the following:

- ✔ Not having the right cable between your computer and your modem. It needs to be a standard RS-232 serial cable or modem cable. You cannot use a serial printer cable or a null modem cable.

- ✔ Not having the modem connected to the correct port on your computer. Most PCs have two serial ports, COM1 and COM2. Most communications programs assume you use COM1. If not, tell your software you're different and are using COM2.

- ✔ Using a modem that is not fully Hayes compatible. Your communications software assumes your modem to be Hayes compatible. If it's not, you need to select a proper modem driver or just sit in a pile of ash and weep bitterly because some bozo sold you an incompatible modem.

Chapter 25

Servicing Your PC

· ·

In This Chapter

▶ Determining if the problem is hardware or software

▶ Checking cable connections

▶ Checking various power sources

▶ Listening for strange noises

▶ Checking your disk drives

· ·

*T*he best way to handle trouble is to let someone else deal with it. Often, there is no one else. In fact, most computer trouble happens at the absolute worst time: the weekend. Why is it most computer stores close on Sundays? Maybe it explains why everything is so hectic on Monday mornings. Anyway, you shouldn't be working on the weekends — not when it's sunny outside or especially when they're having that Russ Meyer Film Festival at the Revival House.

Figure Out Whether It's a Hardware or Software Problem

Your guru, or even you, may be able to fix hardware problems, but most times they require taking the computer to the shop. Software problems, on the other hand, can generally be cured by your guru or by a phone call to the developer's technical support hot line (or wait-on-hold line). But which is which? It's important to know because computer doctors get irked when you hand them a PC with a software problem. Here are the clues:

1. **Does the problem happen consistently, no matter which program you're running?**

   For example, do Word, Excel, and your accounting package all refuse to send stuff to the printer? If so, it's a hardware problem. Take it to the doctor.

2. **Did the problem just crop up?**

   For example, did the page preview mode work last week but not today? If so, it could be a hardware problem — provided that nothing has been changed on your computer and no new software added since the last time the program worked properly. Take it to the doctor.

3. **Does the problem happen with only one application?**

   For example, does the computer always reset when you try to print using Notes? If so, it's a software problem. Call the developer.

Generally speaking, if the problem only happens in one program, it's software. If it's consistent across all your applications or it happens at random times, it's hardware.

Check Cable Connections Yourself

Loose cables can be the bane of existence — and not just in elevators. If your keyboard goes dead, your mouse freezes, or the monitor blinks out, it may be a loose cable. Here's what you should do to check:

1. **Turn the computer off.**

   Shut everything down — *everything*. Refer to Chapter 4 for proper shut-down procedures.

2. **Check all the cables behind the computer.**

   Wiggle each one to make sure it's in the connector nice and snug.

3. **If something is loose, plug it back into its socket gently.**

   If the cable is stretched, move whatever it is that's stretching it so that you can plug it back into the socket.

   Some cables attach to the computer's console with handy thumb screws. Some use tiny annoying screws that require a tiny annoying screwdriver to tighten them. Others may just plug in limply. The network hose usually twists as it plugs in. Printer cables have two wingdings and slide into clips on the printer.

4. **After everything is checked out, turn on the computer again and check for the same problem.**

   If it persists, take the computer to the doctor.

"How much of my PC do I take into the shop?"

If you really can't nail down the problem, should you box up every last jot and tittle by your computer, all the cables and whatnot, and send it all off to the shop? Probably not. But then again, they may ask you to.

I once had a printer problem, and they wanted me to bring the console, printer cable, and printer down to the shop. I didn't have to bring my monitor, keyboard, or mouse since they had those already and didn't suspect them to be guilty of any mayhem.

Always ask what you need to bring and what should stay home. If you do bring several things to the shop, double-check to ensure they have those items written down on your receipt. You want to get each of them back. It also pays to write your name and driver's license number or some other ID on the *inside* of the console case, under the keyboard, beneath the printer, and so on.

Some Things to Try When the Sucker Just Won't Turn On

Nothing fills thy heart with dread like flipping the PC's on-off switch and hearing *click*. "Hey! The mouse is supposed to go *click!* The PC is supposed to warble to life and entertain me!"

The following sections offer some wholesome suggestions for things to try yourself before phoning the repair shop in a dead panic.

Plug the computer into a different outlet

Sometimes wall sockets go dead. If the computer won't turn on, consider plugging it or your power strip into a different wall socket.

A doohickey you can buy at Radio Shack tests wall sockets. It sells for about $5. You just plug it into a wall socket, and little lights will come on if the socket is supplying juice. Tell the Radio Shack people what it is you want, and they'll cheerfully steer you over to it.

Bypass the power strip

If you think the power strip (your computer command center) is broken, try plugging the computer directly into the wall. If it works, the problem is with your power strip. Buy a new one.

Check the circuit breaker

Of course, the only time you really need to check the circuit breaker is when nothing else in the room comes on either. If the lamp is on and your PC sits there dumb, it's probably a wall-socket or power-strip problem. Otherwise, saunter down to the power box and look for one of the switches that's halfway on. Turn it off and then all the way on.

The reason your circuit breaker *trips* is that something on the line overloaded the circuit. This overload could be caused by faulty equipment or, more likely, too much of a power drain. If you're in an older building, your computer (or laser printer) may be pulling too much power from the line. Solution: Consider buying a new house.

Help Out the PC Doc by Listening for Noises

Computers make a cacophony of sounds: The hard drive whirs, and its chipmunks squeal when you access data; the power supply's fan constantly hums; monitors make a high-pitched noise that only those under 30 can hear; and the keyboard goes clackity-clack as you type on it. If something goes wrong, can you still hear the noises you're supposed to? Is any noise missing? Or are there new and frightening noises?

Although you can't do anything to cure the noise problem, you should make a note of it and tell the computer technician. Unlike car noises, computer noises generally don't go away when you get to the shop.

One noise that increases over time is the hard-drive hum. At first, the sound can barely be noticed. But, as you use the computer, the hum gets louder and louder. This increase is caused by wear on the hard drive's bearings, and there's nothing you can do about it. When the noise becomes unbearable, you should consider buying a new hard drive (although the loud noise doesn't always indicate impending doom).

Determine Whether a Disk is Damaged

Like wine, disks age. Unlike wine, older disks lose their flavor and quickly turn to vinegar. Also, disks become damaged with wear and tear. When they wear out, you can't use them again. Ask your guru if he or she can resuscitate the disk (sometimes that's possible).

You can check any disk yourself using one of the Windows marvelous disk tools. Follow these steps:

1. **Open My Computer.**

   Double-click on the My Computer icon to open it and reveal that window full-o-disk drives.

2. **Click on a suspect disk drive in the list.**

3. **Choose File⇨Properties.**

   The drive's Properties dialog box appears.

4. **Click on the Tools tab to bring that panel forward.**

5. **Click the Check Now button.**

   This starts the ScanDisk program, which checks the health of your disk drive like a doctor listens to your ticker. Figure 25-1 shows the ScanDisk dialog box.

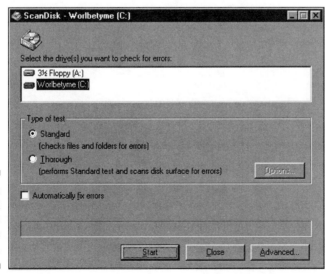

Figure 25-1:
ScanDisk listens to your disk's ticker.

6a. **If you haven't been having major disk disasters, check the** Standard **radio button.**

6b. **If disk disasters is your PC's middle name, check the** Thorough **button.**

7. **Click the** Start **button.**

ScanDisk checks your drive and, hopefully, will find nothing wrong.

The scanning takes longer if you check the Thorough button.

After scanning is completed, you see a summary dialog box chock-full of meaningless statistics. Hopefully, no errors were found.

If errors were found, ScanDisk will offer to fix them. Direct it to do so. Don't bother with the safety or recovery disk in drive A; it's a waste of time. ScanDisk will fix your hard drive up as best it can under the circumstances.

8. **Click the** Close **button (twice).**

You're done.

✔ If ScanDisk reports a lot of disk errors, it might be a sign that your hard drive's days are up. Do a full backup of all the files on the hard drive and buy a replacement immediately.

Part VII

The Part of Tens

The 5th Wave   **By Rich Tennant**

"FOR OBVIOUS REASONS WE DECIDED NOT TO USE AN ACRONYM."

In this part...

They say that Anne Boleyn had six fingers. No, she wasn't missing four; she had six fingers on each hand— twelve total. I just have five fingers on each hand, thank you very much. And because of that, I decided to end this book with a big part containing lists of tens — important information, rules, do's and don'ts, and other trivia I could conveniently stick into various lists. Poor Anne would've had to do lists of twelve.

Yes, I know that there aren't always ten items in each chapter. Sometimes there are more, and sometimes there are less. Still, all the information is good and organized to help you find it quickly. Now get your mind off Henry's wife and back to computers.

Chapter 26
Ten Common Beginner Mistakes

●●

In This Chapter

▶ Buying too much software

▶ Buying incompatible hardware

▶ Not buying enough supplies

▶ Not saving your work

▶ Using a floppy disk instead of the hard drive

▶ Not backing up files

▶ Keeping the monitor up too bright

▶ Turning the computer rapidly on and off again

▶ Not labeling your floppy disks

●●

Sure, there are a million mistakes you can make with a computer, whether it's deleting the wrong word or dropping the monitor on your toe. But I've narrowed the list down to ten (OK, there are nine of 'em). Now, these aren't the classic boners (see the sidebar "Some classic PC boners"), but they're closely related. These are the day-to-day operating mistakes that people tend to repeat until they're told not to.

Buying Too Much Software

Why would I advise against buying too much software? I'd be a hypocrite if I did because I have hundreds of pieces of software. (Of course, I'm a nerd, so it's all right.)

What I'm really advising against here is buying too much software *at the same time*. Buying software's a lot different from buying CDs at the music store. You can listen to a stack of CDs in three days. They're enjoyable the first time, and they age well.

But software is gruesome on the first day, and the enjoyment curve rises slowly after that. It can take months to learn the basics of a single piece of software. Even after a year, you'll still be finding features, shortcuts, and new tricks.

So have mercy on yourself at the checkout counter and buy software at a moderate rate. You learn it faster and won't have the headache of installing five programs in one night, finding out your computer no longer works, and then having to narrow down a list of five suspects at the scene of the crime.

Buying Incompatible Hardware

A computer must be put together like a happy family from a '50s TV show. All the parts must live together in a dreamy, happy way. A computer's separate pieces all affect each other, and if one of them is belligerent, the whole show can go off the air.

For example, when buying a new monitor, you must make sure that the monitor matches your video adapter card (the thing inside your computer that sends the information to the monitor). Likewise, you can't use an old XT keyboard with a newer computer. It just won't work. Sometimes, even the simplest things go wrong: You've bought ED disks, and you only have a high-capacity drive.

There are two ways to avoid these type of errors: First, always have someone else upgrade your hardware. Second, pay attention to everything you buy. Never buy anything — especially floppy disks — in haste.

Not Buying Enough Supplies

People buy toilet paper in big eight-roll packages because they know they're going to use it. The same goes with floppy disks and printer paper. Sooner or later, they'll all be used up.

You don't have to sit down and format an entire case of floppy disks. But when you open a box, format all the disks in that particular box. That way, you always have a formatted disk handy when you need to copy something in a hurry.

Paper's cheaper by the case, too, and it ages well as long as it's kept away from wet garage corners.

Not Saving Your Work

The first time you lose something on your computer, it's frustrating but expected. After all, you're a beginner. About the third or fourth time, however, it moves from frustration to aggravation. Eventually, it reaches the despair level.

Whenever you write a blazingly original thought, select the Save command and save your document to the hard disk. When you write something dumb that you're going to patch up later, select the Save command, too. The idea here is to select Save whenever you think about it — hopefully, every four minutes or sooner.

You never know when your computer will meander off to watch the *MacNeil-Lehrer Report* while you're hoping to finish the last few paragraphs of that report. Save your work as often as possible. And always save it whenever you get up from your computer — even if it's just to grab a Fig Newton from the other room.

Using a Floppy Disk instead of the Hard Drive

Floppy disks have worth. You need them to move files from one PC to another. You need floppies for backups. And floppies are used to distribute software. But one thing you don't need a floppy for is saving your work; always save your work to the hard drive.

I got a letter from a reader once who was frustrated that he couldn't save a large graphics file he created on his floppy disk. It turned out he had never used his hard drive at all — not even once since he bought the computer. He was afraid it would overflow or something. So he used only floppy disks instead. It drove him bonkers.

Please, use your hard drive. Fill it up. Buy another if it gets too full. Only use your floppy disks for backups. Speaking of which . . .

Not Backing Up Files

Saving work on a computer is a many-tiered process. First, save the work to your hard drive while you're creating it. Then, at the end of the day, back up your work to floppy disks. Always keep a safety copy somewhere, because you never know.

Backup programs are a pain, but backing up to a tape drive can be painless. Around my office, the computers are scheduled to begin backing up files daily at 2:00 a.m. This process happens automatically to a backup tape stuck in the mouth of every PC.

Keeping the Monitor Up Too Bright

There's not much explaining to do here. Keeping the monitor turned up too bright is bad for the eyes, and it wears out the monitor more quickly.

To adjust the monitor to pink perfection, turn the brightness (the knob by the little sun) all the way up and adjust the contrast (the knob next to the half moon) until the display looks pleasing. Then turn the brightness down until the little square outside the picture's edges disappears. That's it!

Turning the Computer Rapidly On and Off

People who turn the computer on and off again rapidly, flicking the switch like a kindergartner at a shopping-mall kiosk, can actually damage their computer. If you must turn off the PC, give it at least a 20-second rest before switching it back on again.

Sometimes you may not be responsible for turning the PC off and on again quickly. A half-second power outage at my office one day cost me the life of my hard drive. It cost $1,000 to replace (back in 1989). An uninterruptible power supply (UPS) now guards all my PCs in case of another violent attack.

Not Labeling Your Floppy Disks

Floppy disks require a proper label for identification. Even if the label just says "Stuff," it's great (unless you label all your disks "Stuff"). And use the disk labels, not a Sticky Note.

I once had to grab a disk at the office for a home assignment. The disk had a sticky label on it that fell off. So there was a stack of 20-or-so disks. I took 'em all home since I'd rather waste time there looking for the right disk than examining each disk at an office PC.

Write on the sticky label *before* you stick it to the floppy. Or use a soft, felt-tipped pen to write stuff. Your data will thank you. And when you stick the label on the floppy, be careful not to cover any moving parts: that little window where the disk shows through, that little sliding metal cover, or anything else that looks important.

Chapter 27
Ten Things to Avoid

● ●

In This Chapter

▶ Don't reset to quit your programs.

▶ Never boot from an unknown diskette.

▶ Don't force a floppy disk into a disk drive.

▶ Don't format a disk to a different capacity.

▶ Avoid cheesy CD-ROM software.

▶ Avoid freebie software.

▶ Never plug the keyboard into the PC with the power on.

▶ Don't open anything you're not supposed to open.

▶ Always quit Windows properly.

● ●

*Y*our mother loves you very much. OK, she may not treat you like you were the Lord Almighty, but she loves you. That's important. Before you left the house, Mom would typically give you some rules: Don't run around, don't step in any water, don't pick up anything dead, don't eat dirt, stay away from the junk yard, don't throw rocks at crazy Mrs. O'Malley's house, and don't play with that awful Thompson kid. And, of course, you'd promise everything, and then rush off to Billy Thompson's house for a trip to the junk yard via old Mrs. O'Malley's.

This chapter contains a list of things to avoid doing, looking at, or stepping in while using your PC. Your mother would probably tell you the same things, had she written this book.

Resetting to Quit a Program

Never reset your PC to quit a program. This method was popular in the old days and may still be done in back offices across the land: You were done word processing so you'd punch the reset button. This was the way the person before you did it, and the person before them, and before them, and all the way back to Moses.

Always properly quit any program you're running. Never use the reset button for anything other than a cold, sweaty computer panic.

Booting from an Alien Disk

The number one way to get a computer virus is to start your computer from a strange floppy disk. I'm not talking about starting the PC using a boot disk you create or one that comes in a hermetically sealed software box. I'm talking about that — wink, wink — *game* Vern slipped you last week. You know the one. (Heh, heh.) Boot from that disk and you're inviting who-knows-what into your PC. Don't.

Forcing a Floppy Disk into the Disk Drive

Floppy disks only fit into your floppy drive *one way*. If the disk won't go in, you have one of two problems:

Problem 1: You're putting the disk into the drive the wrong way.

Solution 1: Reorient the disk and try again.

Problem 2: A disk is already in the drive.

Solution 2: Remove the disk from the drive before you put a new disk in the drive.

Formatting a Diskette to Different Capacity

You probably have one or two high-capacity floppy drives in your PC. If so, you must heed the Four Don'ts of formatting floppies:

- Don't mess with low-capacity disks.
- Don't format a high-capacity disk to a low-capacity. No computer on earth needs such a disk.
- Don't format a low-capacity disk to high-capacity.
- Don't buy low-capacity disks and *notch* them to magically convert them into high-capacity disks.

The only time you need to buy low-capacity disks is if (and only if) you need to format a disk for a person who uses only that capacity. These people are dropping like flies, so the odds are you'll never have to do that.

Cheesy CD-ROM Software

A lot of the stuff sold on CD-ROM discs is pure junk. Oh, I could rattle off a list of it for you here, but I won't. Most CD-ROM games are OK, especially the interactive, multimedia kind.

CD-ROM encyclopedias are OK. I can vouch for *Encarta, Cinemania, Dinosaurs,* and the various *Mozart* and *Beethoven*-type CDs. Everything else is iffy at this stage.

If you have a CD-ROM drive, always pick up the CD-ROM version of a software package. It will save you mountains of installation time.

Freebie Software (for the Most Part)

This is why they have uninstall programs: A lot of the freebie stuff you may get in the mail is junk. Don't waste hard drive space with it.

Plugging the Keyboard into the PC while It's On

```
The sizzling sound you just heard is your motherboard's last gasp.
You need to buy a new one. Or you need to replace your keyboard.
Always turn the PC off before you plug anything into it. You've been
warned.
- Your Computer
```

Opening Things You're Not Supposed To

Not everything inside or around your PC has the words "Don't open" on it. Some stuff is meant to open. New console cases actually have flip top lids for easy access. The old cases had six screws on them. Why the improvement? Because lots of people open up their PCs for upgrading.

Your monitor? Don't open it. It says so right by the screws. Same goes for some items inside the console, such as the power supply. Don't open them.

Don't open your printer ribbon and especially a laser printer's toner cartridge.

There is no need to open a modem or any other external device on the PC.

If you are bold enough to open your console for upgrading or just poking around, *always* turn off and unplug your PC first. It's good for you and good for your electronics.

Not Properly Quitting Windows

When you're done with Windows, shut it down. Choose the Shutdown command from the Start menu, click OK, and wait until the screen says it's safe to turn off your PC.

Don't just flip the power switch when you're done. Heavens! That's worse than throwing a rock and breaking old Mrs. O'Malley's window. Sheesh.

Chapter 28

Ten Things Worth Buying for Your PC

I'm not trying to sell you anything, and I'm pretty sure that you're not ready to burst out and spend, spend, spend on something like a computer (unless it's someone else's money). But there are some nifty little things you may want to consider buying for Mr. Computer. Like ten things worth buying for a dog (leash, cat-shaped squeeze toys, pooper-scooper, and so on), these ten things will make working with the beast more enjoyable.

Software

Never neglect software. Jillions of different types of software programs are available, each of them designed to perform a specific task for a certain type of user. If you ever find yourself frustrated by the way the computer does something, consider looking for a piece of software that does it better.

Mouse Pad

Rolling your mouse on your tabletop may work OK, but the best surface is a mouse pad, a screen-sized piece of foam rubber with a textured top ideal for rolling mice around. Avoid the mouse pads with a smooth finish. You pay more for pads with cute pictures or the new mood pads that react to temperature. The best mouse pad is one with your computer's logo on it, a picture of a frightened cat (which makes the mouse happy), or some clever sayings in Assyrian.

Wrist Pad

Like a mouse pad, the wrist pad fits right below your keyboard. It enables you to comfortably rest your wrists while you type.

"Sloppy, sloppy," you hear your typing teacher, Mrs. Goodrich, scream from across the room. "Good typists raise their wrists, striking each key with a deliberate stab!" Before she waddles on over to whack the undersides of your palms with a ruler, tell her this: "Stop, you hulking bruja! Your archaic typing methods aren't needed for the delicate computer keyboard. I can lay my wrists sloppily on a colorful wrist pad and type with reckless abandon. Go make thy husband suffer!"

Antiglare Screen

Tawdry as it may sound, an antiglare screen is nothing more than a nylon stocking stretched over the front of your monitor. OK, these are professional nylons in fancy holders that adhere themselves to your screen. The net result is no garish glare from the lights in the room or outside. It's such a good idea, some monitors come with built-in antiglare screens.

Glare is the number-one cause of eyestrain while you're using a computer. Lights usually reflect in the glass, either from above or from a window. The antiglare screen cuts down on the reflections and makes the stuff on the monitor easier to see.

Some antiglare screens also incorporate antiradiation shielding. I'm serious: They provide protection from the harmful electromagnetic rays that are emitted from your monitor. Is this necessary? No. A lot of alarmists out there claim that monitors induce nuclear madness. This premise can't be disproved (after all, look at your typical computer geek), so they keep at it. Buy a nuclear-proof shield if it makes you feel better or if you notice your hair falling out in fist-sized clumps.

Keyboard Cover

A keyboard cover is a protective cover for your keyboard. If you're klutzy with a coffee cup or have small children or others with peanut butter-smudged fingers using the keyboard, the keyboard cover is a great idea. You may have even seen them used in department stores: They cover the keyboard snugly but still enable you to type. A great idea, because without it all this disgusting gunk falls between the keys. Yech!

In the same vein, you can also buy a generic dust cover for your computer. This item preserves its appearance but has no other true value. Only use a computer cover when the computer is turned off (and I don't recommend turning it off). If you put the cover on the PC while it's on, you create a mini-greenhouse and the computer will — sometimes — melt. Nasty. This result doesn't happen to the keyboard, which is a cool character anyway.

More Memory

Any PC will work happier with more memory installed. There is an upper limit of anywhere from 32 to 128 megabytes or so (which is ridiculous). Still, upgrading your system to 8 or 16 megabytes of RAM is a good idea. Almost immediately you notice the improvement in Windows and various graphics applications. Make someone else do the upgrading for you; you just buy the memory.

Larger, Faster Hard Drive (When You Need It)

Hard drives fill up quickly. The first time it's because you've kept a lot of junk on your hard drive: games, things people give you, old files, and old programs you don't use anymore. So you can delete those or copy them to floppy disks for long-term storage. Then, after a time, your hard drive fills up again. The second time, it has stuff you really use. Argh! What can you delete?

The answer is to buy a larger hard drive. If you can, install a second hard drive and start filling it up. Otherwise, replace your first hard drive with a larger, faster model. Actually, buying a faster model is a great way to improve the performance of older PCs without throwing them out entirely.

Modem

A modem is a fun and interesting thing to have on a computer. Although it's not really necessary in most cases, you open up a whole new world when you buy a modem. Suddenly, your single computer becomes one of many. You can use the modem and your phone to dial up other computers, chat with other modem users, and call national networks like Prodigy. Maybe even the Internet. It can be fun and addicting.

One other thing you need if you have a modem is an extra phone line for it. This purchase has the same logic as when you get a separate phone line for your teenager: Modems are notorious phone hogs. When you're on the modem, no one can call in or dial out. It's just best to get an extra line specifically for the modem. The phone company doesn't charge extra for using a modem, and the calls are billed like any other phone call.

Adjustable, Swiveling Monitor Stand

Some monitors have built-in swivel stands. They enable you to adjust the way the monitor points, primarily so that the monitor points right at your face — not at your chest or over your shoulder. If your monitor is static, don't stick a manual under one edge to line it up; get a swiveling stand.

Some monitor stands are actually mechanical arms. These lift the monitor up off the desk and enable you to position it in the air in front of you. Mechanical arms are great but expensive.

Power Strip

Computers use more power plugs than anything you find in the garage or kitchen. You need at least three plugs for the basic computer setup: one for the console, one for the monitor, and another for the printer. Everything else you add — a modem, a scanner, speakers, a desk lamp, or your clock — requires another power socket. To handle them all, buy yourself one of those six-socket power strips.

Some power strips are more expensive than others. They usually offer protection against some electrical nasties that can flow through the power lines. If that happens often in your area, consider the heavy-duty power strip as an investment. For just about everyone, however, the basic $15 model will do.

Chapter 29
Ten Things You Should Always Remember

In This Chapter

▶ You control the computer.

▶ Upgrading software isn't an absolute necessity.

▶ If you backed up your files, you lost only a day's work.

▶ Most computer nerds love to help beginners.

▶ Life is too important to be taken seriously.

*W*hat! More things to remember? Stuff to remember besides pressing the F1 key for help? Pressing Ctrl+F4 to close a window? Hitting the printer on the side when it jams?

Yeah, but these things aren't as hard to remember. And they're more fun, too. Keep these ideas floating in the back of your memory for an easier, more trouble-free session while computing.

You Control the Computer

You bought the computer. You clean up after its messes. You feed it floppy disks when it asks for them. You control the computer, simple as that. Don't let that computer try to boss you around with its bizarre conversations and funny idiosyncrasies. It's really pretty dopey; it's an idiot.

If somebody shoved a flattened can of motor oil in your mouth, would you try to taste it? Of course not. But stick a flattened can of motor oil into a disk drive, and the computer will try to read information from it, thinking it's a floppy disk.

You control that mindless computer just like you control an infant. You must treat them the same way, with respect and caring attention. Don't feel like the computer's bossing you around any more than you feel like a baby's bossing you around during 3 a.m. feedings.

They're both helpless creatures, subject to your every whim. Be gentle.

Upgrading Software Isn't an Absolute Necessity

Just as the models on the cover of *Vogue* change their clothes each season — or maybe that should be change their *fashions* each season — software companies issue perpetual upgrades. Should you automatically buy the upgrade?

Of course not! If you're comfortable with your old clothes, you don't buy new ones just because the season changed. And if you're comfortable with your old software, there's no reason to buy the new version (unless you're a nerd).

The software upgrade probably has a few new features in it (although you still haven't had a chance to check out all the features in the current version). And the upgrade probably has some new bugs in it, too, making it crash in new and different ways. Feel free to look at the box, just as you stare at the ladies on the cover of *Vogue*. But don't feel obliged to buy something you don't need. (And I apologize for all the parentheticals.)

If You Backed Up Your Files, You Only Lost a Day's Work

Backing up files is about as exciting as vacuuming under the couch. You know it should be done, but it's boring, and chances are it won't really matter whether you do it or not.

But accidents happen. Cats can drag dead roaches out from beneath the couch when Grandma's over. And your software can crash, leaving you with nothing but a blank screen.

Back up your files every time you're through working with your computer. If you back up your files every day, at the very worst you have lost only one day's worth of work. And train the cat to not only drag out the roaches but to toss them in the trash before Grandma arrives.

Most Computer Nerds Love to Help Beginners

It's sad, but most computer nerds spend most of their waking hours in front of a computer. They know that's kind of a geeky thing to do, but they can't help it.

It's their guilty consciences that usually make them happy to help beginners. By passing on knowledge, they can legitimize the hours they whiled away on their computer stools. Plus, it gives them a chance to brush up on a social skill that's slowly slipping away: the art of actually talking to a person.

But, remember, computer nerds are more accustomed to computers, not people. When a nerd gives a command to a computer, the computer acts on it. So when the computer nerd has answered your question, write down the answer on a sticky note. Keep the answer handy so you won't have to bother the computer nerd again with the same question. Don't try to keep them away from their computers for too long.

Life Is Too Important to Be Taken Seriously

Hey, simmer down. Computers aren't part of life. They're nothing more than mineral deposits and drab plastics. Close your eyes and take a few deep breaths. Listen to the ocean spray against the deck on the patio; listen to the gurgle of the marble Jacuzzi in the master bedroom.

Pretend you're driving the convertible through a grove of sequoias on a sunny day, with the wind whipping through your hair and curling over your ears. Pretend you're lying on the deck under the sun as the Pacific Princess chugs south toward the islands with friendly, wide-eyed monkeys that eat coconut chunks from the palm of your hand.

You're up in a hot-air balloon, swirling the first sip of champagne and feeling the bubbles explode against the underside of your tongue. Ahead, to the far left, the castle's spire rises through the clouds, and you can smell Chef Meisterbrau's waiting banquet.

Then slowly open your eyes. It's just a dumb computer. Really. Don't take it too seriously.

Glossary

• •

386: This *number* refers to all computers that have an 80386, 80486, or any higher-numbered 80_86 microprocessor or brain in their computer.

80486: This number refers to the brains found in an 80486 computer. It's a notch better than an 80386 system.

accelerated video adapter: A video adapter with special circuitry to make its graphics hustle on the screen. It says "I paid a lot to watch Windows work even faster!"

accelerator: A hardware device that makes something work faster.

Alt+key: A key combination involving the Alt key plus some other key on the keyboard, typically a letter, number, or function key. When you see Alt+S, it means to press and hold the Alt key, type an S, and then release both keys. Note that Alt+S doesn't imply Alt+Shift+S; the S key by itself is fine.

applications: A term applying to computer programs, generally programs of a similar type. For example, you can have word processing applications, spreadsheet applications, and so on. Several computer programs fit into each application category. And everything is generally referred to as *software,* which makes the computer do its thing.

arrow keys: Keys on the keyboard that have directional arrows on them. Note that some keys, such as Shift, Tab, Backspace, and Enter, also have arrows on them. But the traditional arrow keys are used to move the cursor. See *cursor keys*.

ASCII: Used to refer to a plain text file, one that can be viewed by a human without mental incapacitation.

backslash: The \ character, a backward-slanting slash. The backslash character is used as a symbol for the root directory, as well as a separator between folders in a pathname.

back up: A method of copying a whole gang of files from a hard drive to a backup tape or series of floppy disks. It could also refer to a duplicate of a single file — an unchanged original — used in case anything happens to the copy you're working on.

Baud: A modem's speed is often referred to as baud, though that term is technically incorrect. The speed is really measured in bits per second, or bps, which is defined below. There's no reason to bring this up other than I'm granting you license to correct anyone who refers to bps as a *baud rate*. Baud comes from the 19th century French telegrapher, J. M. E. Baudot. See *bps*.

BBS: An acronym for an electronic bulletin board system. This is a local, typically hobbyist-run online computer system. BBSs have more of a neighborhood or community flavor than the big, impersonal national systems.

binary: A counting system involving only two numbers, which in a computer are one and zero. Humans, which includes most of us, use the decimal counting system, which consists of ten numbers, zero through nine.

BIOS: An acronym for Basic Input/Output System. The BIOS is actually some low-level instructions for the computer, providing basic control over the keyboard, monitor, disk drives, and other parts of the computer. When the computer is on and running, Windows is actually in charge. But to use the computer, Windows itself uses the BIOS to talk with other parts of the PC.

bit: A contraction of *binary digit,* a bit refers to a single tiny switch inside the computer, which contains the values one or zero. Millions of such switches, bits, are inside the typical PC. They form the basis of all the memory and disk storage.

boot: The process of turning on a computer that, surprisingly enough, doesn't involve kicking it with any Western-style footwear. When you turn on a computer, you are *booting* it. When you reset a computer, you are *rebooting* it or giving it a *warm boot* (which sounds kind of cozy, you must admit).

bps: An acronym for bits per second, the speed at which a modem can communicate. A speed of 9600 bps roughly translates into 960 characters per second, which is almost 9600 words per minute that can be sent between two computers.

byte: A group of eight *bits*, all clustered together to form one unit of information inside a computer. Conceptually speaking, a byte is one single character stored inside a computer. The word *byte* would require four bytes of storage inside your PC. Bytes are also used as a measure of capacity. See *kilobyte* and *megabyte*.

capacity: The amount of stuff you can store; the total number of bytes that can be stored in memory or, more likely, on a disk. Some hard disks have a capacity of 600 megabytes. Floppy disks have storage capacities ranging from 360 kilobytes on up through 2.8 megabytes. Some closets have a capacity for 24 pairs of shoes, though many women find miraculous ways to put more shoes into that tiny space.

carrier: This term refers to the tone that two modems sing to each other. You hear it used most often when someone says they "dropped the carrier." Although an impressive mental image of the U.S.S. Nimitz splashing down into the Caribbean appears, think of it instead as hanging up the phone.

CD-ROM: An acronym for Compact Disc-Read Only Memory. It's a special optical storage device that contains millions of bytes of information. Like the musical CDs, you can use the appropriate CD-ROM hardware to have access to the volumes of information stored on a CD disc. And just like a musical CD, you cannot record any new information on the disc; it's *read only*.

Centronics port: See *printer port.*

CGA: An acronym for Color Graphics Adapter. The CGA was the first video system for the PC that offered both color text and graphics. The text was lousy and the graphics were only good for the chintziest of games. CGA was soon replaced by the *EGA* graphics standard.

chat: To type at someone else while you're online with a modem. This can be a lot of fun. It can also be boring to sit and watch some of the slowest typists in the world — and then experience the agony as they backspace over the whole line of text to correct one tiny spelling mistake.

circuit breaker: A safety device installed between a power source and delicate electronic equipment, such as a computer. If the power going through the line is too strong, the circuit breaker *blows*. This shuts off the power, but in the process it stops nasty electrical things from invading your computer.

clock speed: The measure of how fast a computer's microprocessor, or brain, can think. It's measured in millions of cycles per second or megahertz (see *MHz*). The faster the clock speed, the faster the computer (and the more it costs).

clone: *Oh give me a clone, yes a clone of my own, with the Y chromosome changed to the X. And when I'm alone, 'cause this clone is my own, she'll be thinking of nothing but ...* a term used to describe an imitation of an original. You won't find clone PCs today like you used to in the past, but nearly all PCs are clones of the first IBM microcomputers, the original PC and PC/AT systems.

CMOS: This acronym refers to special memory inside the computer. The CMOS memory stores information about your PC's configuration and hard drive, and it keeps track of the date and time. This memory is all maintained by a battery, so when the battery goes, the computer becomes terribly absentminded. CMOS. See MOS run. Run, MOS, run.

communications settings: This phrase refers to the modem's speed and data word format, which must be tailored to each online system you call.

compatible: A term referring to a computer that can run DOS software. This used to be an issue a few years ago. But today, nearly all PCs are completely compatible with DOS and all its software.

console: The main computer box, the thing that all the other parts of your computer plug into. The console is typically a flat slab sitting under your monitor, though tower models sit next to the monitor or on the floor. Note that this word is a noun, not the verb *console* — which is something few people associate with any computer.

console device: Nerd talk for your screen and keyboard.

conventional memory: Memory DOS formerly used to run programs. Also called *DOS memory* or *low DOS memory*.

conventional memory: This is a common term, so I've listed it twice.

CPU: An acronym for Central Processing Unit, CPU is another term for a computer's microprocessor. CPU. Don't step in the PU. See *microprocessor*.

Ctrl: The name of the Ctrl key as it appears on the keyboard. Don't pronounce it *Sitral*.

Ctrl+key: A key combination involving the Control (or Ctrl) key plus another key on the keyboard, typically a letter, number, or function key. When you see Ctrl+S, it means to press and hold the Control (Ctrl) key and type an S, after which you release both keys. Note that Ctrl+S shows a capital S, but you don't have to press Ctrl+Shift+S.

cursor: A blinking underline, bar, or block on the screen. The cursor marks the position on the screen where any new text you type will appear. Cursor comes from the Latin word for runner.

cursor keys: Special keys on the keyboard used to control the cursor on the screen. The four primary keys are the up-, down-, left-, and right- arrow keys. Also included in the cursor key tableau are the PgUp (page up), PgDn (page down), Home, and End keys.

data: Information or stuff. Data is what you create and manipulate using a computer. Data can really be anything: a word processing document, a spreadsheet, a database of bugs your daughter has collected, and so on.

data word format: A technical part of modem communications. The data word format includes three elements: the word length (8 or 7), the parity (Odd, Even, or None), and the number of stop bits (1 or 0). The most common data word format in PC communications is 8, N, 1. The second most common is 7, E, 1. These settings must match those of the computer you're dialing.

default: A nasty term computer jockeys use to mean the standard choice, the option or selection automatically taken when you don't choose something else. They should really use the term *standard choice* instead. *Default* is a negative term, usually associated with mortgages and loans.

desktop: The Windows background. It's the ethereal pasteboard on which you stick windows and icons.

DIP switch: A tiny switch inside a computer, on the back of a computer, or on a printer. DIP switches are used to control the way a computer or printer automatically behaves, to tell the system about more memory, or to configure some doohickey to work properly. This switch only needs to be set once, twice if you weren't paying attention the first time.

directory: The old DOS term for a folder. See *folder*.

disk: A storage device for computer information. Disks are of two types: hard disks and floppy disks. The floppy disks are removable and come in two sizes: $3^1/_2$-inch and $5^1/_4$-inch.

diskette: A term applied to a floppy disk, usually to distinguish between it and a hard disk (which isn't removable). Diskettes are often referred to as disks. See *disk*.

display: The computer screen or monitor. The term *display* is rather specific, usually referring to what is displayed on the screen as opposed to the monitor (which is hardware).

document: A file created by a word processor, though the term *document* is used in Windows to mean anything you created.

DOS: An acronym for Disk Operating System. DOS was the main program that controlled your PC before Bill Gates killed it off and Windows took the throne. A Greek tragedy is in there somewhere.

dot matrix: A type of printer that uses a series of pins to create an image on paper. Dot-matrix printers are a cheap, quick, and noisy way to print computer information — not as slow as the ancient daisy-wheel printer, and not as fast, as expensive, or as cool as a laser printer.

download: To copy a file or program to your own computer from the computer you're calling.

duplex: This term refers to how characters appear on the screen when you're communicating with a modem. Full duplex means you send characters to the other computer, and everything you see on the screen comes from the other computer. This process is also known as *no echo*. Half duplex means the characters you type appear on your screen directly. This is also known as *local echo*. This term can be freely ignored. Only when you can't see what you're typing should you go into local echo mode.

eek! eek!: This is the noise a computer mouse makes. See *mouse*.

e-mail: Electronic mail — personal, private messages you can send to other people who dial into the same computer you do. This is perhaps the most rewarding part of online communications: getting lots of mail. (But please don't beg for others to send mail to you; participate and you'll get mail.) By the way, the Post Office is thinking of starting an e-mail delivery system. The problem is that they can't figure out how to slow it down.

Escape: The name of a key on the keyboard, usually labeled Esc. The Escape key is used by many programs as a Cancel key.

expansion card: A piece of hardware that attaches to your computer's innards. An expansion card expands the capabilities of your PC, enabling you to add new devices and goodies that your computer doesn't come with by itself. Expansion cards can add memory (such as *expanded memory*); a mouse; graphics; a hard disk; or external devices like CD-ROM drives, scanners, plotters, and so on.

expansion slot: A special connector inside most PCs that enables you to plug in an expansion card (see preceding entry). The typical PC has room for five to eight expansion cards, allowing you to add up to that many goodies.

extended memory: Memory in a computer. The reason it has a name is because DOS had so many different types of memory that someone had to do something to keep them all straight.

file: A collection of stuff on disk. Your PC stores information on disk in a file. The contents of a file could be anything: a program, a document, a database, a spreadsheet, a graphics image of Alicia Silverstone . . . you name it.

fixed disk: An old, IBM word for a hard disk. The word *fixed* refers to the fact that a hard disk cannot be removed, unlike the floppy disk. See *hard disk*.

floppy disk: A removable disk in a PC, usually fitting into a 3 ½-inch or 5 ¼-inch disk drive. See *disk* or *diskette*.

folder: A storage place for files on disk. A folder can contain any number of files, or even folders with files in them as well (called subfolders).

form factor: A heavy-duty term that really means the size of something. Typically, you see form factor used to describe a disk drive. Essentially, it means what size the disk drive is, what kind of disks it eats, and how much information you can store on the disks. When you see form factor, just replace it mentally with the word "dimensions."

format: The process of preparing a disk for use by the PC. All disks come naked out of the box. Before your computer can use them, disks must be formatted and prepared for storing files or information. That's done in Windows somehow, probably explained in the main body of this book.

free: Nothing is free.

function keys: Special keys on the keyboard, labeled F1 through F12. Function keys perform special commands and functions, depending on which program you're using. Sometimes they're used in combination with other keys, such as Shift, Ctrl, or Alt. (WordPerfect takes this to the max, with up to 42 combinations of function keys to carry out various actions in the program.)

geek: A nerd with yellow Cheetos between his teeth. See *nerd*.

gigabyte: A perilously huge number, typically one billion of something. (And that's billion with a *b*.) A gigabyte is one billion bytes or 1000MB (megabytes).

graphics adapter: A piece of hardware that controls your monitor. The graphics adapter plugs into an expansion slot inside your PC.

hard copy: Something printed. If you want to print your memo, the paper that spews forth from the printer is the hard copy. Often used with the prefix "getmeeya."

hard disk: A high-speed, long-term storage device for a computer. Hard disks are much faster and store lots more information than floppy disks.

hardware: The physical side of computing, the nuts and bolts. In a computer, hardware is controlled by the software, much in the same way an orchestra plays music; the orchestra is the hardware and the music is the software, and the musicians (especially the violas) are under-appreciated.

Hayes-compatible: A type of modem that works like the original Hayes Micromodem, or at least that shares similar commands. Getting a Hayes-compatible modem guarantees that your communications software will work with it.

Hewlett-Packard: HP makes calculators and special scientific devices, but it's their computer printers that make them popular with the PC crowd. A Hewlett-Packard laser printer will be compatible with just about every piece of software out there.

host: Another term for the computer you're calling with a modem. The host is the computer that answers the phone.

IBM: International Business Money or something like that. They made the first original IBM PC, which formed the platform on which the modern PC industry was launched. Some 180 million PCs later, IBM no longer plays a leading role in the industry, but it still makes quality computers (mostly for the Mercedes crowd).

I/O: An abbreviation for Input/Output, the way a computer works. Computers gobble up input and then spit out output. This is also what the Seven Dwarfs were singing when they went down into the mines.

icon: A religious symbol or painting. However, when you run Windows, an icon is a teensy, tiny picture that represents a program. For example, Microsoft Word uses a pretty icon that looks like a big, blue *W* stamped over a newspaper. That's how Windows presents programs and files to you: pretty pictures or icons. (DOS used ugly text and — heck — the Phoenicians were doing that 7,000 years ago!)

impact printer: A type of printer that produces an image on paper like a typewriter. Not a laser printer, these printers are commonly referred to as *dot matrix* printers, though that's only a specific type of impact printer.

jack: Slang for a connector. Can be either the part that plugs in or the hole it plugs into.

K, KB: Abbreviations for *kilobyte*. See *kilobyte*.

Kbps: Same as bps, but 1,000 times greater. So 14,400 bps is really 14.4 Kbps. Nerdy thing. See *bps*.

keyboard: The thing you type on when you use a computer. The keyboard has a standard typewriter-like part, plus function keys, cursor keys, a numeric keypad, and special computer keys.

kilobyte: One thousand bytes or, more accurately, 1024 bytes. This is equal to about half a page of text. Note that kilobyte is abbreviated as K or KB. So 24K is about 24,000 bytes (more or less).

laptop: A special, compact type of computer, usually running off of batteries, that you can take with you. Laptops are popular additions to a desktop system, allowing you to compute on the road. They are, however, considerably more expensive than regular computers.

laser printer: A special type of printer that uses a laser beam to create the image on paper. Most laser printers work like a copying machine, except that they use a laser beam to help form the image instead of smoke and mirrors. Laser printers are fast and quiet, and they produce excellent graphics. Be sure never to set your laser printer to *kill*; use only the *stun* setting.

load: Another, older term for opening a file. See *open*.

log in: In computer communications, or even when using a PC network, this means to identify yourself to the host computer or network. You log in by entering your name, a special nickname, or an ID number.

M, MB: An abbreviation for megabyte. See *megabyte*.

magneto-optical drive: A special type of optical disk, like a CD-ROM disc, but one you can write to as well as read from. These drives hold a mountain of information. They are a little slower than hard drives but can be removed just like floppies.

mainframe: A larger, behemoth of a computer. The kind you may have heard about in old 1960's educational films. Man in white lab coat to small boy, "No, Billy. This is merely the console. The computer (*mainframe*) sits in that large room back there. Think of it! The technology that can squeeze all that processing power into one single room." Small boy: "Wow!"

megabyte: One million bytes, or 1024K. A megabyte is a massive amount of storage. For example, *War and Peace* could fit into a megabyte with room to spare. Typically, hard drive storage capacity is measured in megabytes, though a capacity of more than a gigabyte is becoming more and more common.

megahertz: The speed at which a microprocessor does its thing. A hertz is a cycle per second; megahertz is 1,000,000 cycles per second or 1,000,000 rental cars.

memory: Where the computer stores information as it's worked on. Memory is temporary storage, usually in the form of RAM chips. The microprocessor can only manipulate data in memory. Once that's done, data can be saved on disk for long-term storage.

MHz: An abbreviation for megahertz. This refers to how fast a computer's microprocessor can compute. The typical PC zips along at speeds up to 160MHz, higher in Montana. The typical human brain, scientists have discovered, works at about 35MHz — or 40MHz after six cups of coffee.

microcomputer: A derogatory term for a PC, used primarily by those who run the (now outdated) mainframes and larger (now obsolete) computers.

microprocessor: The computer's main chip, where all the calculations take place and the control center for the entire computer. Microprocessors are also called *processors* or *CPUs*. They're given numbers such as 80286, 80386, and so on. (See *386* and *80486* at the start of this glossary.)

minicomputer: An older style of computer, not belittled like a microcomputer or hailed like a mainframe. These minicomputers eventually evolved into *workstations*, which are merely powerful PCs that you don't play Solitaire on.

modem: A contraction of *modulator-demodulator,* a modem is a device that takes electronic information from your computer and converts it into sounds that can be transmitted over the phone lines. Those sounds can be converted back into electronic information by the other computer's modem.

monitor: The computer's display. The monitor is like a TV set, showing you information. It's actually only half of your computer's video system. The other half is the graphics adapter, plugged into an expansion slot inside your PC's console.

motherboard: The main circuitry board inside your computer. The motherboard contains the microprocessor, some memory, and expansion slots into which you can plug additional goodies.

mouse: A small, hand-held pointing device primarily used in graphics programs to manipulate stuff on the screen.

MS-DOS: The long, formal title for DOS, the Microsoft Disk Operating System.

multimedia: Essentially a meaningless buzzword, though it tends to identify hardware and software that use a CD-ROM drive plus sound. Also implies a beefier price tag than the typical PC.

nerd: Someone who enjoys using a computer. No one reading this book should be a nerd, though one day you may become one. There is no cure.

network: Several computers hooked together. When your computer is on a network, you can share printers with other computers, easily send files back and forth, or run programs or access files on other computers. It sounds neat, but in practice a network can be a hassle to set up and a pain to maintain. See *NBC*.

notebook: A special type of laptop computer that weighs less than other models made by the same company. Honestly, I just call all portable computers that fold up and fit on airplane trays *laptops*. Sheesh.

online: To be on and ready to go. When a printer is online, it's turned on, contains paper, and is all ready to print. For a modem, it means you're connected and chatting with another computer.

open: To move information (a file) from disk into the computer's memory. Only after you open something, say a worksheet or document, into memory can you work on it. See *save*.

parallel port: See *printer port*.

pathname: The full, exact name of a file or folder on a disk. The pathname includes the drive letter, a colon, and all folders up to and including the folder in question and a filename. Pathnames are an extremely specific way of listing a file on disk.

PC: An acronym for personal computer. Before the first IBM PC, personal computers were called *microcomputers,* after the *microprocessor*. The *PC* in IBM PC means personal computer and, since the time the IBM PC was introduced, all microcomputers have been called PCs.

Pentium: The official name Intel gave to the 586 microprocessor. This name is to keep all the knock-off goofs from calling their chips the 586 (but they do it anyway), since Intel can't copyright numbers.

peripheral: Any item attached to the outside of the computer, such as a printer, a modem, or even a monitor or keyboard.

pixel: An individual dot on the computer's display, used to show graphics. A graphic image on a computer is made up of hundreds of dots or pixels. Each pixel can be a different color or in a different position, which creates the image you see on the screen. The number of pixels horizontally and vertically on the display give you the graphics *resolution*.

pixel dust: That thin layer of dust that coats your monitor. It's deposited there nightly by the pixel fairy.

plug and play: The ability of computer hardware to self-configure. Software plays a role, too. The idea is that everything should figure out how it gets installed so that you don't have to pull your hair out. It works. Mostly.

port: Essentially, this is a connection on the back of the computer to which you attach various external items (*peripherals*). Two primary ports are on each PC, a *serial port* and a *printer port*, though what the keyboard and monitor plug into could also be considered ports.

printer: A device that attaches to your computer and prints information. A printer is necessary to give you *hard copy,* which is printed output of the information inside your computer.

printer port: The connection on the back of the PC into which you plug a printer cable, thereby attaching a printer to your computer. Most PCs have the ability to handle several printers, though you need to add special hardware to give your system the extra ports. The printer port is also known as the *parallel port*, or sometimes you hear some dweeb call it a *Centronics port*.

processor: See *microprocessor.*

program: A special file that contains instructions for the computer. To run a program, you need to find its icon and double-click to open it. Or you can run the program from the handy-though-unwieldy Start menu.

programmed/programming: Telling a computer what to do. This process requires a programming language and the ability to speak it. Anyone can learn. Programming books, such as *C For Dummies*, will tell you exactly how. That knowledge will really put you in charge!

RAM: An acronym for random access memory, this is the primary type of memory storage in a PC. RAM = memory.

read-only: Something that cannot be changed, added-to, modified, or deleted. A read-only file is pretty much protected from messing with; you cannot alter or delete it. A read-only computer chip, or ROM, contains information that can be read but not written to or deleted. Since a CD-ROM disc cannot be written to or altered, it's read-only as well — which is what the RO stands for in CD-ROM.

redundant: See *redundant.*

resolution: This term refers to the number of dots (*pixels*) on the screen. The higher the resolution — the greater the number of dots vertically and horizontally — the finer the graphics image your computer can display.

ROM: An acronym for read-only memory. These are special chips on the computer that contain instructions or information. For example, the computer's BIOS is stored on a ROM chip. ROM chips are accessed just like regular RAM memory, but unlike RAM they cannot be changed; they're read-only.

root folder: The primary folder on every PC disk. Other folders, or subfolders, branch off of the root. The symbol for the root folder is the single backslash (\).

RS-232: A technical term used to describe a serial port. See *serial port*.

R2-D2: The cute little robot in the *Star Wars* films.

save: The process of transferring information from memory to a file on disk for permanent, long-term storage.

SCSI: An acronym for Small Computer System Interface, it's like a very fast and versatile serial port. I only mention it here because it's pronounced "scuzzy" and I think that's nasty-sounding.

serial port: A special type of *port* into which a variety of interesting devices can be plugged. The most common item plugged into a serial port is a modem (which leads some to call it a modem port). You can also plug a computer mouse, a printer, a scanner, or a number of strange and wonderful goodies into the serial port. Most PCs have two serial ports, obnoxiously called COM1 and COM2.

shareware: A category of software that's not free, yet it's stuff you don't have to buy before you try it. Generally, shareware consists of programs written by individuals and distributed hand to hand through user groups, national software clearing houses, or via modem. Lotsa thumbprints on that stuff. You try the software and, if you like it, you send the author the required donation.

slide rule: Whoever is on top of the ladder gets to go down the slide first.

software: This is what makes a computer worth having. It's the vast collection of programs that control the hardware and enable you to get your work done. Software controls computer hardware.

source: The original from which a copy is made. When you copy a file or duplicate a disk, the original is called the *source*. The *source drive* is the drive from which you're copying. The destination, or the location to which you're copying, is referred to as the *target*.

speed: For modems, see *bps*. For a microprocessor, see *megahertz*.

string: In computer lingo, this term applies to any group of characters. A string of text is a line of text, a command you type, or any other non-numeric information. Don't let the term throw you or force you to insert twine or yarn into the disk drive.

subdirectory: A term for a folder within another folder. Should really be called a subfolder, but a lot of those old DOS users just can't seem to retire this term.

SuperVGA: The current graphics adapter champ for the PC.

SVGA: An acronym for Super Video Graphics Array; the next generation VGA. Turn the computer off and you get mild-mannered Clark Kent VGA.

system unit: See *console.*

tab shooter: A whimpy drink made with tequila and a popular diet cola.

tab stop: Just like on a typewriter, a tab stop on a computer is the location where characters will appear after you press the Tab key. In most word processors, you can set tab stops at specific positions on a line of text.

target: The location of a copy or duplicate of an original file. A target can be a filename, a subfolder, or a disk drive — the final destination of the file. Copying things on a computer is a lot like archery.

taskbar: The gray strip of buttons along the bottom of the Windows desktop. The Start button to the left of the taskbar starts programs for you in Windows. On the taskbar itself you find buttons, one for each program or window on the desktop. Click a button to activate that window or program. Oh, this can be so neat.

text editor: A special type of word processor that creates or edits only text files, often called ASCII, unformatted, or nondocument files. A text editor lacks most of the fancy formatting features of a word processor. Oh, you might want to look up *ASCII* since I mentioned it here. (Not that it helps much.) In Windows, the Notepad program is a text editor.

toggle: Something that can be on or off; a single switch that's pressed once to turn something on and again to turn it off. This term appears when describing something you can do in a program that turns a function on and then doing it again turns the function off.

upload: To send a file by modem from your computer to another computer, the host.

UPS: An Uninterruptible Power Supply, a thing you plug your computer into that supplies Mr. PC with power to either survive a short power outage or give you time to save your stuff and properly turn off the computer when the lights go out. Recommended.

user: The person who operates a computer or runs a program. The computer is the *usee*.

VGA: An acronym for Video Graphics Array.

window: An area on the screen where special information appears.

workstation/work station: A muscle-bound PC that usually does high-carb work (such as graphics) or that dictates over the network as a file server. Pricey.

write protect: A method of protecting information on disk from being accidentally changed or erased. This is done by putting a write protect tab on a 5 $1/4$-inch disk or by sliding the little tile off of the hole of a 3 $1/2$-inch disk. After that task is done, the disk is write protected and you cannot change, rename, delete, or reformat it.

X-MODEM, Y-MODEM, Z-MODEM, and so on: These are file transfer protocols or methods of sending files from one computer to another using a modem. These file transfer protocols allow the files to be received exactly as they are sent, so the nerds call them *error-correcting protocols* (as if file transfer protocol weren't goofy enough).

Programs and files are typically sent from one computer to another by using X-MODEM, Y-MODEM, Z-MODEM, or a number of other methods for sending files without errors. It's a modem thing.

Index

(continued)

   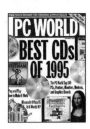

IDG BOOKS WORLDWIDE™

Order Center: **(800) 762-2974** *(8 a.m.–6 p.m., EST, weekdays)*

7/29/96

Quantity	ISBN	Title	Price	Total

Shipping & Handling Charges

	Description	First book	Each additional book	Total
Domestic	Normal	$4.50	$1.50	$
	Two Day Air	$8.50	$2.50	$
	Overnight	$18.00	$3.00	$
International	Surface	$8.00	$8.00	$
	Airmail	$16.00	$16.00	$
	DHL Air	$17.00	$17.00	$

*For large quantities call for shipping & handling charges.
**Prices are subject to change without notice.

Ship to:

Name _____

Company _____

Address _____

City/State/Zip _____

Daytime Phone _____

Payment: ☐ Check to IDG Books Worldwide (US Funds Only)

☐ VISA   ☐ MasterCard   ☐ American Express

Card # _____ Expires _____

Signature _____

Subtotal _____

CA residents add
applicable sales tax _____

IN, MA, and MD
residents add
5% sales tax _____

IL residents add
6.25% sales tax _____

RI residents add
7% sales tax _____

TX residents add
8.25% sales tax _____

Shipping _____

Total _____

Please send this order form to:

IDG Books Worldwide, Inc.
Attn: Order Entry Dept.
7260 Shadeland Station, Suite 100
Indianapolis, IN 46256

Allow up to 3 weeks for delivery.
Thank you!

IDG BOOKS WORLDWIDE REGISTRATION CARD

RETURN THIS REGISTRATION CARD FOR FREE CATALOG

Title of this book: **PCs For Dummies®, 4th Edition**

My overall rating of this book: ❑ Very good [1] ❑ Good [2] ❑ Satisfactory [3] ❑ Fair [4] ❑ Poor [5]

How I first heard about this book:

❑ Found in bookstore; name: [6]

❑ Advertisement: [8]

❑ Word of mouth; heard about book from friend, co-worker, etc.: [10]

❑ Book review: [7]

❑ Catalog: [9]

❑ Other: [11]

What I liked most about this book:

What I would change, add, delete, etc., in future editions of this book:

Other comments:

Number of computer books I purchase in a year: ❑ 1 [12] ❑ 2-5 [13] ❑ 6-10 [14] ❑ More than 10 [15]

I would characterize my computer skills as: ❑ Beginner [16] ❑ Intermediate [17] ❑ Advanced [18] ❑ Professional [19]

I use ❑ DOS [20] ❑ Windows [21] ❑ OS/2 [22] ❑ Unix [23] ❑ Macintosh [24] ❑ Other: [25]_____
(please specify)

I would be interested in new books on the following subjects:
(please check all that apply, and use the spaces provided to identify specific software)

❑ Word processing: [26]

❑ Data bases: [28]

❑ File Utilities: [30]

❑ Networking: [32]

❑ Other: [34]

❑ Spreadsheets: [27]

❑ Desktop publishing: [29]

❑ Money management: [31]

❑ Programming languages: [33]

I use a PC at (please check all that apply): ❑ home [35] ❑ work [36] ❑ school [37] ❑ other: [38] _____

The disks I prefer to use are ❑ 5.25 [39] ❑ 3.5 [40] ❑ other: [41]_____

I have a CD ROM: ❑ yes [42] ❑ no [43]

I plan to buy or upgrade computer hardware this year: ❑ yes [44] ❑ no [45]

I plan to buy or upgrade computer software this year: ❑ yes [46] ❑ no [47]

Name: _____ Business title: [48] _____ Type of Business: [49] _____

Address (❑ home [50] ❑ work [51]/Company name: _____)

Street/Suite# _____

City [52]/State [53]/Zipcode [54]: _____ Country [55] _____

❑ **I liked this book!** You may quote me by name in future
IDG Books Worldwide promotional materials.

My daytime phone number is _____

IDG BOOKS

THE WORLD OF COMPUTER KNOWLEDGE

 **YES!**

Please keep me informed about IDG's World of Computer Knowledge.
Send me the latest IDG Books catalog.

BUSINESS REPLY MAIL
FIRST CLASS MAIL   PERMIT NO. 2605   FOSTER CITY, CALIFORNIA

IDG Books Worldwide
919 E Hillsdale Blvd, STE 400
Foster City, CA 94404-9691